THE SHADOW OF
# BEAUTY

Stephen Talmond Brown has published the most systematic approach to a truly Reformed Christian theory and practice of art attempted in decades. Equal parts devotional, aesthetic theory, church history, and Reformed apologetics, *Shadow of Beauty* rolls along with a spiritual rigor and elegance rare for our age. For the nearly thirty years I've known him, Steve Brown has faithfully groped toward a unified theory of Christian expression. Even if one quibbles with a presupposition here or there, it is impossible to remain unimpressed by the breadth of his accomplishment. *Shadow of Beauty* is a work of pious beauty. S. Talmond Brown now joins the ranks of Seerveld and Rookmaaker as Calvinists who have thought most deeply about how to serve God with our heart, soul, mind, and eyes.

—Tony Norman,
Columnist/Associate Editor, *Pittsburgh Post-Gazette*

# THE SHADOW OF BEAUTY

# THE SHADOW OF BEAUTY

## ART, FAITH, AND THE CULTURE OF FREEDOM

S. TALMOND BROWN

TATE PUBLISHING & *Enterprises*

Published by Tate Publishing & Enterprises, LLC
127 E. Trade Center Terrace | Mustang, Oklahoma 73064 USA
1.888.361.9473 | www.tatepublishing.com

Tate Publishing is committed to excellence in the publishing industry. The company reflects the philosophy established by the founders, based on Psalm 68:11,
*"The Lord gave the word and great was the company of those who published it."*


*Cover design by Tyler Evans*
*Interior design by Stephanie Woloszyn*

Published in the United States of America

ISBN: 978-1-61566-961-5
1. Religion / General 2. Art / General
10.04.12

THIS BOOK IS DEDICATED TO MY CHILDREN:

**NAOMI, MARTHA, AND AARON.**

MAY THEY REJOICE IN GOD'S WAYS AND
BEND THE WORLD TO HIS WILL.

# ACKNOWLEDGMENTS

I am grateful to those who have helped me on my way to discover a distinct sense of assurance with regard to understanding the value of art as a God-ordained ministry. The days of discovery are never completed in the study of aesthetics, but there comes a point of understanding where a world once only imagined comes into view; and that is an exciting time.

I am grateful for the memories I have of Dr. Cornelius Van Til and Dr. John Skilton, two great men of faith who have been called home. They taught me more than they realized. I am grateful to my wife, Susan, to Lee Baxter Davis, James Hilston, and Tony Norman, who have all influenced the outcome of this book. My thanks also to Greg Shull, who has served as proofreader, to my editor, Ashley Luckett, to the rest of the Tate Publishing staff who have worked on this book, and to numerous friends who have helped me in subtle ways.

# TABLE OF CONTENTS

# LIST OF FIGURES

# FOREWORD

*The Shadow of Beauty* comes from the heart of a Renaissance man. Stephen Talmond Brown walks us through halls of culture, history, theology, and philosophy with the enthusiasm of an artist. It is a journey that continually points us toward the purpose and place of enigmatic beauty.

Stephen builds a comprehensive case for the Church to guide the arts toward its proper place as a moral force of truth and beauty. He reminds us that "the arts enshrine sacred values that form the moral substance of free people." The Church needs to be in that battle, yet it has neglected its cultural mandate. The unregenerate mind will only see beauty corruptly. Therefore, it becomes the responsibility of the children of the light to bring art into its true place in our culture.

His chapter "The Myth and Majesty of Art" is worth the price of the book. Here the depth of his training, education, and expertise shines as he clarifies and gives precise meaning to the terminology of art forms. His deep and wide eight-fold explanation of the forms of beauty gives the reader an understanding that is incredibly rich.

He concludes, "Art celebrates the beauty of God's holiness, and it is often the only point of spiritual commonality that lost souls have with God's people. I believe God uses art to draw spiritually dead people into hearing the call to redemption."

He is deeply concerned about the accountability of artists for not only artistic merit of creativity, but also of craftsmanship. He points to the Bible on bringing an objective standard of beauty to bear. The Scriptures promote—even require—excellence in what we produce. He reminds us that real craftsmanship awakens wisdom and creativity.

In the chapter "God's Mysteries—Our Treasures," Stephen shows the depth of his understanding of God's use of art in the Scriptures. He clearly helps us see that God prefers to use enigmatic ways to communicate his truth. He reminds us of Solomon's words that, "It is the glory of God to conceal a matter" (Proverbs 25:2). Pastors and teachers will be enthralled with this section. C.S. Lewis said that George MacDonald baptized his imagination and set him free in his writing. Likewise, Stephen's treatment of the enigmas in Scripture will do the same. Here he finds his title: "God gives us shadows and mysteries that challenge our understanding and lead us through various layers of revelations for answers." He affirms that, "In this journey, we may find principles of enigmatic beauty that energize the Bible's spiritual witness to the world." His challenge is clear: "If the church does not manage the ministry of art for good, the children of darkness will manage it for evil. Whoever shapes art shapes culture." His challenge is not only compliant. He offers solid solutions and realistic evaluations of both art and artists. The author ends with a challenge to the Christian artist to "live and labor in the shadow of an enduring beauty that is the shadow of Almighty."

This is a book that will grow in your mind. It begins as a broad river urging you on to find the deep channel. As he explores many tributaries, you find that they flow ultimately from one true source, the only constant of the universe, God himself. He is truth. He is beauty. And we will find our deepest satisfaction and joy in him.

You are in for an awesome journey.

—Dr. Pete Deison, pastor, Churchwide Ministries
at Park Cities Presbyterian Church,
author of *The Priority of Knowing God,* and teacher

# PREFACE

I have loved art since childhood, but I sometimes thought it to be frivolous compared to other useful and respectable occupations that I might have otherwise considered. My father, Marden Brown, was a World War II veteran who was too preoccupied with the needs of his family to see his own greatness. My mother, Lois, indulged my dreams of being an artist, even though they must have seemed strange to her at times. My parents never disparaged my calling, but I had my doubts. My parents saw difficult times, surviving the Depression and World War II. Their generation made great contributions to a free and prosperous society.

I imagine our ancestors laying the fruit of their life's work at the feet of our Lord—the amazing inventions of industry, the just laws of magistrates, the crowns of conquered tyrants, the testimonies of martyrs, the great polemics of churchmen, and the souls of millions. So it is with great humility that an artist may approach the throne of our Lord with what seems to be a small gift—a thing of beauty.

My father did not want me to follow in his footsteps. He wanted me to chart my own course, and art was fine with him. I had an intuitive sense of the importance of art, but by my college years, I craved a more logical affirmation of my labors as an artist. As a young Christian, I wanted biblical evidence of some enduring good in the labors of my hands and a logical assurance of art's worthiness as a God-honoring career. This book represents the result of my decades-long effort to find that assurance.

I offer a philosophy of aesthetics that is largely informed by the ideals of the Protestant Reformation. However, those who are not persuaded by reformed views should find something of practical value in this book. All Bible quotations are taken from the New King James Version. I have chosen this translation for its literary quality, its consistently good translation, and its agreement with the Greek-majority-text type.

# INTRODUCTION

I wrote this book as a biblical apologetic for the spiritual value of art and its role of preserving the enduring beauty of a Christian culture. My primary goal for this book is to persuade church leaders, theologians, and Christian artists of the need for an aggressive mission to reestablish the church's rightful influence on culture and to view the arts as a distinct ministry of the church. My secondary goal for this book is to encourage a conversation among Christians regarding the distinct and illuminating philosophy of aesthetics that may be found in the Bible. Any knowledgeable student of the Bible can take you to a verse or two that has something inspiring to say about beauty, but many Christians do not think of the Bible as an abundant source of commentary on the subject of aesthetics. I hope that this book can change that view for more than a few people.

I believe that the ministry of art—rightly directed—has the power to vindicate and preserve the culture of Christianity as an indispensable foundation of a free society. Some of what we may learn from the Bible regarding the nature of the ministry of art gives us reason to believe that our generation is not likely to see a spiritual revival until we see a cultural revival. The wisdom of a free society will always be preserved in the pages of books and in the hearts of a remnant of God's people. But without the arts, an enlightened civilization will not be long preserved among the majority of people.

It is the desire of every conscientious artist and craftsman to understand the real worth of his labors. When an artist compares his work to the tangible accomplishments of other fields of endeavor, he can often feel inconsequential. Art can seem frivolous, and yet God has judged whole societies over matters that pertain to art. In Daniel 5, God had Belshazzar killed and his kingdom divided for desecrating the temple artifacts. Also, God devastated the Philistines over their sacrilege of capturing the Ark of the Covenant and setting it before the graven image of their god. (See 1 Samuel 4:10–7:3.) In the Holy Scriptures, God has regulated art and has lavished his people with art. God has appointed artists to direct the production of sacred art. God has used art to instruct and inspire his people, as in the sacred dramas of the Passover, the Levitical ceremonies, and the Feast of Booths. God has used art as a means of grace and of true worship in his use of sacred music and the temple and its furnishings. God has used art to preserve the legacy and substance of true religion, as in the reforms of Hezekiah. God has used art as an instrument of mercy and of judgment, as in the plague sent to the Philistines after they captured the ark, or the bronze serpent that Moses lifted up in the wilderness to heal the children of Israel from the bite of the serpent and, of course, the tabernacle services of atonement. The church must not neglect the arts because art can be a powerful spiritual force for good or evil, and if the church does not harness its potential for good, it will be a force for evil. That is because art has a powerful allure and can easily be used to exploit the corrupt desires of people.

Art is a God-appointed ministry, and those who keep watch over the souls of men should exercise a responsible stewardship of the arts. Yet understanding art from a biblical perspective requires a journey through a constellation of other ideas and principles that relate to the concept of beauty as expressed in the Holy Scriptures. Before one undertakes such a journey, a word of warning is in order: A proper study of the essence of beauty will lead us to confront the most formidable demons of human existence. Solomon, who sought a logical basis for beauty and meaning, found none that could stand in the existential context of mere finite humanity. Pleasure became an illusion, and he could never return to the hedonistic gratification that he enjoyed while in his former state of ignorance. Those who zealously guard their ignorance need not face such unsettling issues in this life. However, with wisdom comes grief. The biblical paradigm is a bitter pill to the mind of fallen man, but it is far more desirable than the deadly alternative. Joy is possible with wisdom, but only on God's terms.

This is perhaps the most important aspect of art's ministry to humanity. Fine art defies any excuse for its existence other than its value as a thing of beauty. It challenges us to grapple with the foreboding question of why something is beautiful. By doing so, it ultimately forces us to ask why *anything* is beautiful. Those who take the issue lightly will surely be taken off guard if they pursue that question to its logical end.

Art as an expression of beauty is also an illuminator of the truth that is foundational to beauty. The most important thing art teaches us is that we are creatures made in God's image. A mouse would as soon live in a rusty can as in a beautiful vase. The fact that we humans value one over the other has to do with our unique nature as creatures made in God's image. The Bible provides for us a view of culture and humanity that supports a logical reason for believing in beauty. Art is the full flower of culture, and culture is an order of values and beliefs that involves every conceivable aspect of human existence. No proper study of art's purposes can be confined to art any more than a gardener can study only blossoms. To raise a beautiful flower, the gardener must tend to the whole plant. He must care about its leaves, its stems, its roots, its soil, its seasons, and its preferred climate. Whether consciously or unconsciously, the artist draws from multiple aspects of culture that inspire the full expression of beauty. In the same way, anyone who desires to understand the purpose of art must first understand the culture from which it grows.

There is a shadow of enduring beauty—a body of things held sacred—that a people must possess in order to maintain a free society. It is the same, I believe, for a people who would hear and believe the gospel in great numbers. There is a foundation of enlightened thought that inspires us to be free from tyranny, including the tyranny of sin. It is the proper role of the arts to create a desire for freedom and a culture in which the hope of redemption becomes palpable. It is for this reason that we see in the ministry of Christ a distinct preparatory period. John the Baptist came to prepare the way of the Lord, and Christ himself spoke in parables to prepare the hearts of men for the gospel that spread like wildfire after Christ ascended. The Messiah changed the culture before he changed the hearts of millions.

I, like most Christians, find great personal value in the writings of Christian authors, but the culture around us continues to decline. Neither this book nor a thousand others will ever mean much to the overall culture apart from the labor of God's people called to action by the unction of the Holy Spirit. For this reason, I regard this book and others like it as a small part of a larger mission of God's people to make a real change in the culture. As one who strongly believes in the divine unction of Christ's church, I have resolved to stir up her duly ordained leaders and invite scrutiny. Any protagonist of ideas should embrace accountability. Art is a mission field, and I hope that church leaders will feel compelled to assess my stewardship in this mission at some point. Perhaps, then, they may also be compelled to act.

Those who would investigate these things from outside the covenant community are most welcome to do so, but what they will find in these pages may largely depend on what they are willing to lose. The Bible offers a reason for the existence of beauty and meaning, but these reasons are only possible in the context of an overall worldview that the predominant culture of our time is sure to find offensive. Let the seekers of truth consider carefully what the truth is worth and what price is acceptable. Let those who are willing loosen their grip on illusions most precious to the mind of fallen man in all of us. Then let them proceed with their quest for a reason to believe in beauty. The spiritual voice that can lead us is willing to be heard, but is the destination worth all that must be cast aside in order to follow it? Yes, it is.

# THE VOICE
## WE FOLLOW

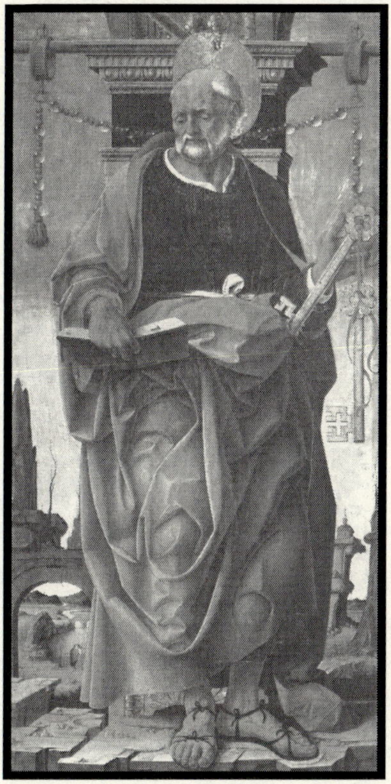

Fig. 1, Francesco Del Cossa, *Saint Peter,* c. 1472

The character and confession of the Apostle Peter illustrates both the true nature of faith and the only sound foundation for true spiritual authority. After the hard sayings of Jesus had driven away many followers, Jesus asked his apostles, "Do you also want to go away?"

Peter answered, "Lord, to whom shall we go? You have

the words of eternal life" (John 6:67–68). The word of truth is revealed in the heart of the devoted seeker. The voice he must follow is clear, and that voice led Peter to declare, "You are the Christ" (Matthew 16:16). For this, Jesus gave him a name that means "rock," saying, "Upon this rock I will build my church" (Matthew 16:18). Del Cossa depicts Peter standing upon a rock. Peter holds in his hands the keys of the kingdom and the book of God's written Word. The power of the keys is apostolic authority, and the book is the unfailing word of revelation. Peter possesses the efficacious power of faith and the solid foundation of all that is knowable and beautiful.

Whatever is pleasing to behold, to hear, or to experience is that which in one sense or another we may call beauty. It is by the light of truth that we perceive the end of all beauty. There is a sort of beauty that is vain and another sort of beauty that is authentic and enduring. To distinguish between the two is a discipline of the mind and of faith to perceive the ultimate end of that which we would call beauty. Therefore, the pursuit of ultimate beauty—that which engenders an ultimate and eternal good for the life and pleasure of mankind—is in reality the pursuit of truth. If the search for enduring beauty is the search for truth, how is truth itself knowable?

In the words of Anselm, "I believe that I may know," is found what many hold to be the only sound foundation for the pursuit of truth. The late Cornelius Van Til taught in the same tradition that without believing in God, one cannot logically believe in anything else. God is the "all-conditioner" who has given us an implicit covenant of reliable order. Thus, we may take natural revelation at face value, assured by faith of the firm boundaries of natural law and of spiritual truth, which is the root of all beauty and wisdom.

Yet simply believing in God is not enough. Believing in God is only useful to us in our search for truth if we also believe that

God has established immutable laws that govern his creation, and that we may discover those laws and trust in their constancy. What if the observable constants of our existence were mere illusions that could be revoked at any time as a sort of elaborate divine joke on humanity? Without faith in God's sovereignty, belief in God would be no better than unbelief as a certain foundation of truth or ultimate beauty.

There is, then, a two-sided premise, which is foundational to all things knowable, and it may be described as follows: (1) there is an all-conditioner (God), and (2) it is God's desire to make his divine order known to us, being earnestly committed to the universal order that he allows us to observe. While this two-sided premise—faith in God and his covenant of constancy—provides us a logical basis for demanding a commitment to evidence in the pursuit of all other truth, it is absurd to subject the premise itself to the test of evidence. Apart from the two-sided premise, evidence itself cannot exist. Apart from the two-sided premise, nothing at all is either knowable or meaningful. If we do not presuppose that God is and that he desires to reveal his truth to us, then logic, order, beauty, meaning, and truth are all rendered nonexistent before our search for any of the above has even begun. Faith in God precedes logic, and those who seek the truth must proceed on that premise. In the language of the epistle to the Hebrews, "He who comes to God must believe that he is and that he is a rewarder of those who diligently seek him" (Hebrews 11:6). This is our guarantor of constancy through which all that is beautiful may be known and through which all that is knowable may be found.

This view is the theology of Dr. Cornelius Van Til. My first introduction to Dr. Van Til's theology was through my Christian friends in college. The chapter leaders of Intervarsity Christian Fellowship arranged for him to come and lecture. As I spoke with Dr. Van Til on topics of theology, I began to see a side of him that is under-represented in his writings. Through the influence of friends, I was becoming enamored with the divines of the Reformation, and Dr. Van Til helped that process along. I wanted to immerse myself in the Reformation culture as much as possible in the twentieth century. Dr. Cornelius Van Til seemed to be a perfect balance of intellect, devotion, and passion.

When someone suggested the classical training of Pennsylvania Academy of Fine Art, I was sold on two levels. I wanted the classical discipline of the oldest art academy in the Western Hemisphere. But more than that, I wanted to become a part of a spiritual community that could produce a man like Cornelius Van Til. I would greet him as "Dr. Van Til," but he later insisted on being called "Casey." My contact with Casey led me into his circle of Christian friends. I became involved with some of the compassion ministries of Dr. John Skilton, who lived in my neighborhood. He became somewhat of a mentor to me, and he, like Casey, preferred not to be called "doctor," and so I called him "John."

John was a retired Westminster Seminary professor. He used his inner-city row house as a base of operation for a number of mercy ministries. He named it Skilton House after his parents. He also hosted a weekly dinner with a Bible study and hymn singing. Skilton House would be packed with a very diverse group of people, and John treated every guest with the same high standard of hospitality. Casey would show up at the Skilton House meetings regularly. During the hymn singing, Casey often requested the children's hymn "Jesus Loves Me" because the lyrics reflect his theology. All knowledge and assurance is from God. We can only have it through childlike faith, trusting God to lead us to all truth. Casey believed that there was no such thing as evidence of anything without first believing in God.

John shared this view with his longtime friend Casey, and he had his own way of explaining it. I once related to John a point that somebody had made regarding Casey's concept of the "all-conditioner" and its importance to the existence of science. John instantly took up the role of a venerable old professor, speaking eloquently regarding the nature of the covenant of Noah. He gesticulated in his characteristic style, moving his hands in a symmetrical fashion, as if conducting a choir, and quoted a passage from Genesis: "As long as the earth endures, seedtime and harvest, cold and heat, summer and winter, day and night will never cease" (Genesis 8:22).

John explained, "Now there is a foundation upon which laws of science can be established." The point, as I took it, is that an assurance of the constancy of seasons is not all God gave to Noah. The larger truth is that there is a reliable order of God's creation that God himself has established with a promise. Embedded in the explicit promises of God's covenant with Noah is an implicit covenant of constancy that precedes all of science. We must believe in the ability and desire of a sovereign God to establish constancy before we can begin to have any logical assurance of the constancy of the laws of physics.

Isaac Newton once said, "In the absence of any other proof, the thumb alone would convince me of God's existence." Yet in his masterwork *Principia,* Newton seems to recognize that evidence is useless without an implicit trust in the sovereignty of God. He says:

> We have ideas of his attributes, but what the real substance of any thing is we know not. In bodies, we see only their figures and colours, we hear only the sounds, we touch only their outward surfaces, we smell only the smells, and taste the savours; but their inward substances are not to be known either by our senses, or by any reflex act of our minds: much less, then, have we any idea of the substance of God. We know him only by his most wise and excellent contrivances of things, and final cause: we admire him for his perfections;

> but we reverence and adore him on account of his dominion: for we adore him as his servants; and a god without dominion, providence, and final causes, is nothing else but Fate and Nature.[1]

All that is knowable comes to us through faith in the implicit covenant of constancy and the divine assurance that leads us to trust in the laws that he has established for our world. So we listen for that voice to follow, knowing that this voice must make itself known to us or there can be nothing of goodness, truth, meaning, logic, or beauty in anything. We accept by faith in this implicit covenant that the basic laws of physics may not at any time be suspended by a momentary intrusion of a fifth or sixth dimension into our well-ordered world. By faith in this implicit covenant we are skeptical of the tales of spontaneous human combustion, levitation, magical transformation of elements, objects passing through each other, or any other strange phenomena one may expect to read about on the cover of some tabloid. The guarantor of constancy makes it possible for us to observe and to trust the laws (constants) he has established. Yet in addition to forming the basis of true science, this also implies that supernatural intervention does have a place somewhere beyond the realm of human understanding. For the guarantor of constancy cannot guarantee anything over which he has no absolute control, and to exercise absolute control over natural law is, by definition, supernatural. Therefore, while it is good theology to seek out natural explanations, it is bad science to rule out whatever explanation may seem to cross the boundaries of natural law. After all, the role of our supernatural guarantor of constancy is essential to the logical certainty of natural law.

Thus, our supernatural guarantor of constancy makes science possible. Also, let us never forget that the boundaries of credibility constantly change. How is science to advance the boundaries of credibility if it denies the very existence of the incredible? How shall we bring that which is incredible into the realm of credibility with new understanding? How shall the highest and most ultimate beauty knowable to man be realized unless we first believe that it may be found?

Our training and cultural indoctrination has made us creatures religiously committed to credibility, but the integrity of scientific scrutiny or artistic pursuit is surrendered at the very point where this commitment becomes obsession. If the biblical worldview seems incredible to some, perhaps it is because the Bible yields nothing to the cultural preferences of contemporary culture. Modern man accepts as reality all that can be perceived with or deduced from the senses. The Bible lays a deeper foundation for truth in which all things knowable are based on the fact of God's role as Creator and a logical construction of reality that is ultimately based on faith. The overarching concern of all Scripture is to teach mankind the walk of faith not of sight so that our world of cognition may not be limited by the narrow walls of perception or even by the slightly less narrow walls of that which we may imagine.

The logician perceives truth not only through what is sensible but also through what can be deduced or imagined. The man of faith believes in a reality that often cannot be sensed, deduced, or imagined. The people of God rest their faith on something far more reliable than the senses or the imagination. That is the guarantor of constancy. Faith in this guarantor of constancy is the foundation of all truth. Faith in this guarantor is not merely logical but is essential to the existence of a logical conclusion regarding anything at all.

All faith must be tested if it is to be found spurious or sound. Truth is not to be feared, for truth is the only logical alternative to fear. Truth itself is sacred. Subverting or denying any truth—religious or scientific—is a form of idolatry. God has ordered his creation to reveal himself to us, and truth itself is one of God's attributes. To shun truth, therefore, is to shun the true God as he chooses to reveal himself and to invent, in our mind, a very different god. That is idolatry. Ultimately, all verity is an act of faith, and understanding the nature of faith as the foundation to all truth is our essential beginning in understanding the nature of beauty and culture and of our purpose for being.

In ancient Gnostic traditions, some aspects of divine truth were considered knowable to only a few persons. Those who were privy to this secret body of knowledge presumed themselves to be members of a higher spiritual class. This secret knowledge was carefully guarded and was not to be disclosed to uninitiated persons who were not considered wise enough to understand and use the gnosis properly.

The Bible repudiates this idea, as it pertains to the realm of basic spiritual truth. The essential principles of righteousness and the basic knowledge of who God is and who we are as creatures made in his image are revealed to all people by the light of nature.

In the words of the Apostle Paul, "Since the creation of the world his invisible attributes are clearly seen, being understood by the things that are made, even his eternal power and Godhead, so that they are without excuse" (Romans 1:19–20).

God clearly reveals himself to all mankind, but mankind suppresses the truth through the effects of sin. The theologian is no more privy to the essential truths of God than any other individual is. His primary role as a theologian is to overcome the spiritual noise of darkness and confusion so that the seed of truth known to all should rise up and penetrate the consciences of those who become futile in their thoughts. Therefore, true theological reasoning has nothing to do with discovering unknown truths. Rather, it is a process by which spiritual leaders evoke the power of exhortation to do battle with the forces of spiritual darkness. It is taking to task those who would, in Paul's words, "suppress the truth in unrighteousness" (Romans 1:18). This is an important service, yet it is not for every person to examine the volumes of intricate theological arguments. This is tedious work, and although one may benefit from the spiritual goading that such a discipline may provide, it is the fear of God, not intellectual prowess, to which all mankind is universally called. In the words found in the book of Ecclesiastes:

> The words of the wise are like goads, and the words of scholars are like well driven nails, given by one Shepherd. And further, my son, be admonished by these. Of making many books there is no end, and much study is wearisome to the flesh. Let us hear the conclusion of the whole matter: "fear God and keep his commandments, for this is the whole duty of man. For God will bring every work into judgment, including every secret thing whether it is good or whether it is evil."
>
> Ecclesiastes 12:11–14

So any firm foundation for culture is based ultimately on faith in God, who speaks to us through his law.

If this is the nature of God's truth, the godless intellectual will never be as close to the truth as the simple man who simply fears God. While it is not for every individual to ponder vast volumes of tedious theological exposition, it *is* for every person to fear God and keep his commandments, for "the fear of the Lord is the beginning of wisdom" (Proverbs 1:7).

Jesus states this principle in the form of a promise: "If anyone wills to do his will, he shall know concerning the doctrine, whether it is from God or whether I speak on my own authority" (John 7:17).

Every individual has an inward sense of good as long as he

seeks God's will. Conversely, it is sin—not a lack of information—that makes us intellectually committed to error, as we have seen eloquently expressed in Paul's epistle to the Romans. Sin obscures the light of natural revelation, and if we are without excuse because of natural revelation, we must conclude that such basic enlightenment proceeds from a heart obedient to God and not mere academic investigation. The theologian may acquire a superior knowledge of history, literature, commentary, and theological jargon. Yet apart from a simple willingness to love and obey God, he has no advantage in perceiving the essential truths of God. The redeemed will of the heart, not the intellect, is the key to perceiving the divine light of true doctrine. It is also the key to discerning true and ultimate beauty because ultimate beauty is the expression of ultimate good.

If truth is the foundation of beauty, then the artist—as the purveyor of beauty—must exercise a role that corresponds to that of the doctor of the law. Bad aesthetic judgment, like bad doctrine, is a manifestation of the overall moral corruption of humanity.

The Mosaic Law forbade a number of "abominable" things that modern society would be quick to pigeonhole as a matter of purely aesthetic judgment. Our disgust for something of poor taste arises from a sense of moral offensiveness. That which offends our aesthetic sensibilities does so because it reveals an island of spiritual darkness. The dynamics of creative expression affect our general progress toward or against the ultimate good. The people of God must test all opinions while seeking God's face, confessing sin, calling upon his grace, and imploring him to remove the secret idols erected in the hearts of humanity, which beguile and obstruct their vision of the truth.

This is what it means to acknowledge that the fear of the Lord is the beginning of wisdom and the foundation of all beauty. The fear of the Lord will not necessarily give us greater skill in explaining or teaching Scripture. It will, however, lead us to believe the truth for reasons that are as sound as the most able scholar may articulate. The doctor of the law is not distinguished by any secret gnosis of truth, but by his ability to defend the truth. Similarly, the artist is not distinguished by any inherently superior sense of beauty but only to clarify that which is beautiful. God's truth and beauty are known to all who seek them even if commonly suppressed. This principle appears in the first epistle of John: "But you have an anointing from the Holy One, and you know all things. I have not written to you because you do not know the truth, but because you know it, and that no lie is of the truth" (1 John 2:20–22).

The Bible is a small book compared with the vast library of inevitable implications that it raises. These implications may be hidden in the hearts of God's people, but they will have an influence upon those who set their hearts to seek God's face. And it is these things that the theologian brings to light. In the words of Jesus, "Every scribe instructed concerning the kingdom of heaven is like a householder who brings out of his treasure things new and old" (Matthew 13:52). Treasures, such as those kept in storerooms, most likely had aesthetic as well as monetary value. Coins and bullion may have been kept safely hidden in the ground, as was the custom in ancient days. Christ speaks of treasures that can be eaten by moths (cloth) and that are subject to rust (iron). The use of such objects of interest to be taken out and shown to others implies a value that is at least partly aesthetic. People do not generally show off common legal tender. This use of art treasures as an analogy of God's various instructions from the law is consistent with the manner in which craft and wisdom are correlated elsewhere in the Bible (see Exodus 31:3 and Proverbs 8:31). The teacher of the law is a lover of wisdom who imparts wisdom to others. In substance, the ministry of the artist is no different from the doctor of the law. Both are ministers of the truth, but the artist ministers the truth in its purest form—beauty.

The teacher of the law must reinforce truths that are already recognized while elucidating those still suppressed in the mind of the hearer. Similarly, the artist must celebrate the beauty that is seen and must also unveil that which is largely unseen. According to the Westminster Divines, the theologian brings forth not only those things expressly stated in Scripture but also those things that "by good and necessary consequence may be deduced from Scripture."[2] But here the seeker of truth must be cautious. Not everything that is to be found in our hearts is inspired by our internal knowledge of God's law. Two opposing voices seek to persuade us, and the purveyor of wisdom can bring out of his storeroom not just the true treasures of the kingdom, but also the ancient household idols. It is ludicrous for the theologian or the artist to claim any exclusive powers of discernment between truth and idolatry, for the willing hearer of truth is fully equipped to discern ultimate truth for himself according to the promise of God (John 7:17). And the simple man who seeks to obey God will discern the ultimate truth as well as any scholar.

When the full counsel of God's revelation is heard and our reasons for knowing truth and cherishing beauty are sorted out, we will find that art plays an important role in the process of sifting out spiritual truth. It is our view of ultimate truth that shapes our appreciation of creation's whole and pleasant forms.

It is the role of spiritual leaders to enlighten us in the knowledge of ultimate truth, which is our perception of beauty. Where do our spiritual leaders get their authority? Where does the Church get her authority? Why is Scripture more authoritative than the Church? Some divines have argued that the Church gives the Bible its authority. But this view is logically untenable since it represents a circular view of what is knowable as ultimate good. Authority is merely the credible witness to truth, and all truth that is knowable must be founded on previously established truth. A foundation for truth cannot be built upon itself alone. For this reason, the reformers held that Scripture's authority is internally evidenced to the individual through the illumination of the Holy Spirit and that every individual is responsible to God for laying hold of God's revealed truth.

This pathway of enlightenment implies a great deal regarding the potential power of art, either as an ally or enemy in our ongoing battle for the cause of truth. Art was used to that end in the ceremonial law. Art has also been a powerful force for evil and has often come in the form of an idol. In art, as in doctrine, one may conclude that we are safer to trust the judgment of more expert guides. Still, it is we who must judge if those guides are worthy of the trust that we place in them. We look to our spiritual leaders to keep watch over our souls. Unless we presume to judge our guide's credentials and competence at some point, we have no alternative but to follow—like imprinted ducklings—the first relatively large, moving authoritarian who happens to pass our way making some claim to authority. This authoritarian may be a false prophet or a true prophet, a man of God or an antichrist, a sincere man or a charlatan. None of this would matter apart from individual judgment. Our measure of faithfulness would be based on how well we follow—not *whom* we follow.

Now, consider our pursuit of ultimate good in context with what has been said regarding discernment and authority, and let the Christian artist consider the implications of these things with regard to his search for a biblical philosophy of aesthetics. First, there is no secret gnosis among the people of God. Second, the duty and power of discerning truth belongs to all men—not just to the doctor of the law or the craftsman who creates a thing of beauty. And third, the teacher of divine truth is distinguished only in explaining the truth, not in discerning it. It is ultimately this internal light of truth that sets the Bible apart as authoritative. There can be no higher authority to interpret the Scriptures than God's own voice speaking to the hearts of those who seek him. The highest vindication of orthodoxy is the general consensus of God's elect. The doctors of the law may express the Bible's authority in eloquent terms, but they have no special authority to determine it as authoritative. Beauty, like authority, may not be established by decree. The responsible truth seeker will recognize a thing of beauty based on his worldview and value structure. This is the inevitable principle contained in the words of Christ, spoken in the manner and context of a promise: "If anyone wills to do his will, he shall know concerning the doctrine, whether it is from God or whether I speak on my own authority" (John 7:17). Any individual who sincerely desires to do God's will has better authority to judge truth than some intellectual giant who does not truly seek the will of God in his heart. Christ repudiated the spiritual darkness of the religious authorities of his day while commending words of truth uttered from the most unlikely sources such as a former prostitute, a Roman soldier, a penitent thief, and an impulsive fisherman named Simon.

The knowledge of ultimate good is the gift of the all-important illumination of the Holy Spirit in the hearts of willing recipients. No elite group of scholars may claim any monopoly upon this knowledge of good. The Holy Spirit is the only indispensable factor that enables sinners to discern the God likeness (his law) that is engraved on our souls, bearing witness to the truth of the written Word. The words of the *Westminster Larger Catechism* express it beautifully:

> The Scriptures manifest themselves to be the word of God, by their majesty and purity; by the consent of all the parts, and the scope of the whole which is to give glory to God; by their light and power to convince and convert sinners, to comfort and build up believers unto salvation: But the Spirit

> of God bearing witness by and with the Scriptures in the heart of man, is alone able fully to persuade it that they are the very word of God.[3]

But this witness of the Spirit to the souls of individuals implies nothing against the concept of well-defined doctrinal standards, or of clear aesthetic standards in art, or of organized religion in general. If anything, it only obviates the need for the organic unity of God's people and for its courts and committed leaders.

Walking in the truth is not a discipline that is learned from the bare facts of doctrine. It is a discipline that comes from having good leaders to exhort, reprove, and lift us up when we fall. We do not need the doctors of the law because we are ignorant of the truth but only because we are reluctant to acknowledge the truth and to walk in it. Nor do we need artists because of anyone's inability to discern beauty but to amplify a form of enduring beauty that is sensible to all who do not suppress wisdom's instruction. Our moral leaders in the church are approved by what individuals recognize as truth in the Holy Scriptures. Therefore, the Scriptures must be a higher authority than any ecclesiastical court. Christians will differ in their reasons for believing that Scripture is without error, and these reasons involve important issues. But for the purpose of judging any church's claim to ecclesiastical authority, it is enough simply to know that the apostolic church acknowledges that the Scriptures are without error. For if the church acknowledges something that is false, that reflects upon the church. But if the Scriptures are without error, the church must submit to them. Either way, the church must be judged by what she embraces as truth. Thus, the preeminent authority of Scripture is inevitable, for the Scriptures cannot be contradicted without contradicting the church.

Scripture's own authority, however, will neither stand nor fall on the judgment and approbation of the church or of any human court. Scripture speaks to the hearts of men. Errors of later councils cannot be used to diminish the credibility of the Scriptures because the Scriptures do not endorse or embrace the teachings of future councils but rather explicitly disavow all teaching contrary to it. This includes the teaching of those who would arise from within the leadership of the church (see Acts 20:28–31). If Scripture is true, one must believe that Scripture is the final authority, or one cannot logically believe that the church has any authority at all.

The authority of Scripture demands ultimate allegiance. Those who are called to follow human authority must judge that authority as worthy of being followed. Scripture lays this responsibility at the feet of every individual. Every authority or pretender to authority must appeal to the judgment of individuals if only to convince individuals to defer to greater authority. Thus, eliminating individual judgment is impossible, for even excessive reliance on outside human authority is itself a choice based on individual judgment. Unquestioning acquiescence to human authority is that beautiful gate and broad way that leads to hell. In this case the basis of judgment is shifted from the promise of God received by an obedient heart to a misplaced trust in a Gnostic-like tradition. It is perverse to discourage private judgment. The job of a spiritual leader is to instruct individuals in the principles of sound moral judgment. One of the most important of these principles is the humility to understand the limits of individual judgment and to know how to recognize those who can lead us better where our own judgment fails. We can say that this involves faith, but what kind of faith? There is the true faith, and there is a worthless faith. We must distinguish here too. Faith in the one true God is one thing, and it is vindicated by conscience. Faith in man or in any other lesser god is another thing; it is idolatry.

Choosing the voice we follow may seem to entail a precarious balance of judgments. However, although sin has obscured human judgment somewhat, it is not so difficult for the genuine truth seeker. God has given the truth seeker some reliable signs in big print, which can be read even by the dim eyes of fallen humanity. These signs clearly distinguish good leaders from blind guides. Jesus teaches, "You will know them by their fruits" (Matthew 7:16). One who has no real desire for righteousness can never be a reliable guide for others, no matter how much he may know. If someone is incompetent to teach the truth, perhaps it is because he has rejected the truth himself. Ignorance can be the product of simply ignoring the truth, for with regard to the knowledge of divine truth, the root of ignorance is to ignore something that is clearly revealed.

The summary of scriptural council regarding the voice we should follow appears to be this: good spiritual leaders are as useful as bad leaders are dangerous. No single person's judgment—including one's own—should be trusted too much. Because of the subtle guile of sin, the vindicators of truth must be many and persuasive, demonstrating a wisdom that is vindicated by deeds. One should honor and value those leaders who articulate the truth well and who are known by their good fruit. We should seek God's Word in their words. Even though good spiritual leaders are fallible, they must never be dismissed lightly or capriciously. And even when they are wrong, they must be respected. God will use them to lead us notwithstanding. If we submit to God in faith with a whole heart, we will know the proper place of leaders, of conscience, and of individual judgment. In the end we will not fail to receive God's truth. But a word of caution applies even here. We must be willing to receive God as he reveals himself and not some god of our own invention. We must seek the God who is however he may choose to reveal himself. It is anyone's good pleasure to see God as a loving father, but it is the hard discipline of the people of God to also acknowledge God as a holy judge whose wrath and eternal damnation we deserve as sinners.

Judging what is knowable with regard to the voice we choose to follow is essentially the same walk of faith whether one is looking for that body of spiritual knowledge called aesthetic truth or for spiritual knowledge in general. Those we chose to follow must speak in a voice that we recognize as that of our creator who makes himself know to us. There is, ultimately, no way to relegate the entire weight of this responsibility to any higher authority, either as artists or as Christians. We are all personally responsible to search out the truth. All pretenders to absolute spiritual authority must be summarily dismissed.

# THE FOUNDATION **OF BEAUTY**

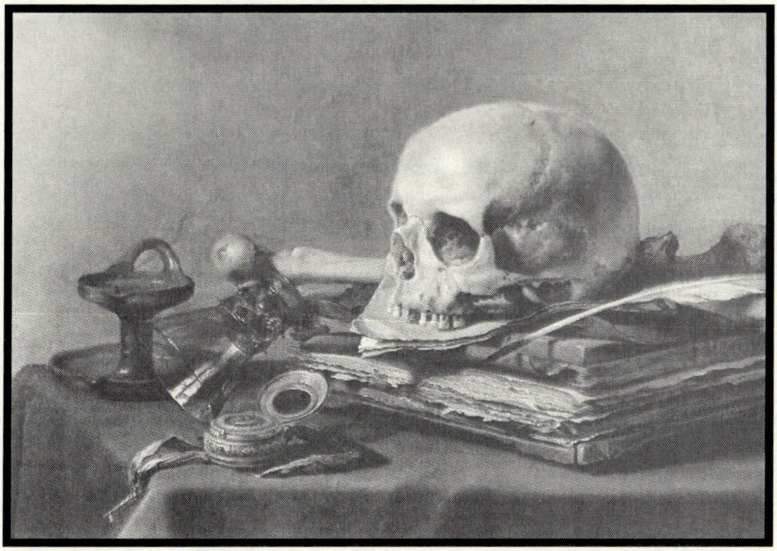

Fig. 4, Pieter Claesz, *Vanitas*, 1630

A *vanitas* is a traditional form of still-life painting that contains certain poignant reminders of the message of the book of Ecclesiastes. In the *vanitas* by Pieter Claesz, the book and the ink font represent knowledge and wisdom. The skull represents the shared fate of the fool and the wise man. It is a reminder of the uselessness of wisdom in the worldview of the godless. Life's lamp is snuffed out. The splendid wineglass is inverted and empty. The single key represents earthly treasures once closely guarded. These are all the elements of vanity with no beauty and meaning apart from God's eternal purpose.

There is a season appointed by God for all things, and God makes everything beautiful in its season (Ecclesiastes 3:11). The decrees of God are the basis of all beauty. We participate in God's eternal purpose by obedience to God's revealed will, which is his law. If God makes all things beautiful in his season and God's season is in turn revealed in God's law, then the law is a compass for beauty as well as morality. The conclusion of Ecclesiastes is, "Fear God and keep his commandments" (Ecclesiastes. 12:13). This is our essential basis for the discernment of beauty. The Bible speaks of wisdom as the expression of beauty and order in God's works of creation. Wisdom is also the expression of man's works of creation. Craftiness is the essence of craft. God said of Bezaleel:

> I have filled him with the Spirit of God, in wisdom, in understanding, in knowledge, and in all manner of workmanship, to design artistic works, to work in gold, in silver, in bronze, in cutting jewels for setting, in carving wood, and to work in all manner of workmanship.
>
> Exodus 31:3–4

This endowment of wisdom from the Holy Spirit to create artistic works is mentioned several other times in Exodus. Scripture again associates wisdom with skill and artistry in Proverbs 8 where wisdom describes herself as a master craftsman saying, "And I (Wisdom) was beside him (God) as a master craftsman; and I was daily his delight, rejoicing always before him" (Proverbs 8:31). Now, wisdom is the sense of order and that awareness of ultimate and eternal good that promotes the cause of life and beauty. Wisdom, like beauty itself, has an essential foundation in the order of creation, which is conspicuously set forth in the law. Scripture declares, "Behold, the fear of the Lord, that is wisdom, and to depart from evil is understanding" (Job 28:28). The basis of beauty and of wisdom is God's law. The artistic expression of beauty is the expression of ultimate good. Art, therefore, is the expression of wisdom. Beauty is closely related to wisdom and law and cannot properly be understood without first understanding the nature of wisdom and of God's law. And from here the study of the nature of beauty can easily lead the serious student into a wide range of other topics. Beauty relates to the nature of our Creator and his creation. It relates to the nature of man as one created in the image of the Creator and to man's fall from the divine order of creation. It relates to the nature of revelation and of redemption. All of these relate, in turn, to principles that govern our perception of beauty. So an in-depth study of art is a study of many other things in relation, which is why an in-depth study of aesthetics can seem so confounding. That which a culture perceives as beautiful is influenced by its beliefs or attitudes concerning all of the above. That perception is, in turn, governed by man's view of himself, his Creator, and his place in creation. Art is the distilled essence of culture and can be studied in context with every aspect of culture. It can inspire areas of investigation that could fill libraries. It is a study that demands context, or it will forever elude understanding. One might as reasonably strip a rosebud of its roots, branches, leaves, and soil and expect it to bloom.

*Beauty* is a word used often enough in Scripture. But what can we learn from Scripture about the nature of beauty itself? This is the question that is best answered in Solomon's statement, "He has made everything beautiful in its time" (Ecclesiastes 3:11). This indicates something of the origin of beauty, does it not? But consider the compelling reasoning that precedes this statement: "'Vanity of vanities,' says the Preacher; 'Vanity of vanities, all is vanity.' What profit has a man from all his labor in which he toils under the sun? One generation passes away, and another generation comes; but the earth abides forever" (Ecclesiastes 1:1–4). Vanity is manifested in the passing of generations. Nothing man does is of any consequence because it has no lasting advantage. All is swept into a vast natural cycle that is ultimately uninfluenced by man's coming and going. The cycle is eternal and infinite. Man, by contrast, is transient and finite. Man's life and everything he does is destined to become utterly inconsequential, absorbed into the endless ocean of nature's indifferent and unstoppable cycle. Solomon writes:

> The sun also rises, and the sun goes down, and hastens to the place where it arose. The wind goes toward the south, and turns around to the north; the wind whirls about continually, and comes again on its circuit. All the rivers run into the sea, yet the sea is not full; to the place from which the rivers come, there they return again. All things are full of labor; man cannot express it. The eye is not satisfied with seeing, nor the ear filled with hearing. That which has been is what will be, that which is done is what will be done, and there is nothing new under the sun. Is there anything of which it may be said, "See, this is new?" It has already been in ancient times before us. There is no remembrance of former things, nor will there be any remembrance of things that are to come by those who will come after.
>
> Ecclesiastes 1:3–11

Solomon renounces the value of every accomplishment that is eventually forgotten. Conversely, as we see later in Ecclesiastes, Solomon attributes the essence of beauty to things of eternal consequence. But this is a contingency that Solomon has not yet introduced. Meanwhile, the existential monotony described above has hatched a profound sense of futility and dissatisfaction. Note the nature of Solomon's lament. There is no inherent joy or satisfaction to be found in anything that is seen or heard in all this vast ocean of existence. The reason is based on the premise that there is no lasting remembrance of anything. Solomon also reminds us that he is speaking from the vantage point of a king who has vast resources for investigating the meaning of existence. This is to assure those of lesser station—everyone—that there is not the slightest hope of finding meaning in our finite existence. Solomon declares that he was a king over Israel, and with that in mind, he says:

> And I set my mind to seek and to search out by wisdom concerning all that is done under heaven. It is a grievous task that God has given to the sons of man, by which they may be exercised. I have seen all the works that are done under the sun, and behold, all is vanity and striving after wind.
>
> Ecclesiastes 1:13–14

Increasing wisdom increases pain. Solomon searched for wisdom and found that it led to nihilism and grief. We might avoid the anxiety of knowing that we are at the end of our rope by simply not noticing. In the same way, one might imagine that there is a purpose to existence if the proposition is never challenged. Solomon's unrewarded search for meaning was not a failed aspiration, as if he might yet attain his goal in the future. No, his failure was of a terminal nature in that he achieved the opposite of what he had hoped to find. What he found was the assurance that there is no inherent meaning to be found in any aspect of man's finite existence. What is crooked cannot be straightened, and what is lacking cannot be counted. The fact of human mortality erases all meaning to human existence, and there is not the faintest hope for any cure. Man's life is incurably meaningless because that which would make it otherwise is utterly unattainable.

Although this logical revelation of meaninglessness is a bitter sorrow, Solomon sought to find some small gratification in temporal pleasure. Solomon went on an all-out, conscious search for hedonistic and materialistic pleasures (see Ecclesiastes 2:2–15).

He looked for pleasures from every pleasure source he could find. He found shallow, temporary pleasures, but his pleasures faded. Solomon found out, no doubt to his horror, that even mirth and pleasure could no longer gratify him. He declared that laughter was madness and that mirth was useless, implying that the value and desirability of laughter and mirth, even as existential experiences, were not inherent. Solomon perceived that even the transient value of mirth and pleasure is contingent upon some eternally efficacious end, implying that the importance of pleasure is a thing ordained by God. Although many godless people are able to derive gratification from mirth and pleasure, this does not negate the need for some perceived eternal benefit. Solomon would no doubt say that there must be some intuitive realization of the existence and eternal purpose of God for anyone who is able to find pleasure in life. Yet Solomon had uncovered the existential absurdity of life, which comes with a godless frame of reference. He saw some temporal advantage in having wisdom, but in the end, why bother? Both the wise and the foolish die, and there is no lasting remembrance of anything. So he hated life and all the fruit of his labor (Ecclesiastes 2:18–24). Having posterity gives no lasting meaning either. He was sure that his labors would count for nothing in the future. His posterity would eventually squander his legacy of wealth and wisdom (Ecclesiastes 2:19–21).

Then the writer suddenly takes on a different tone: "Nothing *is* better for a man *than* that he should eat and drink, and *that* his soul should enjoy good in his labor" (Ecclesiastes 2:24). One can imagine this statement spoken with a deep sigh of relief because it is so contrary to all that precedes it, indicating that the writer does not intend to leave us wallowing in that preceding quagmire of nihilism. Solomon proceeds to show the way out, saying, "This also I have seen, that it is from the hand of God" This is the source of our meaningfulness. Solomon continues, "For God gives wisdom and knowledge and joy to a man who is good in his sight; but to the sinner he gives the work of gathering and collecting, that he may give to him who is good before God. This also is vanity and grasping for the wind" (Ecclesiastes 2:26).

This last statement describes all of life as good and meaningful from the perspective of one who fears God. Simultaneously, the evil man continues to perceive that all is vanity while his hard labors become a providential source of good for those who fear God. This statement reveals an important principle in discerning the nature of meaningfulness: God does not consign the ungodly to a life of meaninglessness. Man simply lacks the ability to perceive the meaning that is in everything. "The Lord has made all for himself, yes, even the wicked for the day of doom" (Proverbs 16:4). This principle helps us to perceive another level of truth contained in the axiom "Beauty is in the eye of the beholder." Discerning God's hand of providence is the key to perceiving the beauty and meaning that is in all things. Solomon elaborates:

> To everything there is a season, a time for every purpose under heaven: a time to be born, and a time to die; a time to plant, and a time to pluck what is planted; a time to kill, and a time to heal; a time to break down, and a time to build up; a time to weep, and a time to laugh; a time to mourn, and a time to dance; a time to cast away stones, and a time to gather stones; a time to embrace, and a time to refrain from embracing; a time to gain, and a time to lose; a time to keep, and a time to throw away; a time to tear, and a time to sew; a time to keep silence, and a time to speak; a time to love, and a time to hate; a time of war, and a time of peace. What profit has the worker from that in which he labors? I have seen the God-given task with which the sons of men are to be occupied. He has made everything beautiful in its time. Also he

> has put eternity in their hearts, except that no one can find out the work that God does from beginning to end.
>
> Ecclesiastes 3:1–8

God has given to man a desire to see God's purpose in all things. Yet in many ways, God's ultimate purpose remains inscrutable. Solomon writes again, "I know that nothing is better for them than to rejoice, and to do good in their lives, and also that every man should eat and drink and enjoy the good of all his labor—it is the gift of God" (Ecclesiastes 3:9–13).

This is what gives meaning to human existence. Note that the focus has shifted from that which man does to that which God does. Consider this in context with the previous passage regarding the season for all things. The words "every purpose under heaven" seem mostly relevant to man's deeds and actions, yet it is God who makes all these things beautiful in their season. God is providentially working his own will through the instrumentality of man. If the work of man is indeed God's work by providence, then the source of man's meaning becomes clear. Remember that it is precisely the apparent lack of eternal efficacy that is set forth as a reason why the preacher of Ecclesiastes first declares all things as "meaningless." He says, "For there is no more remembrance of the wise than of the fool forever, since all that now is will be forgotten in the days to come. And how does a wise man die? As the fool!" (Ecclesiastes 2:16). Factoring in the existence of the eternal God changes all of this. Man's labors are ultimately God's doing, and whatever God does shall remain forever. Man's labors have now taken on a certain eternal efficacy through God's eternality. The search for enduring beauty is inevitably the search for meaning, and meaning can only be found in the context of God's eternal purpose. This presumes heavily upon faith in God's ability to establish his eternal purpose. Art as an expression of beauty leads us to acknowledge a whole body of truth regarding God's character and attributes. It is for this reason that art will always be a powerful ministry for truth seekers.

# ART AS LIFE
## AND DEATH

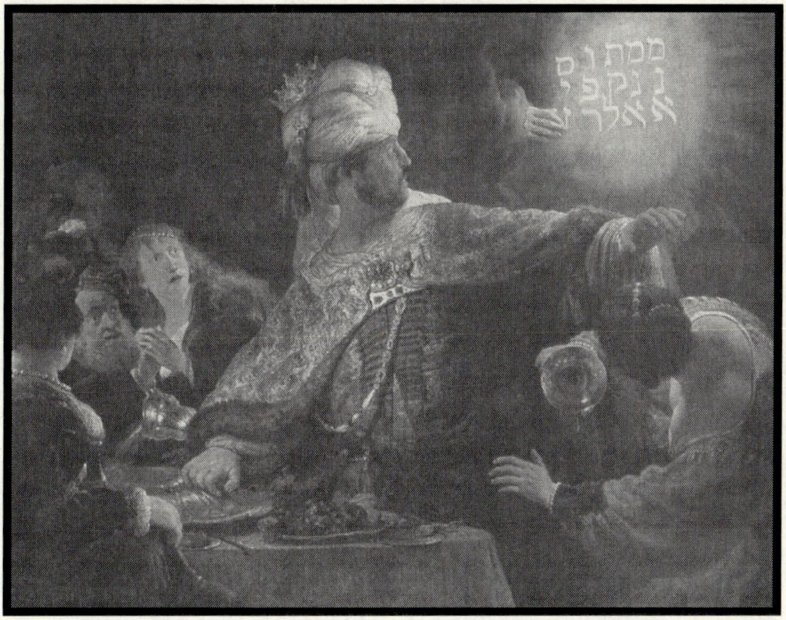

Fig. 5, Rembrandt van Ryan, *Belshazar's Feast,* c. 1630

While the previous chapter provides a foundation for understanding the nature of beauty and the importance to the artist's ministry, it is instructive to know just how deadly serious the subject of art seems to be in God's eyes. Art is not a frivolous thing. It is an instrument of both life and of death, both of grace and of judgment. The purpose of this chapter is to examine biblical evidence of this and (just as importantly) to examine *why* this is true. There was death in idols and in the sacrilegious use of sacred art, and there is life found by faith through the service of atonement and through the bronze serpent that Moses lifted up in the wilderness.

Some instruction regarding the nature and importance of art comes by way of direct statements or examples in the holy text. Yet some of the more valuable lessons about art and its rightful use by God's people can be found in the ways that art is applied in the Holy Scriptures and how God responds to the creative efforts of his people.

In *The Feast of Belshazzar,* Rembrandt depicts the king turning his head about in fear to behold the terrifying apparition of a hand writing something on the wall. It is the herald of his imminent demise. Belshazzar's father, Nebuchadnezzar, destroyed the temple in Jerusalem and pillaged its furnishings and artifacts. Belshazzar served false gods and held captive the people of God. Yet Belshazzar lived and reigned until the day he used the artifacts of the temple at his feast. For this sacrilege, God arranged his assassination, but why only then? What was it about profaning the art of the temple on that day that crossed the line in God's eyes? Though his father destroyed the temple in Jerusalem, Nebuchadnezzar was God's servant sent as an instrument of judgment upon Judah. The faith of God's people had degenerated into a superstitious trust in religion without moral substance. The temple itself had become an idol, and Nebuchadnezzar was God's agent appointed to destroy it. Yet Belshazzar was not acting as God's minister of justice when he used the splendid vessels of the temple at his feast many years later. The time of Judah's chastening was almost complete by the reign of Belshazzar. By this time, the crucible of the Babylonian captivity had consumed much of the dross of idol worship from the hearts of the children of Zion. This was one of God's objectives. Belshazzar may have deserved God's judgment for any number of reasons besides his idolatry and sacrilege, but it is his sacrilege with the temple artifacts and the idols on which God focuses here—the sacred art and the profane art. God often chooses to act on symbols after long withholding his judgment for ongoing offenses. Art objectifies ideas, and the idea of a one true God had returned to the children of Judah. Now it was time for God to avenge the prolonged insult to his holy name and to set the stage for rebuilding the temple.

Sacred art can be misused in other ways. The Church has not been well served by the extravagant excesses of the past when the pure gospel was subverted for power and avarice of a corrupt papacy. The Church did not need Saint Peter's basilica, however beautiful it is. The reformers saw such extravagance as an offense against the gospel of grace, having been largely subsidized by the selling of indulgences. The sheer artistic genius showcased by the basilica represents a legacy of good that can be judged independently of the corruption from which it was born. Yet most Protestants were determined to seek a more enduring, if less opulent, legacy. In the end, they gave us a more beautiful one—an age of gospel prosperity and a revived vision of a godly order in the affairs of mankind.

The nature of medieval or Renaissance cultures may arguably justify much of what we might today see as extravagant, but there is no comparable need for modern people. Today's church can certainly make her own positive contributions to the arts, yet in the short term, she might best be served by knowing what she should remove: the cheap, mahogany paneling in the foyer, the obligatory plaster knockoff of Albrech Dürer's praying hands, a poster of an effeminate-looking Jesus holding a lamb, and so on. Biblical principles should inform the Christian's aesthetic sensibilities. Aesthetics, an area of study that should not be neglected among God's people, has everything to do with creating a suitable environment for worship and spiritual instruction.

Aesthetics has little to do with extravagance. A good aesthetic environment does not require grand edifices of worship or gilded iconography. Our Puritan ancestors finally did built grand edifices of their own, but they were mostly edifices of a different sort. Harvard, Yale, Princeton, and other great institutions were established by generations of faith-inspired Christians seeking to establish and protect an enlightened free society. These were children of the Reformation. Yet their spiritual successors have been largely dispossessed. Those who profess a different religion have taken over those institutions. Today, the children of the Reformation have been all but banished. The rightful heirs of Western culture have been forced to break new ground so that the essential message of that faith might continue to be heard somewhere. It is no doubt a painful loss for those who are old enough to remember the former glory of that world. Perhaps they, like the returning exiles of Ezra's day, have seen the first temple and wept when the foundation of the second temple was laid before their eyes (Ezra 3:12).

But if our new foundation must be small and humble, it should at least be straight. The church should seek some guidance in developing her aesthetic sensibilities. The church should examine her hymns for artistic merit as well as sound theology. Rather than uninspiring stained-glass windows, perhaps plain glass would be aesthetically preferable. Instead of econo-art, perhaps a more discriminating selection of art objects donated by members of the congregation would be aesthetically preferable. There are compelling theological arguments for such aesthetic decisions that the church should learn to understand and articulate. Aesthetics is a field of study that is ripe with spiritual instruction. With a little guidance, a more beautiful sanctuary is not necessarily a more costly one. Extravagance is by no means synonymous to beauty, nor is simplicity synonymous to artlessness. Biblical principles and codes of ethics are to govern any chosen field, and art is no exception. The difficulty of understanding the importance of art has to do with the intangible nature of its ministry. It is easier for the church to assert the relevancy of her beliefs regarding law, medicine, and business. We can point to the victims of bad legal council, unethical medical practice, and the like, but where are the victims of bad art? Would we know them if we saw them? Although the consequences of neglecting God's ministry of art are largely intangible, we can find enough reason from Scripture to say that art is important and to act on faith in scriptural wisdom rather than sight. It is, after all, the walk of faith not of sight to which the church is called. If we are to trust Scripture's judgment regarding the potential importance of art, we will inevitably come to see how import this subject is from God's perspective. Art is one of the few designated ministries that God has established directly, having called by name Bezalel and Oholiab for overseeing the production of the art of the tabernacle. If God in his infinite wisdom chose to place such an emphasis on art, do we not neglect it to our peril?

God commanded a lavish use of art in the facilities and institutions of Old Testament worship. God directed the production of sacred art and established laws to regulate its proper use and handling, forbidding the common use of sacred things as well as the sacred use of common things. God also forbade the use of idolatrous images, as shown in the Ten Commandments (Exodus 20:4–6).

This prohibition of the use of images pertains as much to the *means* of worship as it does to the proper *object* of worship. This is evident in Israel's fall into idolatry at the very time in which Moses was given the law. The object of worship through the golden calf was ostensibly, though not in fact, Jehovah. When Israel sinned with the golden calf, the people declared, "This is your god, O Israel, that brought you out of the land of Egypt!" (Exodus 32:4). In truth, the point implicit in this story is that no god who is worshiped through an image could ever be the one true God. When God appeared to Moses, he said, "You cannot see my face, for no man can see me and live!" (Exodus 33:20). God then placed Moses in a cleft of the rock and covered him with his hand as he passed so that Moses would not see his face.

The Apostle Paul described Jesus Christ in similar fashion as one who is "dwelling in unapproachable light: whom no man has seen or can see" (1 Timothy 6:16). Throughout the Bible, the criticisms of the prophets with regard to idols consistently focus on how inherently opposite a created image is to the one true God. God is all-powerful, all-knowing, and all-seeing. By contrast, an idol can do nothing, can know nothing, can see nothing, and is all that God is not. Most importantly, a created thing is created. The most conspicuous and distinctive attribute of the one true God is specifically that he is uncreated. God has communicated other divine attributes to creation, such as wisdom, love, power, and beauty. But who other than God himself is in any sense uncreated? God's role as the uncreated Creator is the very thing by which he identified himself to Moses, saying, "I AM WHO I AM" (Exodus 3:14). God is introduced in Genesis as the Creator of all things (Genesis 1:1).

Throughout the Bible, the one true God is distinguished as the God who is without beginning. Since being uncreated is God's most distinct and conspicuous attribute, a created thing represents precisely what God is *not* in the most significant way we can imagine. In truth, a cabbage may more closely represent a whale than can any creation of man represent he who is uniquely uncreated, existing from eternity past.

## WHAT KIND OF ART PLEASES GOD?

The Bible does not restrict his people only to "sacred art," but clearly commends visual adornments and artistry in general. The

Bible validates art that has nothing to do with any divine mandate for facilitating public worship. Such examples include the treasures that God gave to Solomon to reward his desire for wisdom (2 Chronicles 1:10–12), the embroidery of Dorcas, which was her legacy (Acts 9:36–39), and the excellent wife whose household was clothed with scarlet (Proverbs 31:21). God is described metaphorically as lavishing jewels and fine clothing upon his people as one of several forms of blessing (Ezekiel 16:10–12). The Song of Solomon is a love song. The Song of Deborah is a ballad, which includes some rather biting satire celebrating the defeat of Sisera, the enemy of Judah (see Judges 5:24–31). David wrote a ballad honoring both Saul and Jonathan (2 Samuel 1:17–27). All these artistic expressions have received the ultimate validation by being incorporated as portions of God's inspired word. Yet the primary intent of these portions of Scripture seems to have little to do with formal corporate worship.

God's ministry of sacred art is a calling to which God gave great emphasis in the Mosaic Law. God's instructions with regard to the artistic designs of the tabernacle were given in great detail. In the book of Exodus, 464 verses are related to the craftsmanship and use of the tabernacle. This is about double the 230 verses devoted to all moral and civil laws combined. Another three chapters are devoted in the first book of the Kings to the building of Solomon's temple. Sacred art was obviously of great importance in the mind of God, and it is important for us to examine the reasons why.

The writer of the epistle to the Hebrews notes the instructive significance of these things as types and shadows of a greater heavenly reality. Their specific pedagogical importance is evidenced by this command: "See that you make all things according to the pattern shown you on the mountain" (Hebrews 8:5 and Exodus 25:40). While the tabernacle artists were given some important guidelines from the mouth of God, they were also given God's

Spirit for exercising individual artistic expression. These artists were inspired. In the book of Exodus, God commands Moses, saying, "See, the Lord has called by name Bezaleel... and he has filled him with the Spirit of God in wisdom and understanding, in knowledge and all manner of workmanship, to design artistic works" (Exodus 35:30–36:3).

The literal meaning of the name *Bezaleel* is "in the shadow of the Almighty."

As the creator of such types and shadows of heavenly things, Bezaleel's name was appropriate to his ministry, living, and working in the shadow of the Almighty. Bezaleel's name is also appropriate with regard to the form of God's visible presence among his people. The pillar of cloud by day provided shade for Israel in the wilderness and filled that holy tabernacle, which was built by Bezaleel and his company of artisans.

The book of Exodus describes it in this way:

> Then the cloud covered the tabernacle of meeting, and the glory of the Lord filled the tabernacle. And Moses was not able to enter the tabernacle of the meeting, because the cloud rested above it, and the glory of the Lord filled the tabernacle.
>
> Whenever the cloud was taken up from above the tabernacle, the children of Israel would go onward in all their journeys, but if the cloud was not taken up, then they did not journey till the day that it was taken up. For the cloud of the Lord was above the tabernacle by day, and fire was over it by night, in the sight of all the house of Israel, throughout all their journeys.
>
> Exodus 40:34–38

Although some basic proportions, images, and conventions of the tabernacle were carried over to the building of the temple, some changes were made that were appropriate to the nature of a permanent structure. Some added features appeared with obvious religious and symbolic significance, such as the freestanding pillars named Jachin and Boaz and the four pairs of oxen that held the bronze sea. No divine mandate can be found regarding the pillars and oxen, yet God's approval of the temple was unquestionable. For in the first book of the Kings, it is again recorded, "The glory of the Lord filled the house of the Lord" (8:11). Through Solomon, God once again put art to sacred use and gave it a major role in the pedagogical services of worship. God's zeal for the proper use of sacred art has been quite severe. A good example of this may be found in the case of the offering of the strange incense of Nadab and Abihu when fire went out from the LORD and devoured them (see Leviticus 10:1–3). The offense of Nadab and Abihu was a form of idolatry since they did not have a proper regard for the holiness of the one true God. By their offering of strange incense, they were worshiping a god whom they evidently regarded as somewhat less holy than the one true God. There was something about their notion of deity that was contrary to the true nature of God. In truth, they did know God. In the words of Saint Paul, they "suppressed the truth in unrighteousness," and they turned to worshiping a god that was very different from the one true God. This was reflected in their disregard for the sanctity of the form of worship. If God's people have such a propensity for stumbling over art and ceremony, why did God give his people so much of it? God's copious use of art sometimes looks like a trap to us. The irony does not stop here.

The first artists mentioned in Scripture were of the cursed lineage of Cain. These were Jubal, a musician, and Tubal-Cain, a craftsman in bronze and iron (see Genesis 4:19–22). The cursed lineage of Cain developed skills that were to become important to the cultural and religious life of the covenant people. The Bible gives us no example of the craft of Jubal that is inherently offensive to God. But the recurring abuse of Tubal-Cain's craft appears in the form of idolatry again and again. Pagan cultures universally seemed to consider an idol as the worthiest use of a craftsman's skills.

Perhaps this reveals a key difference between the nature of sacred music and the visual forms of sacred art. Music is transitory, existing in the moment and occupying time. Music is a common grace that speaks universally to all cultures, and it is hard to corrupt. Visual sacred art is much different. It occupies space as something that offers a perpetual vigil and a timeless testimony to the presence and majesty of God. But the aesthetic benefits of visual art are often dependent on what the viewer brings to it from the broader context of his culture. Visual art forms are a special grace to enlightened cultures, and yet they are a potential source of stumbling to others.

## SYMBOLS, FAITH, AND IDOLATRY

An interesting encounter between holy and profane art is found in the account of the Philistines' capture of the ark of the covenant. Yet when the Philistines presented the ark to their god, the idol twice fell prostrate before the ark and a plague of hemorrhoids and rats broke out against the Philistines, killing many.

Here is another duel of symbols—the idol and the ark—through which God gave the Philistines a prelude of the judgment to come. The Philistines returned the ark, along with a peace offering to the God of Israel. This peace offering was five golden rats and five golden hemorrhoids, corresponding to the five lords of the Philistines (1 Samuel 4:10–7:3). God, with the symbol of his presence, defeated the nation of the Philistines and toppled their god without one man of Israel to do his bidding.

There is a lesson in this Old Testament duel of symbols regarding the handling of sacred art. This story of idolatry, holy artifact, and plague may seam enigmatic to creatures of a new and better covenant, but the God we serve is the same God that waged this war of symbols. Our symbols are different, but they are nevertheless holy, and God still punishes those who do not regard his symbols rightly. Saint Paul warned the saints in Corinthian, "He who eats and drinks in an unworthy manner eats and drinks judgment to himself, not discerning the Lord's body. For this reason many *are* weak and sick among you, and many sleep" (1 Corinthians 11:30).

Baptism, like the Lord's Supper, can also be a means of judgment for those who do not discern its meaning rightly. John the Baptist said of Christ, "[H]e will baptize you with the Holy Spirit and Fire" (Matthew 3:11). The context of John's statement makes it clear that the fire refers to judgment.

A wrong-minded view of God not only inspires the creation of an idol, but it can also transform a thing of genuine divine inspiration into an idol. We find an example of this in the creation of the bronze serpent by Moses. The bronze serpent began as a good use of art as a symbol of mercy in the midst of God's judgment. We are told:

> So the LORD sent fiery serpents among the people, and they bit the people; and many of the people of Israel died. Therefore the people came to Moses, and said, "We have sinned, for we have spoken against the LORD and against you; pray to the LORD that he take away the serpents from us." So Moses prayed for the people. Then the LORD said to Moses, "Make a fiery serpent, and set it on a pole; and it shall be that everyone who is bitten, when he looks at it, shall live." So Moses made a bronze serpent, and put it on a pole; and so it was, if

> a serpent had bitten anyone, when he looked at the bronze serpent, he lived.
>
> Numbers 21:6–9

God, who chose spectacular means for delivering his people from Egypt, here chooses art. Why did he not simply remove the serpents and heal those afflicted by them? Unlike the judgments designed to put the gods of Egypt in their place and to distinguish God's people, the bronze serpent seemed to have an ongoing pedagogical use that went further. Like other things retained for pedagogical usage (the tabernacle and religious ceremonies), the bronze serpent ministry of healing involved the participation of those whom it was designed to heal. The fact that God himself commanded the creation of this image implies a great deal regarding the appropriate use of art and images in the conveyance of spiritual truth. The bronze serpent was not a means of worship in any sense that would make it iconography. On the contrary, the serpent image was created with an opposite end in mind. It was the image of something from which the people were delivered. It was an effigy and token of surrogate judgment.

God's choice of an artist's image as a vehicle for mercy amid judgment could perhaps teach us something regarding the ministry of art in general for God's people and for society as a whole. The serpent, while relieving the children of Israel of the temporal judgment of God, contained a deeper spiritual truth. Jesus said, "As Moses lifted up the serpent in the wilderness, even so must the Son of man be lifted up, that whoever believes in him should not perish but have eternal life" (John 3:14–15). During the reforms of King Hezekiah, the king destroyed the serpent that God commanded Moses to create. It had become an idol. We are told that Hezekiah "broke in pieces the bronze serpent that Moses had made; for until those days the children of Israel burned incense to it, and called it Nehushtan" (2 Kings 18:4).

This demonstrates that images need not be inherently idolatrous by design in order to become idols. Even an image inspired and commanded by God can become an idol simply by being received or interpreted in an idolatrous way. The name *Nehushtan* means "the bronze thing," which indicates that the people did not know or care enough about the original significance of the image to give it a real name. Yet they worshiped the image capriciously. This reveals a strong predisposition of fallen human nature toward idolatry.

If there is such great potential danger in the use of artistic images, why did God lavish so much of it on his people? Without question, God considered the potential benefits of sacred art to be far greater than its dangers. Certainly art, like a gun, is dangerous. It can be an instrument of idolatry, extravagance, lust, hatred, false doctrine, or any number of other evils. But art is also a weapon of spiritual warfare, and God's people are at war. We do not give guns to children, but we would not have our army without them. In fact, what we want for our army is more guns, better guns, and better marksmen to shoot those guns. Likewise, the church needs art if it is to conquer and subdue the fallen culture of Adam and transform it into one that obeys God.

It is one thing to take away a people's land, place of worship, and freedom. It is much more difficult to take away a people's song. Even in captivity, God's people have had their instruments of music, even if they were not in the mood to use them. This is the case described in the book of Psalms:

> By the rivers of Babylon, there we sat down, yea, we wept when we remembered Zion. We hung our harps upon the willows in the midst of it. For there those who carried us away captive asked of us a song, and those who plundered us requested mirth saying, "Sing us one of the songs of Zion!" How shall we sing the Lord's song in a foreign land? If I for-

> get you, O Jerusalem, Let my right hand forget its skill! Let my tongue cling to the roof of my mouth—If I do not exalt Jerusalem above my chief joy.
>
> Psalms 137:1–6

Notice what self-imposed penance is established here for severity's sake. The psalmist declares, "May my right hand forget its skill!" If such were indeed the case, the psalmist would never play a harp again. If his tongue clings to the roof of his mouth, he will never sing again. This is the curse he would call upon himself if ever he forgets Jerusalem. Yet even while he remembers Jerusalem, his acute grief makes the thought of singing unbearable. We are told elsewhere in Scripture, "Like one who takes away a garment in cold weather, and like vinegar on soda, is one who sings songs to a heavy heart" (Proverbs 25:20). God has made everything beautiful in its season; there is a time to mourn and a time to dance. But what can be said of those who will neither mourn nor dance?

Those who will neither mourn nor dance are spiritually dead. Jubilation is one of the "vital signs" of those who are spiritually alive. So is mourning in due season.

## HOW MOVES THE SPIRIT

In the account of David and his harp, we have a biblical example of music as a means of keeping a vexing spirit at bay. It was providentially David's ministry of music—the use of his harp to soothe Saul's torments from a distressing spirit (see 1 Samuel 16:14)—that first brought him to the court of Saul, later to become Israel's king and the only person in the Bible ever called "a man after God's own heart." There are three biblical examples of music related to prophesy. One of these has to do with Saul after he was anointed as king. He was told by God through Samuel,

> It will happen, when you have come there to the city, that you will meet a group of prophets coming down from the high place with a stringed instrument, a tambourine, a flute and a harp before them; and they will be prophesying. Then the Spirit of the Lord will come upon you and you shall prophesy with them and be turned into another man.
>
> 1 Samuel 10:5–6

In the second example, Scripture describes how "David and the captains of the army separated for the service some of the sons of Asaph, of Heman and of Jeduthun, who should prophesy with harps, stringed instruments and cymbals" (1 Chronicles 25:1). In the third example, Jehoram, king of Israel, asks Elisha to prophesy. Elisha then called for a musician. When the musician played, the hand of the Lord came upon him (2 Kings 3:14–17).

All of these examples validate the use of music as a means approved by God of facilitating communion with God and, for the prophets, prophetic revelation. Hymns are used as ballads in the context of rejoicing. Hymns were also sung in the confrontation against Moab in which God delivered Israel by miraculous means. The book of Joshua gives an account of how Jehoshaphat "appointed those who should sing to the Lord, and who should praise the beauty of holiness, as they went out before the army and were saying, 'Praise the Lord, for his mercy endures forever'" (2 Chronicles 20:21). After Israel followed these instructions, the army of Moab miraculously turned against itself.

Dancing was often added to music in the spiritual life of Israel. Like everything else under the sun, there is a time to dance (Ecclesiastes 3:4). Dancing was a natural and expected response of rejoicing, thanksgiving, and praise. It is seen as an impromptu response of the Song of Miriam the prophetess after Israel's deliverance from the army of Egypt. It is recorded how Miriam, as she sang the Song of Moses, "took the timbrel in her hand, and all the women went out after her with timbrels and with dances" (Exodus 15:20).

## ART AS INSTRUCTION AND PROPHECY

Drama was yet another art form that had an important place in the religious life of God's people, although it took a different form than that developed by the Greeks. Biblical drama is in all cases pedagogical or prophetic, telling what God has done or what God will do. Drama is interwoven in the ceremonial law in ways that make it a form of worship or religious celebration. God instituted the Passover feast as a celebration of deliverance that was in every respect a sacred drama. The drama of Passover was intended to lead children to ask, "What do you mean by this service?" (Exodus 12:26). The Remembrance of the circumstances and events surrounding God's deliverance of his people from Egypt was played out and told in great detail (Exodus 12 1–28). A similar example is found in the feast of booths. This drama was a remembrance of the wilderness wanderings. Israel was commanded:

> You shall keep it as a feast to the Lord for seven days in the year. It shall be a statute forever in your generations. You shall celebrate it in the seventh month. You shall dwell in booths for seven days. All who are native Israelites shall dwell in booths, that your generations may know that I made the children of Israel dwell in booths when I brought them out of the land of Egypt: I am the Lord your God.
>
> Leviticus 23:41–43

Drama was also used in connection with prophecy, as we see in the case of Ezekiel's prophetic ministry. God instructed the prophet saying:

> You also, son of man, take a clay tablet and lay it before you, and portray on it a city, Jerusalem. Lay siege against it, build a siege wall against it; and heap up a mound against it; set camps against it also, and place battering rams against it all around, moreover take for yourself an iron plate, and set it as an iron wall between you and the city. Set your face against it, and it shall be besieged, and you shall lay siege against it. This will be a sign to the house of Israel.
>
> Ezekiel 4:2

Another example of drama in the context of prophecy is found in Acts where we are told that

> [A] certain prophet named Agabus came down from Judea. When he had come to us, he took Paul's belt, bound his own hands and feet and said, thus says the Holy Spirit, "So shall the Jews at Jerusalem bind the man who wears this belt, and deliver him into the hands of the Gentiles."
>
> Acts 21:10–11

## SUMMARY

In all these examples, art in the Bible is either an expression for truth or a conduit to truth. In some cases, art is a catalyst for truth and for divine intervention. Does a thing of beauty renew a man's spirit? Does it revive man's love for his Creator or his fellow man? Does it fill him with a wholesome hatred for injustice or inspire him with a fresh resolve for good? Society as a whole is well served if any of its members are served in this way. Art in one form or another has always been a catalyst for social progress. Yet even that which may be called "good art" in some respects can serve an unholy end. Desire and passion can be corrupt, and like the love a harlot, some of what sinful flesh finds beautiful must be rejected. There are many useful governing principles to be discovered for understanding, defending, and producing good art. These are things that God himself has judged important to humanity. The task is clearly an important one, involving life and death consequences in the eyes of God. Yet to understand how art affects us for good or evil requires an explanation of the nature of art's ministry to humanity, and this requires a fundamental understanding of humanity itself and of the intricate tapestry of divine likeness that God has woven into the life and being of mankind. All of this governs our perception of truth, beauty, and meaning.

# THE PRIMEVAL **CULTURE**

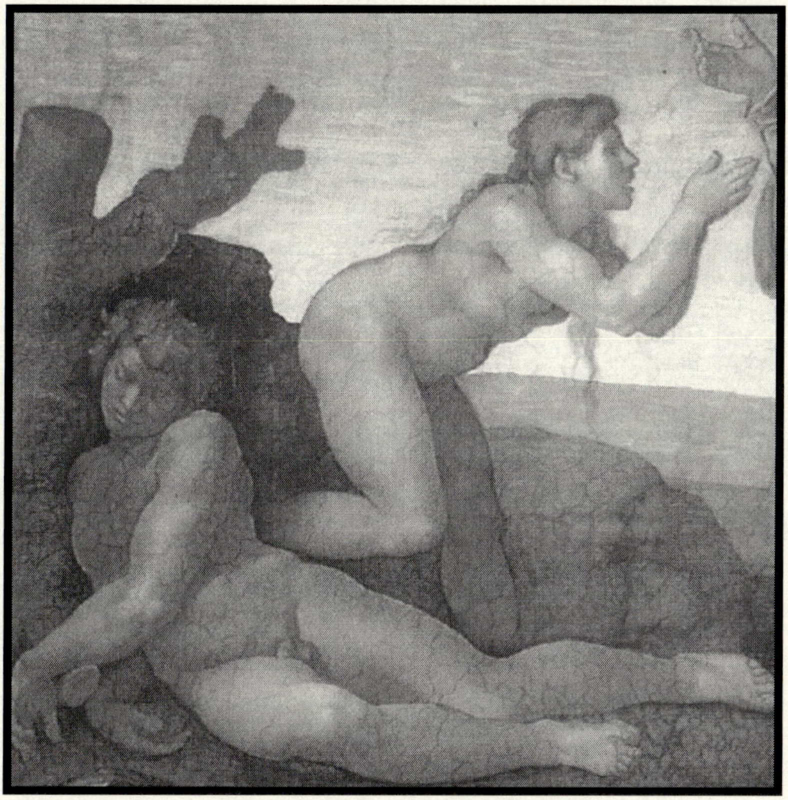

Fig. 6, Michaelangelo, *The Creation of Eve (detail),* Sistine Chapel ceiling, c., 1510

## THE ESSENCE OF A CULTURE

Michelangelo depicts Eve in a gesture of prayer giving homage to her Creator, even as she is still emerging from the side of Adam.

God has put Adam into a deep sleep. The creation of Eve is an essential part of that which makes man created in God's image. Eve was created to be a helper suitable to Adam, and that relationship was the centerpiece of God's cultural mandate to "fill the earth and subdue it." What does it mean to be created in God's image? When all the specifics provided in the Bible are sorted out, the image of God relates mostly to the nature of the family of man. This includes the extended family of man as a primeval culture ordered around a divine mandate of procreation and dominion in accordance with God's will. This primeval culture was established by God and corrupted by the fall. It was designed to reveal to the soul of man the ineffable and profound truths of God and the astonishing wisdom and beauty of his divine order.

What is the real essence of culture? The dictionary definitions of culture are diverse, long, and complicated, but they can be reduced to this: Culture is a community's shared body of beliefs, behavior, and values or the artistic expressions of the same. The opulence of a culture should never be considered its greatest asset. We can find times and places in history where the arts are magnificent, and yet the culture is blighted by injustice and corruption.

Two people living together in peace is a culture. Jesus says, "For where two or three come together in my name, there am I with them" (Matthew 18–19). Why does Jesus attach this provision to such a promise? Surely God can make his presence felt by those who seek him in solitude. Does Jesus imply that he is not with us when we are alone? No, he wants us to understand that our coming together is important because he chooses to pour out his divine unction through the community and culture of his people.

# THE IMAGE OF THE INVISIBLE

God reveals himself through correlative earthly types. Familial relationships create a vast network of pedagogical roles that supply a vast wealth of revelation. The closer mankind conforms to the primeval culture of righteous conduct toward one another, the greater is God's light of revelation. Somewhere, embedded in this web of revelation, is the distinct ministry of the artist. The artist's ministry, well beyond sacred art, speaks to the nature of man's own Creator, who is God. This is the ministry of art within the broader context of the cultural mandate given to the family of man. The primeval culture still exists in a corrupted form. The objective of God's people—even today—is to restore the primeval culture. The cultural war waged against God's people threatens to corrupt the culture further. God's light shines through the culture of mankind, and the purer the culture, the more of God's light shines through to those who live in darkness. Yet even in mankind's imperfection, God's revelation of his own character is clear.

This is a principle that Christ treats as an accepted premise: the nature of earthly fathers gives evidence to the nature of our heavenly Father. Jesus says, "If you then, being evil, know how to give good gifts to your children, how much more will your Father who is in heaven give good things to those who ask him!" (Matthew 7:10–11).

This logic appears in various other places in Scripture where God's nature is revealed through corresponding earthly types. In the Gospel of Luke, Jesus also presents the analogy of a good shepherd as proof of something significant regarding the relationship between God and the lost sinner. These types are more than analogies. They are presented to us as proof of God's nature. These types can also be very imperfect, yet remain effective as a means of revelation.

In the Gospel of Luke, we find the story of a persistent widow seeking legal protection of an unrighteous judge. Jesus says:

> There was in a certain city a judge who did not fear God nor regard man. Now there was a widow in that city; and she came to him, saying, "Avenge me of my adversary." And he would not for a while; but afterward he said within himself, "Though I do not fear God nor regard man, yet because this widow troubles me I will avenge her, lest by continual coming she weary me." And the Lord said, "hear what the unjust judge said. And shall God not avenge his own elect, who cry out day and night to him, though he bears long with them? I tell you that he will avenge them speedily. Nevertheless, when the Son of man comes, will he really find faith on the earth?"
>
> Luke 18:2–8

Jesus makes the point that despite the corruption of man, God's attribute of justice is manifested even through a corrupt and unwilling minister of justice. If a little justice can be obtained through corrupt and unwilling humanity, surely perfect justice may be expected from the hand of God who is quite willing to grant justice. It is God's design to reveal his nature through correlative earthly types. The nature of earthly shepherds, fathers, and judges reveal something of the nature of our heavenly Shepherd, heavenly Father, and heavenly Judge.

The writer of Hebrews describes the tabernacle and its ceremonies as a copy and shadow of the heavenly things, reminding us that God told Moses, "See that you make all things according to the pattern shown you on the mountain" (Hebrews 8:5–6). All of this foreshadowed a better covenant through Christ.

## CORRELATIVE EARTHLY TYPES

In art, as in the very fabric of humanity, God reveals spiritual truth through correlative earthly types—those that are established in the form of human relationships, as well as those that are established in sacred art. Through this, God provides a shadow of enduring beauty—a broad and abiding imprint of divine truth upon the life of humanity. The writer of the Epistle to the Hebrews sees types and shadows not just in terms of humanity and sacred art but also in sacred history. He describes one such type, Melchizedek, who by his name, his office, his actions, and his lack of recorded ancestry all prefigure Christ. Most notably, it is asserted by the writer of Hebrews, "[H]ere mortal men receive tithes, but in that case one receives them, of whom it is witnessed that he lives" (Hebrews 7:8). The writer of Hebrews is referring to his earlier quote from the Psalms: "[Y]ou are a priest forever according to the order of Melchizedek" (Hebrews 7:17). The writer of Hebrews seems to be saying that Melchizedek was immortal. Some theologians suggest that Melchizedek was a theophany and more specifically the pre-incarnate Christ. The writer of Hebrews speaks of Isaac as another type of Christ, being offered as a sacrifice by his father, Abraham, who believed that God would also raise Isaac from the dead (Hebrews 11:17). God uses this same typological relationship as a more general means of natural revelation.

This principle of types implies a great deal with regard to the importance of good family and social relationships. Correlative types of wholesome interpersonal relationships are the means by which God reveals his attributes to us. Conversely, unwholesome relationships constitute a pantomimic lie by which we teach ourselves falsehoods concerning God's nature and attributes. What we perceive concerning the nature of God as Father comes by way of observing the nature of fathers in general. If we perceive the general nature of fathers to be unloving and uncaring, we will transfer this perception onto our heavenly Father in particular. Those who are indifferent to their own children will find it hard to believe that God is not indifferent to his children—to us. We will never be able to walk by faith in God as long as we believe that God is indifferent. To understand the power and importance of typological revelation as it relates to art and craft, consider God's use of it in the book of Jeremiah. The book of Jeremiah gives us this account:

> "Arise and go down to the potter's house, and there I will cause you to hear my words." Then I went down to the potter's house, and there he was, making something at the wheel. And the vessel that he made of clay was marred in the hand of the potter; so he made it again into another vessel, as it seemed good to the potter to make. Then the word of the LORD came to me, saying: "O house of Israel, can I not do with you as this potter?" says the LORD. "Look, as the clay is in the potter's hand so are you in my hand O house of Israel!"
>
> Jeremiah 18:1–5

Here is an example of a prophet who hears the audible voice of God. But God chose to use the typological revelation of a craftsman to press his point, and he directed Jeremiah to go to the potter and watch him work. Saint Paul wrote, "All Scripture is given by inspiration of God, and is profitable for doctrine, for reproof, for correction, for instruction in righteousness" (Timothy 3:16). But it is also this apostle's lament that for some,

> [T]heir minds were blinded. For until this day the same veil remains unlifted in the reading of the Old Testament, because the veil is taken away in Christ. But even to this day,

> when Moses is read, a veil lies on their heart. Nevertheless when one turns to the Lord, the veil is taken away.
>
> 2 Corinthians 3:14–15

Perhaps there is some aspect of God's typological revelation that has the effect of lifting that veil through art and through interpersonal familial relationships.

## THE LIKENESS OF GOD

As creatures made in God's image, we share in a number of communicable attributes that may be called God's image in that they reflect important aspects of God's character. But with regard to the distinct, incommunicable attributes of God, any created being will be everything God is not. Can a portrait of a woman with blond hair and a round face be a likeness of Abraham Lincoln? Such a face would not be called a likeness of Abraham Lincoln, even though the portrait does share certain common attributes—having hair, two eyes, two ears, a mouth, and a nose—all distinctly human. Yet in spite of such clear similarities, nobody would call this woman's face a likeness of Lincoln. Such a face—whatever its basic human similarities to Lincoln—does not reflect the *distinct* attributes of Lincoln. It is, in fact, distinctly *unlike* Lincoln in all the ways that count when speaking of a person's likeness. This same principle applies when speaking of God's likeness in the strictest sense. Since God is invisible, he is only knowable by his distinct character attributes—omnipotence, omniscience, omnipresence, eternality, and immutability—all of which are absent in any created being. No created thing can be like God simply by representing communicable attributes such as beauty or strength or wisdom. Such attributes may describe men, angels, animals, or flora, but God is distinguished by his unique attributes that are included in his role as Creator. Yet humanity is considered God's image because there are communicable attributes that only humanity shares with God. And in some analogous ways, humanity seems to reflect even God's incommunicable attributes. Although we are finite beings, God has put eternity in our hearts.

God gave the family of man a cultural mandate to fill the earth and subdue it as a creature of dominion, and this is a task that is realized through marriage and procreation. Human beings are designed to reflect God's attributes as they obey God's moral law and interact with others in the vast depth of human interpersonal relationships. Humanity's mastery over creation includes his mastery over art and craft, in which the relationship between creature and creator is revealed.

Mankind is the only created thing in Scripture that is said in some sense to be made in God's image and yet not in any sense as to justify either the image of man or man himself as a proxy for worship. This is emphatically forbidden in Scripture. God's image must be revealed by means other than that which captures the mere form and beauty of man. God's revelation of himself is through the life of mankind, and it is an image of divinity that is full, intricate, and profound. Nothing created by man can reflect God's attributes so completely as a life lived in obedience to God. Thus, God says, "You shall be holy, for I the Lord your God *am* holy" (Leviticus 19:2). This is an image that cannot be captured in the lifeless work of an artist's hands however cleverly it is crafted. It is in the act of living over the years and decades of a man's life that the image of God is revealed.

# THE ARTIST AND THE CREATOR

If God's nature is revealed through an intricate web of corresponding earthly types, what can we conclude with regard to the role of the artist? The implications are enormous. Just as the knowledge of our heavenly Father is derived from observing the nature of fathers in general, so is the nature of the great Creator revealed through the corresponding earthly types of those who create things. If God's role as Creator is communicated through corresponding earthly types, then the most fundamental aspects of God's nature may be revealed—or obscured—in the product of a man's hands and in the creative process itself. The significance of this typological relationship appears in the Scriptures.

Again and again, the relationship of a craftsman to his craft is set forth by Scripture to depict something of the nature of God's relationship to man. The Creator/creature relationship is spoken of in Scripture in terms of a potter to his pot, a goldsmith to his gold, an architect to his architecture, and the like. If we perceive that creators in general perform their work with love, skill, and integrity, we are predisposed to believe the same concerning the great Creator in particular. One who creates becomes a visible pantomime of the great Creator and as such bears a heavy responsibility toward society. This principle applies not just to art but to every effort in which creative energy is applied. But the artist, whose focus and ministry is more purely that of the creative gift, has an even weightier responsibility in this regard. He should take care to be a worthy reflection of the divine likeness, whatever that entails artistically as well as in personal morality. If the artist fails in his responsibility as a positive creator type, he does so to the spiritual peril of mankind.

Bad art is morally offensive, and one of the most notorious examples of morally offensive art is idolatry. If creators of images bow down to and serve the work of their own hands, this implies the ultimate lie concerning the relationship between God and man. Nothing turns the Creator/creature relationship on its head so completely as idolatry. Other questions of aesthetic and artistic judgment are moral issues for reasons that relate to the same principles that make idolatry such an affront to God. Shall we perform the work of our hands with love, skill, and integrity, or with indifference, ineptitude, and artlessness? The model we establish will shape our view of the great Creator. One model is a form of praise, and the other is a form of blasphemy.

## DESIGNED FOR FAITH

We were created to walk by faith, for our inherent lack of self-sufficiency is conspicuous. We are not bestowed with formidable strength, sharp teeth, or claws. We are not swift or large, and we have little tolerance for heat and cold. After the fall, Scripture consistently associates nakedness with frailty, poverty, and helplessness. Yet Adam and Eve were naked and unashamed (Genesis 2:25). Adam and Eve walked by faith and knew God perfectly as their all-sufficient strength and their provider in all things. Their inherent creaturely weakness and insufficiency was not an issue since they were not autonomous, but they derived perfect strength and sufficiency from God. As creatures who lived in perfect obedience to God, our first parents were able to see in their own beings, both soul and body, all that was sufficient for doing the will of God. They found beauty and meaning in all they did toward fulfilling God's cultural mandate and his eternal purpose—a way consistent with the lesson of Ecclesiastes. Adam and Eve's being "naked and unashamed" describes a whole and harmonious existence, which again relates to the lesson of Ecclesiastes. God makes all things beautiful in his season.

# THE TRINITY OF MANKIND

In the creation account of Genesis, *man* clearly refers to mankind or to the family of man, which is made "in the image of God." God said:

> Let Us make man in Our image, according to Our likeness; let them have dominion over the fish of the sea, over the birds of the air, and over the cattle, over all the earth and over every creeping thing that creeps on the earth." So God created man in his own image; in the image of God he created him; male and female he created them. Then God blessed them, and God said to them, "Be fruitful and multiply; fill the earth and subdue it; have dominion over the fish of the sea, over the birds of the air, and over every living thing that moves on the earth.
>
> Genesis 1:26–28

God refers to himself in the plural *"Us"* as he states his resolve to make man in his image. Man is likewise referred to in the plural as *"them."* What follows is an elaboration of just what it means to be "made in God's image." Man is not only a plurality, but he is male and female and has been given dominion over creation. The book of Psalms describes mankind as "a little lower than the angels," which again is linked to the dominion God has given to man (Psalms 8:5–6). Moreover, this dominion is specifically commanded to Adam through the raising up of posterity in the words, "Be fruitful and multiply; fill the earth and subdue it" (Genesis 1:28). In the post-fall epoch of our first parents' legacy, God again refers to himself in the plural. It is written: "Then the Lord God said, 'Behold, the man has become like one of Us, to know good and evil'" (Genesis 3:22). The book of Genesis later states in summary fashion: "In the day that God created man, he made him in the likeness of God. He created them male and female, and blessed them and called them mankind in the day they were created" (Genesis 5:1–2). Note also for a second time the link between God's image and man as plurality, being made male and female.

So then, God's image in man consists of being a plurality, with being male and female and with exercising dominion over the earth through posterity. These aspects of God's likeness pertain to principles of what humanity is inherently, a plurality of male and female. This also pertains to a principle of action that is commonly called the cultural mandate—humanity's marching orders. It is that task that God has called mankind to perform. We, as creatures of dominion, have been given the institution of marriage and a charter for the family of man through which dominion is to be realized. Thus, marriage, procreation, and dominion are all interrelated aspects of the divine likeness in man.

The marriage relationship itself—even apart from procreation—is based upon a mutual goal for dominion. Here is how the book of Genesis describes it:

> "It is not good that man should be alone; I will make him a helper comparable to him." Out of the ground the Lord God formed every beast of the field and every bird of the air, and brought them to Adam to see what he would call them. And whatever Adam called each living creature, that was its name. So Adam gave names to all cattle, to the birds of the air, and to every beast of the field. But for Adam there was not found a helper comparable to him.
>
> Genesis 2:18

Note that God's solution for man's loneliness was not just a cohabitant but a helper. Adam first looked for a suitable helper among the animals over which he exercised dominion. But mere cohabitation is not the solution to loneliness. It was this lesson that God was determined to teach Adam. One of the qualifications for a helper was that the creature had to be *comparable* to Adam. Eve was uniquely qualified as a creature comparable to Adam and thus uniquely qualified to be his helper. Eve was an indispensable partner in fulfilling God's plan for man's place of dominion. God's cure for loneliness is a relationship that is centered on a mutual God-given goal. Thus, the solution to loneliness is not primarily companionship but performing God's appointed purpose.

The book of Genesis records Adam's first response to the creation of Eve:

> The man said: "This is now bone of my bones and flesh of my flesh; She shall be called Woman, because she was taken out of man." Therefore a man shall leave his father and mother and be joined to his wife, and they shall become one flesh. And they were both naked, the man and his wife, and were not ashamed.
>
> Genesis 2:23–25

Scripture describes a web of interpersonal relationships that correspond to the three persons of the Holy Trinity and the relationship, also, between God and man. The divine likeness is reflected in God's communicable attributes as exhibited in man.

## THE LAWMAKER

Fathers reflect the attributes of God's care, authority, and providence. Husbands are to lay down their lives for their wives as Christ laid down his life for the Church. As the Holy Spirit is coequal with God the Father and the same in substance, so the woman is flesh of her husband's flesh and bone of his bone—the same in substance. As the Holy Spirit is in submission to God the Father yet equal to him, so the wife is in submission to yet coequal with her husband under God.

Fatherhood envelops the ministry of both genders. We are taught by Christ to pray, beginning with, "Our *Father* in heaven" (Matthew 6:9). *Father* is by no means an arbitrary designation. It reflects an entire order of creation, with an elaborate web of pedagogical and subliminal associations built into it since the dawn of time. The husband's authority is by nature broader than that of his wife. He is the lawgiver who establishes guiding principles of order for his household and accepts the ultimate responsibility for all that is done under his oversight. He exercises dominion over his estate and provides for his entire household. He is called upon to be the responsible leader of his household, not because of any one attribute to which he has an exclusive claim, but because he excels in certain attributes typical of humanity in general. It is precisely because Eve was created to be a creature comparable to Adam that she was deemed a suitable helper. It is precisely because manhood and womanhood share so much that a man is able to play the part of a representative or "federal head" for his entire family. This makes manhood, in the larger scope of human effort, the seat of authority, the progenitor and impetus of creative energy, and the director of that which is called the cultural mandate. It is what women will by nature find beautiful in manhood.

Understanding the nature of the cultural mandate yields a treasury of wisdom for Christian artists with regard to understanding their own aptitudes as designed by God. As an artist or craftsman, a man's creative efforts are most likely to reflect a critical or cerebral view of the world, and that has everything to do with a man's place in the primeval culture. He has a great capacity for being objective, judicious, and brutally honest. He can communicate positive and uplifting themes in his art, but does it best when these things communicate a broad and far-reaching vision. It is not just the man, but mankind that is called "him" in Genesis. The ,word *him* (mankind) is clearly used in a non-gender-specific sense where God creates "him" both male and female. There is also the issue of federal headship to be considered. As head of the household, a father represents more than himself. He represents his wife too, and the two are one flesh. He represents all posterity born to or adopted to this union. This gives the male, by nature, a broader perspective, a tendency to look to the horizon, and propensity for serving the larger issues and the bigger pictures in everything he does.

He can appreciate tenderness and sentiment, but he must generally look to the help of a woman to find access to these attributes. The lack of a woman in his life can leave him without direction in this regard. Absent the influence of a woman, a man may throw himself into his work with intense resolve. This can be good or bad, but for a man to understand his own nature according to God's design, can be a great help.

## LIFE GIVER AND COMFORTER

Women have a propensity for a form of creative genius that is hard for men to achieve. The creative gifts of women tend to be more conspicuous because they seldom overreach, stay focused, and tend to complete what they begin. This has everything to do with a woman's place in God's primeval culture. Scripture describes the ministry of the Holy Spirit in female-analogous terms. A mother conceives, gives birth, comforts, leads, and instructs her child in wisdom. The Holy Spirit also quickens

(Genesis. 1:2), gives spiritual birth (John 3:6–8), comforts (Isaiah 66:13), and leads and gives instruction (Proverbs 1:20–23). In Proverbs 8, Wisdom is personified in the female gender and sounds like the Holy Spirit. Wisdom's presence in the work of creation implies divinity, and the description of Wisdom's rejoicing in the works of God's creation implies personhood (Proverbs 8:22–36).

Yet it is improper to refer to God as *she.* When the Bible refers to the works and attributes of God—using female typology—it is with respect to his attributes. God, in reference to his personal being, is never directly called *she.* This distinction is consistent with the nature of biblical typology. The word *she* is gender specific and refers to womanhood. The biblical concept of womanhood and the words used to designate womanhood specifically describe a created being. *Woman* is the name given to Eve because she was "taken out of man," having a point of beginning and thus being finite. God is from everlasting. He is not created. Adam was obviously created too, but the word *he* has no specific association with the fact that Adam was a finite creature.

If manhood is defined by extra endowments of attributes that define humanity in general, womanhood may be distinguished by attributes unique to womanhood such as the ability to bear and nurse children. The biological realities of a woman also influence her psychological nature and her general outlook on life. All of this dramatically shapes the woman's role in society and makes her the central player in God's design for dominion as set forth in the cultural mandate. The means to dominion is to fill the earth, and the means to filling the earth is to be fruitful and multiply. Mankind's chief means for exercising dominion is through the bearing of children. The Apostle Paul, in the context of making a case for the male's authority in the household (including the household of faith), states that the woman is saved by the bearing of children (1 Timothy 2:15). Perhaps the woman is said to be saved in the sense that she is "set aside" for exercising her dominion in a special way. While it is given to the father to act as head of the household, she is given a special kind of authority over her children. Her ministry, her wisdom, and her mentoring of her children represent the most direct work of the cultural mandate. The father's role as the head of the household is in some sense a supportive role to the woman's ministry. She, like the male, is a creature made in God's image with a natural God-given instinct to fulfill God's cultural mandate to fill the earth and subdue it. God has given her specific attributes for a specific and important task. While the father typifies God the Father, the woman, in the exercise of her special authority over her children, is a type of the Holy Spirit. To her children, the woman is the comforter, the nurturer, the counselor, and the confidant.

She is an independent, moral being, accountable to God and obligated to resist all that is contrary to God's law. Yet a woman's authority is best exercised by proxy as that of her husband. It is to her advantage not to be looked upon as the final arbitrator of law. If the mother assumes the role of ultimate lawgiver in her household, it will be at the expense of her role as counselor. This typifies the ministry of the Holy Spirit, who makes intercession for us with "groanings which cannot be uttered" (Romans 8:26). The woman tends to have a greater sensitivity to nuance. She is better able to find sermons in rocks and to see her visual world as a slate of expression for the continual praise of her Creator. Everything she touches is absorbed into her extended world of being, and she becomes its guardian. Her art can express sentimentality with convincing authenticity. She can appreciate the cerebral world of her husband and has no problem sharing in its grand and far-reaching ideas. Yet she sees her husband's world as a ship in danger of crashing on the rocks of a more focal reality that she perceives clearly. To her husband and her children, she is a lighthouse.

This is not to say that fathers do not exercise grace and comfort or that mothers do not administer justice. It is only to say that fathers and mothers tend to fall into their roles by natural design and that their roles are symbiotic. Fathers do show grace and comfort, but they do so most effectively in the context of the social dynamic created by the mother's pervasive ministry of grace. Mothers do administer justice, but they do so most effectively in the context of the social dynamic created by the father's pervasive ministry as lawgiver. Conversely, a father will find it difficult to fill his role as lawgiver without the mother's complementary ministry of grace, and a mother will find it difficult to administer grace to her children without the father's complementary ministry as lawgiver. The lack of either ministry is potentially devastating to the peace of a household and to a child's spiritual development.

## CONQUEROR AND REDEEMER

It is helpful to understand the identity and instincts of a youth as he strives for redemptive value in his creative works. It is frustrating for a youth to not know what it is he must redeem, but if he is not given a cause, he will try to find it. The instincts of male headship or nurturing womanhood manifest themselves early in childhood, but these instincts are largely eclipsed by the instinct of progeny to subdue the world. This is an instinct that God has placed in the heart of a youth. A wise parent or art instructor will channel the power of this instinct by supplying a clear need and a clear vision. The posterity of mankind is the backbone of the cultural mandate. The posterity is set forth as a centerpiece of the covenant of promise in the cultural mandate to "be fruitful and multiply; fill the earth and subdue it" (Genesis 1:28). The Noetic

Covenant, Abrahamic Covenant, and Davidic Covenant are in spirit and substance the same covenants of grace. All of these covenants inculcate various expressions of the cultural mandate (see Genesis 9:7, Genesis 15:5, 2 Samuel 7:12, and Acts 2:39). In all of these covenants—as in the cultural mandate itself—the posterity is set forth as the major focus of all God's promises to man and of humanity's service to God. How then does the posterity reflect the second person of the Godhead? The posterity is the visible and abiding manifestation of the parents who are the analogous earthly types of the Father and the Holy Spirit. Character attributes are learned mostly from one's parents.

Moreover, the children are the very substance and identity of the parents. They are the parents' likeness, their heirs, and their representatives. In the words of Christ, "He who has seen me has seen the Father" (John 14:9). It is through the children that the parents are honored, vindicated, and remembered. The child is the chief legacy of the parents. The posterity has a distinct duty to conserve the most positive legacies of parents and to refine, adjust, and apply all the wisdom of his parents to the needs of his own age. Yet if he finds anything short of heaven in the world of his parents, he will seek to find it in something new. The instinct of youth is to find a frontier and subdue it. Even with a healthy respect for tradition, what is known and passed on from parents is simply not enough. He must find something better. This is a desire God has placed within him, and he will see it as his mission to subdue new frontiers. It is his duty to God and to his fellow man. It is through the children and successive generations that the work of the kingdom is fulfilled, with each generation adding to the work of the previous generation. This creative role of the posterity parallels the description of Christ in the first chapter of the Gospel of John: "All things were made through him" (John 1:1–2).

Siblings are also a reflection of the divine likeness to one another. The Apostle Paul calls Christ "the firstborn among many brethren" (Romans 8:29) and speaks of our sibling relationship to Christ as providing an example or "first fruit" of God's resurrection for all the elect—Christ's brethren. In practical terms, good parents treat their children as equals under the law of the Father, and all siblings are subject to the same laws.

The relationship of a child to his older sibling provides a visible model of obedience as fellow subordinates to the will of the father. The obedience of the eldest sibling and the subsequent rewards of honor and authority given to such provide the younger siblings with a model of hope for the fruits of obedience and good character. Christ is the ultimate example of obedience to us. He is, like us, born under the law of the Father and is our example of obedience to it. As our older brother, he is our protector, vanguard, and advocate before the Father. He works within the same context and restrictions of the law as we do and succeeds in obtaining glory, honor, and dominion from the Father. He too has tasted of the weaknesses, temptations, distractions, and frustrations of childhood and can sympathize with our weaknesses, yet he has prevailed through it all. It is one thing to hear assurances from the Father that the walk of faith and obedience leads to life, joy, and prosperity. It is another thing to look upon an older brother as a living, flesh-and-blood testimony of the same.

## A TAPESTRY OF REVELATION

If we understand the general principles of biblical typology as manifested in Scripture, it is easy to see the importance of God's revelation of himself through the family of man. In addition to the all-important nuclear family, comparable avenues of divine revelation are at work through the various social dynamics of in-laws, cousins, friends, magistrates, and neighbors—ad infinitum. Indeed, the Apostle Paul teaches us that God is revealed in all his works of creation. Yet it is mankind that is said specifically to be the very image of God. For this reason, it is necessary to study the nature of the family of man as God has designed us. The light of natural revelation is born of the life experience that thrives on godly devotion. Such a life emanates its sublime message to the mind and heart in ways that cannot always be uttered with the tongue. The obedience of mankind to the law of God is what gives this tapestry of revelation its exquisite clarity to the mind and heart of man. Our Creator has taken us in his hands and formed us with great love in his image. In the very process of our coming to be, and in the entirety of life lived in service to him, is the ongoing utterance of his name.

# THE PRIMEVAL **REVOLUTION**

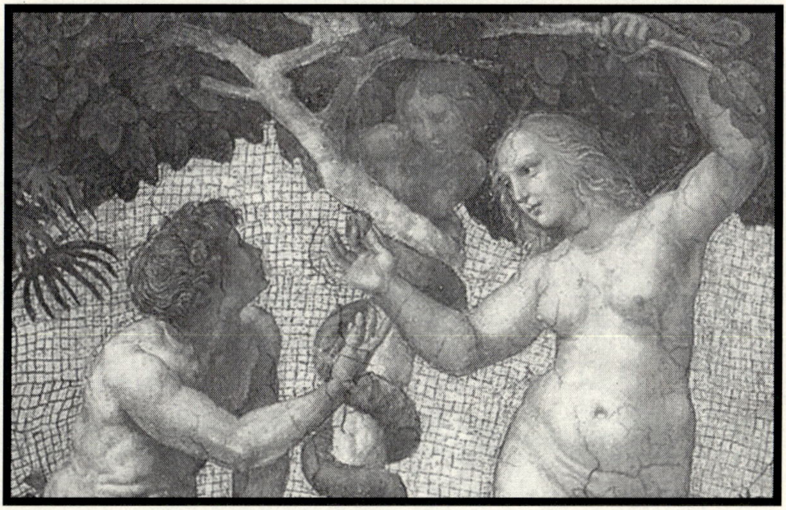

Fig. 7, Raphael, *Adam and Eve* (detail), c. 1510

Humanly speaking, to know good and evil would seem to be a good thing. After all, are we not taught from childhood to judge between right and wrong and to choose what is right? Raphael has given the serpent a face of innocence. The serpent looks into the eyes of Adam. Eve holds the forbidden fruit in her line of vision as she looks to Adam. He is looking at the serpent, as if to confirm something just told to him by Eve. What issue was Adam considering? What change was about to occur with this first sin of mankind? The primeval culture was God's ideal order of creation in which mankind acknowledged God as God and enjoyed life and happiness within that order through obedience to God. The fall, by contrast, was a primeval revolution by which our first parents, created in the likeness of God, sought to be like God in a specific way forbidden to them.

This sin of Adam and Eve was the usurping of the place of control in the moral code by which they lived. The knowledge of good and evil is the autonomous determination of good and evil as a standard established apart from God. It is basic to the nature of all sin. The notion may be best illustrated in the form of an important question: is God good because God consistently does that which is good, or is goodness defined by whatever God decrees? How this question is answered determines which side one takes in the primeval revolution: Lucifer's or God's. Adam and Eve were created with their faith in God written into their frame of thinking. "Good" to the unfallen mind of man was whatever God decreed, and "evil" was whatever God forbade. What God expressly forbade before the fall was essentially that mankind must never presume to know good and evil apart from God. But then came Lucifer to seduce our first parents into a corrupt way of thinking. This was the essence of the primeval revolution that resulted in the fall of mankind.

Satan sought to introduce a way of thinking into the untainted mind of Eve, who had no concept of good and evil other than what was spoken from the mouth of God or written by God into her pure heart and sinless conscience. She had no independent concept of good and evil by which she could ever find cause to be angry with God. Satan had to construct that point of reference. To understand Satan's strategy for establishing this point of reference in the mind of Eve, it is necessary to analyze not only what Satan said but also what he implied.

He said, "Has God indeed said, 'You shall not eat of every tree of the garden?'" (Genesis 3:1). This was a twice-removed implication against God. Satan implied some injustice on God's part, which implied a law that is above God—one to which even God is obligated to conform. The serpent was said to be crafty, but what can be less subtle than to speak a false charge to one who had firsthand knowledge of its falsehood? Surely Satan had no expectation to convince Eve of his first charge. On the contrary, Satan wanted to have this idea quickly rebutted while luring Eve into a tacit acceptance of a deadly underlying premise. Therein lies the nature of Satan's craftiness. By implication, Satan led Eve to accept the premise that God is good *because* he had not decreed anything contrary to that which she as an independent judge of right and wrong would call "good."

The serpent said, "You will not surely die. For God knows that in the day you eat of it your eyes will be opened, and you will be like God, knowing good and evil" (Genesis 3:4–5). Lucifer stops speaking at this point, and Scripture tells us that Eve perceived the fruit "was pleasant to the eyes, and a tree desirable to make *one* wise." Did Eve not notice until then that the fruit was beautiful, or was Eve's perception of beauty born spontaneously with her false perception of the fruit as an instrument of ultimate and eternal good? Satan's assurance to Eve was that she would not die because eating the fruit of the knowledge of good and evil would open her eyes, causing her to become like God, knowing good and evil. (See Genesis 3:4.)

After our first parents took of the fruit, we are told, "The eyes of both of them were opened, and they knew that they were naked; and they sewed fig leaves together and made themselves coverings" (Genesis 3:7).

God is the only true author of law. In taking of the fruit of the knowledge of good and evil, man seeks to declare his own standard of good and evil separate and distinct from the decree of God and to usurp God's role as lawmaker. Partaking of the knowledge of good and evil is to be like God and usurp the place of control. This account of the fall reflects the nature of Lucifer's rebellion as described in the words of Isaiah, who prophesied against Babylon: "For you have said in your heart: 'I will ascend into heaven, I will exalt my throne above the stars of God... I will be like the Most High." Yet you shall be brought down to Sheol, to the lowest depths of the Pit (Isaiah 14:12–15).

Satan introduces to the mind of Eve the concept of a separate standard of determining good and evil—a standard apart from God's decree. She was so beguiled by the smelly red herring of an outrageous accusation that she accepted Satan's implied premise of autonomous law. She did so haplessly and for the ostensibly laudable purpose of rebutting Satan's accusation against her God. All that mattered for Satan was that Eve accepted his premise. By doing so, Eve had already unconsciously practiced a working knowledge of good and evil. She had made her fledgling flight with the wings of an insidious Luciferian worldview. She let into her mind a notion that she no doubt would have rejected outright if offered in explicit form. This relates to the warning of Proverbs: "Do not answer a fool according to his folly, lest you also be like him" (Proverbs 26:4). Wrong ways of thinking are infectious. We can absorb them unwittingly if not identified and resisted. Eve answered Satan in accordance with Satan's own folly, and she began to think like him.

Since we are born into this fallen way of thinking, it is difficult for us to imagine anything else, but it is an aspect of fallen nature that redeemed sinners learn to overcome by faith. The minds of our first parents were different. They had to be taught this autonomous knowledge of good and evil. Satan's lie was more than untrue to the sinless mind. To them, it would have seemed irrelevant. God is good regardless of what he commands of us. God did not command our first parents to abstain from all the fruit of the garden, but if he had done so they would have simply obeyed and continued to declare that God was just because God was God and goodness was whatever God does. To believe that God's decrees could be anything other than just is to partake of the one fruit of the knowledge of good and evil that God forbade. The Apostle Paul provides a better response than that of Eve with regard to the issue of God's fairness:

> What shall we say then? Is there unrighteousness with God? Certainly not! For he says to Moses, "I will have mercy on whomever I will have mercy, and I will have compassion on whomever I will have compassion." For the Scripture says to the Pharaoh, "Even for this same purpose I have raised you up, that I may show my power in you, and that my name might be declared in all the earth." Therefore he has mercy on whom he wills, and whom he wills he hardens. You will say to me then, "Why does he still find fault? For who has resisted his will?" But indeed, O man, who are you to reply against God? Will the thing formed say to him who formed it, "Why have you made me like this?" Does not the potter have power over the clay, from the same lump to make one vessel for honor and another for dishonor?
>
> Romans 9:14–21

Note that in answering the anticipated objections, Paul does not proceed to justify God in terms of human concepts of fairness, but to underscore the utter impropriety of a created being calling into question his Creator. The Bible consistently uses the relationship of a craftsman to his craft as a type of God's relationship to man. The prerogatives of an earthly creator over his creation are no different from that of God's prerogatives with regard to man. Having bluntly dismissed the whole question as improper, Paul then proceeds to offer us a look at the issue from God's perspective, not by way of justifying God's decree, but by way of affirming God's eternal attributes. In the mind of Paul, to declare that God is good, just, and patient is to say that God is consistent with his own nature and cannot act contrary to it. This has nothing to do with God's actions being consistent with our notions of what is good, just, and beautiful.

Adam's fallen race now takes its knowledge of good and evil for granted, even though death and paradise hang in the balance. With the benefits of Scripture and retrospection, we may, with some difficulty, come to understand the full significance of the issue that Eve was confronted with in the garden. But how could we expect Eve, having neither Scripture nor retrospect, to understand all of this? Eve was no fool. Pre-fall innocence was not of such a nature as to render one stupid or gullible. On the contrary, the unfallen mind must have been quite astute. Consider the task God gave Adam and Eve as the keepers of Eden, exercising dominion over every living thing.

Moreover, we should remember that the Luciferian way of thinking was not yet habitual to Eve as it is to us who are born into it. The serpent is described as "crafty" because that which was unsaid was more important than all that was said. Satan used a seminal acquiescence to seduce Eve into haplessly practicing the autonomous knowledge of good and evil in an effort to rebut Satan's temptation. Before she had made the conscious determination to partake of the actual fruit, she was already seduced into Lucifer's way of thinking. Satan manipulated Eve to justify God on Satan's presupposition terms, and that is precisely how Eve responded. Satan implied to Eve that having her eyes opened would result in life autonomous from God. He said, "You will not surely die. For God knows that in the day you eat of it your eyes will be opened, and you will be like God, knowing good and evil" (Genesis 3:4–5). Adam and Eve did, in a sense, become "like God," and their eyes were indeed opened. God himself declared, "Behold, the man has become like one of Us, knowing good and evil" (Genesis 3:22). But what their eyes were open to was their own nakedness or insufficiency. The manner in which they became like God was only death to them.

This revolution in man's thinking is key to understanding the nature of the struggle between the people of God and the pervasive culture. The result of this revolution was the death of all mankind. Man's spiritual death is reflected in the very nature of this dramatic revolution in man's perceptions of himself, of God, of creation, and of law (good and evil). He sees in the context of this new paradigm that he is naked and is ashamed. Some essential aspect of man's own being—though created good—has become loathsome to him and devoid of beauty. This revolution is the cornerstone of all false religion and of every cultural standard that is contrary to the life and wellbeing of man and the law of God. Understanding the nature of the fall in these terms helps us to understand the contrary and relentless theme of Scripture—faith. The essence of all true faith consists of surrendering back to God the unlawfully usurped knowledge of good and evil. This spiritual surrender to God is the key to true religion and true obedience to God's law. It is the ultimate path to true meaning and true beauty.

This is the spiritual testing of Job, who serves as a concrete biblical example of what it means to yield back to God the knowledge of good and evil. The writer of the book of Job gives us a window into the mind and actions of God in a way that explodes the Luciferian criteria for judging God as good. In the end, God will not allow himself to be called righteous for any reason given by Job's friends. God will insist on being called righteous because he is God, the Creator of mankind and of all things. God confronts us with the issue of who he is and with the most central aspect of our own fallen nature that separates us from God. We may presume ourselves to be on God's side and yet, in the end, find ourselves serving a god of our own making rather than he who is truly our Maker. We are warned of two ways of blasphemy: (1) that of accusing God as if God were not just and (2) that of justifying God as if he needed an advocate before the court of mankind. To do either is to become the unwitting advocate of Lucifer's teaching, for both imply that there is some man-made determination of good and evil to which even God must conform. To speak rightly of God entails surrendering back to God the unlawfully usurped knowledge of good and evil and confessing God as just for only one ultimate reason—that he is God. Whatever God does defines all that is just, all that is right, and all that is beautiful.

# THE INEVITABLE **DICHOTOMY**

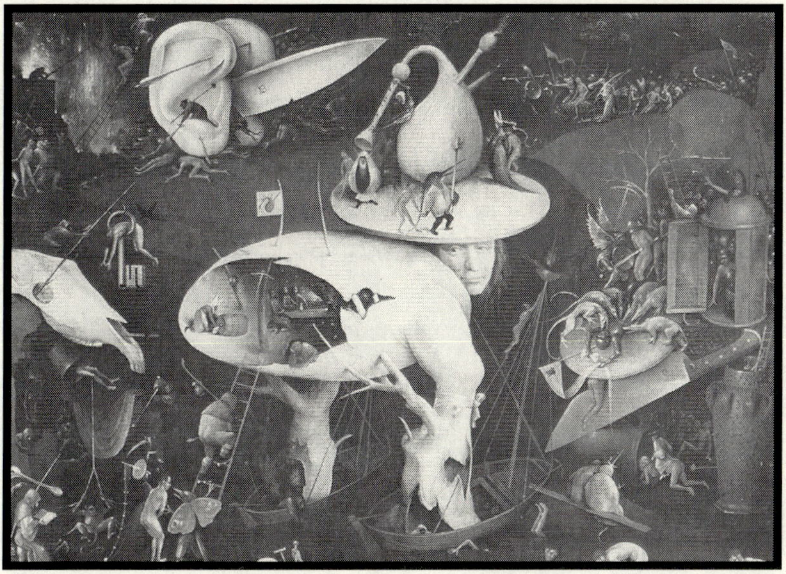

Fig. 8, Heironymus Bosch, *Garden of Earthly Delights (detail)*, c. 1500

The unredeemed soul will always perceive part of himself as inherently unredeemable while treating another aspect of himself as his god. The work of Heironymus Bosch depicts numerous manifestations of a dichotomized (Adamic) worldview including gluttony, promiscuity, debauchery, hedonism, and asceticism. This is far different from the biblical assurance that mankind is totally depraved as a result of the fall and yet is also totally redeemable. All that is basic and essential to humanity is good because it is created in God's image. Yet all of man's being is tainted so that he cannot find salvation through any native island of goodness within himself. He can only find it outside of himself, through the mercy and righteousness of the God of all creation.

The primeval revolution infected all of mankind with, among other things, a corrupt cosmology. It led to an inevitable dichotomy that will never allow the human soul to find true wholeness in this life. This chapter was written to explain this cultural pathology that Lucifer's doctrine has inflicted on Adam's fallen race.

In our search for a culture that honors God's ways, it is important to understand how ideas affect our ability to resist evil and promote good. Only then can we construct a correct view of the culture God has designed and know our rightful place in that culture. This is especially important for the Christian artist as he seeks to apply his vocation to the needs of the imperfect culture in which he lives. Humanly speaking, it's a daunting task because our view of the world shapes our perceptions of beauty, and the world sees things very differently. The Christian artist must promote a vision of enduring beauty shaped by a truthful understanding of ourselves and of the God we worship.

God is not some part of us, and we can never find redemption in any god that can be imagined as such. God has established a holy law that cedes nothing to the approbation of man. That is to say, God alone may declare what is good and what is evil. We as God's creatures must accept God's decrees by faith.

Man's pre-fall relationship to the I AM was one in which man acknowledged God alone as the author of law. God alone determined good from evil, and mankind was intended to follow the will and providence of God as the ultimate guide to preserving the life and pleasure of mankind. But this walk of faith is inconsistent with the will of fallen man, who aspires to determine the means of life for himself. Satan assured Eve that she would *not* die because her eyes would be opened, knowing good and evil. As lawmaker, man was an immediate and profound failure, but the nature of his spiritual death would allow him no ultimate moral authority outside of himself. Fallen man is darkened to natural revelation by sin. He is guided by the presumptions and desires of his own sin nature, and he has attempted to reconcile the problem of his own existence apart from God. Fallen man is a self-proclaimed judge of good and evil and yet manifestly a victim of the latter. Because he cannot admit any external god as his sovereign, he is left to explain good and evil as opposing aspects inherent in his own existence. Man is both lawmaker and lawbreaker, and he is locked into a dichotomized existence.

Since the essence of the Adamic rebellion centers around man's presumption of his own ability to be "like God, knowing good and evil," autonomous man cannot admit his state of total depravity, the idea that there is no aspect of man's being that is not subject to error. This would leave him without any reliable reference for declaring authoritatively what is good and what is evil. The essence of man's rebellion is that he is the author of law, acknowledging no higher law than that of his own making. This presumes the existence of an infallible guide as an aspect of man's being. If man is both lawmaker and lawbreaker, he is manifestly imperfect. This limits his moral authority to whatever aspect of his humanity contains the seed of perfection and is thus competent to be the author of law and to judge between good and evil. He cannot truly consider the problem of evil in terms of transgressing God's law or the solution to evil in terms of mere obedience to God's law. Autonomous man may speak of God's law in reverent-sounding ways, but this is ultimately a reverence for whatever he independently approves as God's law.

Such an ostensible reverence for God's law is different from God's true ideal for man, which is an unconditional submission to all that God decrees, whether favorable or unfavorable to human judgment. The autonomous man could never obey God's law simply as an external objective standard because man, not God, must be the lawmaker. Man as lawmaker ultimately determines and decrees good and evil. If man is the ultimate judge of good and evil, he must choose which one of the several internal voices he will follow. Inner conflicts arise from opposing aspects of his being, each seeking to dominate. Passion may entice him in one direction, but reason may cause him to fear the consequences. If his mind has led him into bad choices, he may resolve to follow passion next time and abandon reason. A man cannot serve two masters. He will learn to love one and hate the other. One voice he will follow, and the other he will suppress and call evil. Thus fallen man inevitably creates a dichotomized view of himself. Those dedicated to the Luciferian knowledge of good and evil can only banish or suppress that side of human nature that seems to lead him into bad choices, treating it as inherently evil. The best he can hope for is the destruction of that internal source of imperfection to the triumph of whatever part of himself he determines to be good.

This dichotomizing dynamic has created different arrangements but all with an equal, usually unconscious allegiance to the Luciferian premise that humanity is the ultimate author of law.

Christians are not immune to the corrupt cosmology of Adam. Many Christians in the spiritualist and pietist movements rejected academic reasoning to follow pure conscience as their only guide. The mystic John Tauler quotes Dionysus as saying, "The light of faith requires that a man should be raised above the apprehensions of reason,"[4] and again, "No contradiction or mishap shall have power to move or constrain him so that it separate him from the truth."[5] Thomas Aquinas, who had profound contributions to Western thought, held to an opposite view, seeing reason as the one aspect of humanity that is not tainted by the fall. Such dichotomies can be found in numerous systems of theology, but the cosmological foundation for this comes from our fallen nature. There is no major philosophy in the world that does not identify some aspect of human existence that must be suppressed or destroyed. Gnostics see all that is physical as evil and all that is spiritual as good, while Stoics seek to escape passion in favor of reason as the ultimate good.

The different philosophies of the world find different devices, but in the end, they all dichotomize some aspect of basic humanity. The religion of the Bible—rightly understood—Declares man "very good." Every aspect of man's being is good. Body, soul, intellect, passion, conscience, reason, instinct, intuition, appetite, and emotion are all good. All senses, faculties, pleasures, and gratifications are good when they are ordered according to God's will. Every aspect of humanity that is essential to humanity was created and ordained by God, who has made everything beautiful in its season, according to God's purpose.

Platonism and Neoplatonism have long been established in Western culture as the predominant forms of the dichotomized worldview that is basic to all societies shaped by the mind of fallen man. These principles have in turn been interpreted and applied in differing ways. The Platonic ideal of "pure spirit" is based on the idea that all creations of a man's hands are inferior to pure thought. In a perfect, Platonic society, art could not exist. The idea in the world of the mystic is a purely subjective and personal experience. To some mystics, reason is an implement of the flesh. Pure thought is intuitive thought, both spontaneous and immediate. Reason, therefore, which is neither spontaneous nor immediate, is a fabrication of man, falling short of the Neoplatonic ideal of pure thought. This is the legacy of Platonic thought that has led the Church to devalue art with undue devotion to abstract ideas. It has led much of the church to value art only to the extent that it serves an abstract thought, such as a pretty background for a Scripture verse or an illustration in a Bible story. It has led some Christians to forsake art and the sacraments altogether, as if these things are mere distractions to the pure abstract ideas of biblical truth. The dichotomy of the Luciferian paradigm is largely unconscious to most people, but it has been recognized as a problem by some. Some students of Kabbalah or secular mystics—like Blake—have offered monism as an alternative. Close inspection of monism, however, reveals it to be no real alternative. This is most apparent in the worldview of Blake, who exhibits a deep-seated antipathy for the role of reason. Law is the foundation of reason, and Blake disparages both law and reason.

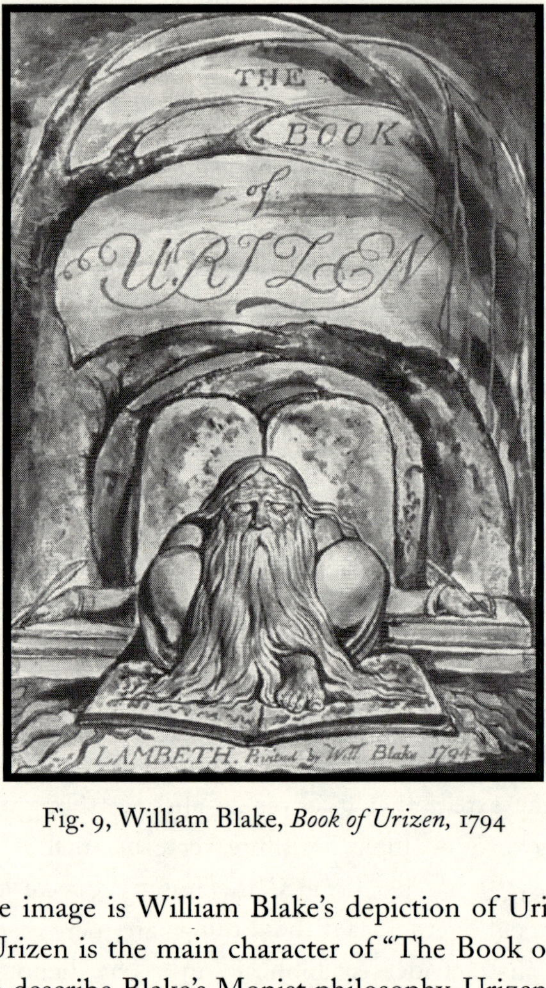


Fig. 9, William Blake, *Book of Urizen,* 1794

The above image is William Blake's depiction of Urizen (your reason). Urizen is the main character of "The Book of Urizen," written to describe Blake's Monist philosophy. Urizen takes the form of an ambidextrous Moses. He is crouched before the stone tablets of God's law, diligently writing. Blake was not fond of the idea of objective revelation. He believed there should be a balance between reason and intuition. But reason, to exist, must provide some absolute basis for reason and some basis for absolute law from which reason derives its essence. Otherwise, reason is not reason. Without some all-conditioning basis of absolute law that reason may proclaim, reason is robbed of its existence and is replaced with subjectivism. The dichotomy found in dualism is still present in monism. Blake assigns to reason a place of obscurity. Yet if a monist rejects objective law, he must still have some criteria for judging good and evil. He chooses to do one thing and not another. He declares one thing good and profitable and another thing not. This is autonomy, or self-law.

Therefore, monism is really a form of dualism. The monist simply dispenses with the classical concept of good and evil and replaces it with his own. Both are equally dependent on the premise of Luciferian autonomy. Since the monist's moral authority for determining good and evil is autonomous and yet manifestly imperfect, and since he must contend with a balance of choices, which is simply good and evil assigned another name, he must dichotomize like any dualist. Man's enemy continues to be an aspect of his own humanity, a condition vividly reflected in the prelude to Blake's *The Book of Urizen,* which reads:

> Preludum–of the book of Urizen, of the primeval priest's assumed power when the Eternals spurned his religion and appointed him a place in the North—cold—shadowy—obscure. Oh, Eternals I hear you call gladly! Dictate swift words and fear not to unfold your dark visions of torment![6]

Blake may distinguish between good and evil a little differently, but he still treats one essential aspect of man's being, Urizen (your reason), as inherently problematic. This shapes his perception of what is good and beautiful in different, if equally imperfect, terms.

The solution to this dichotomy is to surrender back to God

the unlawfully usurped knowledge of good and evil and acknowledge God alone as lawmaker. As long as God is the lawmaker, human concepts of good and evil are mere opinions amendable to that singular "law above the law" to which the people of God seek ultimately to conform. All of society may press, however imperfectly, to one absolute standard. In the Luciferian paradigm, there is no logical hope of redemption and no firm foundation for a just social order.

In the Luciferian way of thinking, beliefs that may otherwise be held as mere opinion become individualized dogma, which differ from one person to the next. Each chooses for himself that which is right. Each opinion becomes a religion by itself, and it is defended with dogmatic zeal. Fallen humanity cannot think in terms of true reform because true reform requires true repentance and acknowledgment of God's external law. If fallen man is his own lawmaker, there is no logical means of appeal to any sacred external standards; only external force. One man's claim to the role of lawmaker is as good any other man's claim. There is no external author of law and no redress or point of reference by which one might be reformed to a right knowledge of good and evil since each individual defines it. In this context of fallen man's thinking, only annihilation can be seen as a reliable solution to human conflict. This is characteristic of man's fallen estate (see Genesis 4:8, Genesis 4:23, and 2 Samuel 24:14).

Contrast this with the liberty that is made possible in biblical redemption. The I AM is sovereign, and his law is binding and absolute. Thus, all things created by God are good, and the Creator's decree is certain. Whatever problems and choices the people of God face need not dichotomize their existence. Their law is God's law. God's law is objective, perfect, sacred, all conditioning, and external. It does not demand the eternal subjugation, annihilation, or demeaning of any aspect of man's essential being in deference to some imaginary seed of perfection within the individual. Jesus Christ neither venerates nor assassinates any aspect of humanity. God's external law nourishes the whole man, body and spirit, in conformity to the lights and perfections of God's law.

Evil exists, but it exists in the same sense in which a vacuum is said to exist. A vacuum is by definition an absence of something. No aspect of humanity is created evil. Evil is by nature something uncreated. God created all things, and he cannot be the author of sin. Therefore, sin is not created at all. Sin is without substance. As darkness is the absence of light and a vacuum is the absence of matter, so sin is the absence of things created and of the law that governs things created. Sin is lawlessness. Thus, the problem of evil as it relates to man's existence is resolved through God's external law. All that God has created is good, and sin is declared void. This is unthinkable in the Luciferian mind because autonomous law does not allow for any external measure of good and evil. Determining good and evil is the essence of deity. Embracing God's external law negates any claim to deity. Embracing God as lawmaker affirms that God is all good and totally distinct from man, whose duty is to obey God's law.

Man is a sympathetic creature, and as such, the impressions upon his physical life will influence his perceptions of the divine nature in harmony with his own condition. He intuitively perceives all relationships as a mirror of the divine nature, and what is true of one is typical of the other. A man who walks by God's law becomes the walking revelation and living image of his heavenly Father when his bodily existence is brought into conformity to God's will. The people of God confess total depravity and may look to God for total redemption. Unlike the dichotomized, autonomous man, the people of God are able to embrace every aspect of humanity as good when brought to conformity to the will of God. When God created man, he saw that what he created was good. To the ascetic, the body represents death and decay. But to the people of God, the life of this body is the slate of the Spirit, upon which is recorded the infinite greatness and eternal attributes of God.

Although we are fallen, every essential aspect of humanity is good, as God has created it. So we confess that we are not just fallen in most aspects, but in every aspect. We are totally corrupt, and yet we have a source of grace completely outside of ourselves where we find total redemption. So let our spiritual leaders and all of those of who seek a better culture consider carefully what we feel compelled to cast aside, and let it never be some aspect of our humanity. That is the way of the world, but God redeems *all* of humanity. And let Christian artists, as advocates of a better culture, remain mindful of the historical doctrines of darkness that have often assailed and corrupted the artist's vocation, even through the church. Let them doggedly follow the wisdom and light of God's Word rather than the philosophies of the world.

# THE GREATER **LIGHT**

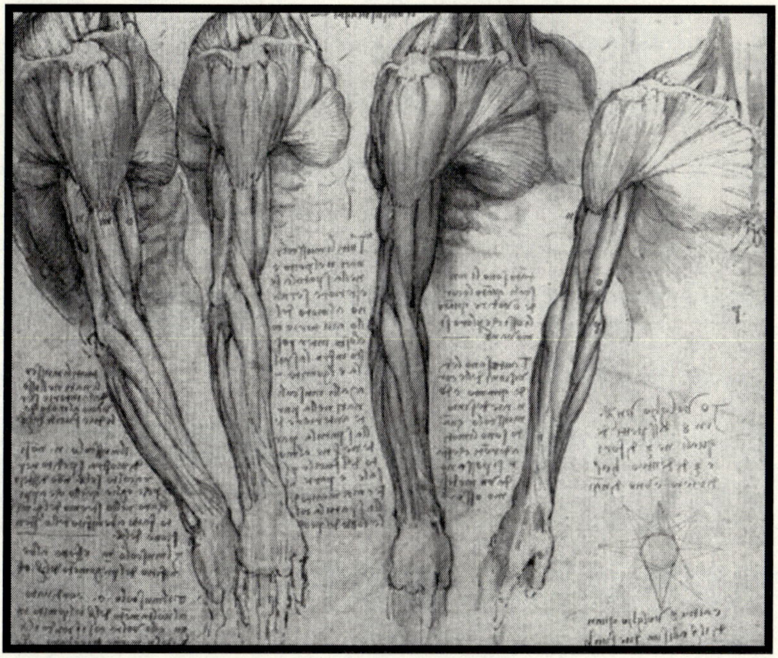

Fig. 10, Leonardo de Vinci, *Muscles of the Neck, Shoulder and Arm (detail),* c. 1509

The above drawing by Leonardo de Vinci depicts more than just artistic studies in form. It shows anatomical details that indicate a deep fascination for human anatomy as a natural science. Leonardo was fascinated with every aspect of God's creation. He thought of creation as a mirror of divine attributes. Leonardo is widely regarded as the symbol of his age—the product of a new economy made possible by the opening of trade routes and commerce. This gave rise to a new wealthy merchant class and a new market for art, science, and revolutionary ideas. This broke the corrupt intellectual monopoly of church demagogues. Although the church was corrupt in Leonardo's days, there were pockets of renewed spiritual enlightenment.

Saint Paul wrote of a light that is greater than that which appeared in the face of Moses after he had spoken with God. He writes, "If the ministry of condemnation had glory, the ministry of righteousness exceeds much more in glory" (2 Corinthians 3:9–11). The Reformation was that ministry of righteousness reborn. It was the greater light and the rebirth of every biblical ideal that would become essential to the foundations of truly free societies.

It seems inevitable that whenever the mind of man is liberated from the oppressive thumb of demagogues, the cleansing light of God's natural revelation begins to awaken souls, inspire the intellect, and wash away the corruption of darkness. Then, as the faith of God's people burns brightly, the darkness is driven back and God's people enjoy that greater light that sanctifies even the most common elements of our world.

This chapter is about the nature and power of that greater light. What connection do Leonardo's works have with this greater light that Saint Paul calls the ministry of righteousness? To answer this question requires a bit of analysis. It is no coincidence that the Reformation came on the wake of the Renaissance. Leonardo de Vinci was one of many people used by God to help advance a view of the world that energized the Reformation. Leonardo had an acute sense of vocational stewardship and accountability. He believed he had a sacred duty to create, invent, and investigate. The medieval church had long represented itself as the sole legitimate mediator for all things pertaining to God and spiritual truth, but all the great minds of the Renaissance sought out knowledge and truth independently of the corrupt church. This outlook elevated conscience and individual moral accountability over dogma and challenged every man as a morally independent creature. It is this attitude of unmediated, independent spiritual responsibility that prepared Europe for the Reformation. This way of thinking set all of Europe on an inevitable collision course with the papacy.

May we say, then, that people like Leonardo helped to prepare the ground for Luther's Reformation? Before the voice of Luther was ever heard, was there already a still small voice speaking to the hearts of the people through the cultural light of the Renaissance? The Renaissance brought raw creative energy to European culture and gave economic empowerment to commoners. Inevitably harnessed to this great wind of cultural change came the Reformation, which brought spiritual freedom. Leonardo s work was received with fanatical enthusiasm in pre-Reformation Germany. Leonardo inspired Albrecht Dürer, Lucas Cranach, and Matthias Grünewald, who all zealously embraced the Reformation.

Not much is known in regard to the personal faith of Leonardo himself. We do not find in his writings the kind of ponderous introspection or detailed theological polemics that characterized the writings of the reformers. Yet he clearly did have his own form of obsession for his Creator. He wrote, "Oh admirable impartiality of thine, thou first Mover; thou hast not permitted that any force should fail of the order or quality of its necessary effects."[7]

Aside from the Platonic language, this sounds much like Cornelius Van Til, who calls God the "all-conditioner." It is God's sovereign ordering of creation that validates the role of science and reason. Similarly, Leonardo saw the laws of nature as God's order of force and effect that God establishes with impartiality (consistency). These are laws of nature that are meaningful and useful because God will not permit them to fail. We may search in vain to find any musing from Leonardo that sound like the

Confessions of St. Augustine, but Leonardo's historical image of a dispassionate intellectual may not be accurate.

The individual piety of such world makers is of no relevance to the overall importance of the Renaissance to the Reformation. They were instruments of the greater light regardless. The Bible provides many good examples of covenant outsiders who advance the ways of God's people. How else should we understand the role of Xerxes, who empowered the Jews to defend themselves? The Bible gives an interesting example of this in a historical chain of events, starting with Pharaoh Necho. God prophesied through Pharaoh Necho and helped him against Carchemish, only to be defeated by Nebuchadnezzar, king of Babylon (see 2 Chronicles 35:20–22). Then God, speaking through Jeremiah, calls Nebuchadnezzar "My servant" and uses Nebuchadnezzar to punish his people with exile (see Jeremiah 27:9–11). Later, Nebuchadnezzar left his kingdom to Belshazzar, whom God had assassinated for profaning the vessels of the temple. King Cyrus then took power and became an agent of restoration for God's people.

All this shows that God's unction has clearly rested upon some who are complete strangers to the covenant, sometimes devouring like a flame those who bear it and leaping to the next unwitting instrument of God's providence. So it was, perhaps, with many of the great minds of the Renaissance. Some were men of faith, and they were all instruments of God's providence.

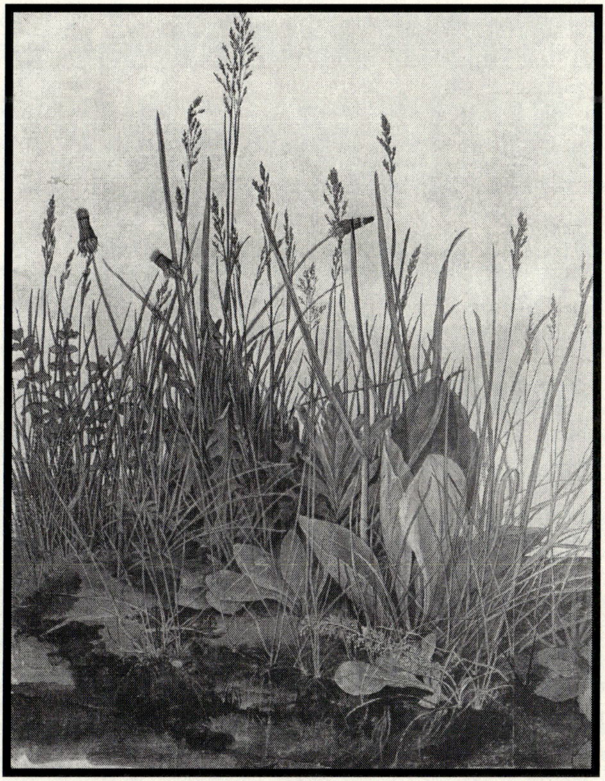

Fig. 11, Albrecht Dürer, *The Large Piece of Turf,* c. 1503]

Artists like Albrecht Dürer saw common things as worthy art subjects. His study *The Large Piece of Turf* almost makes it possible to smell the mingled fragrances of the earth, the grasses, and the gentle summer breeze. His exquisitely rendered studies included small creatures. Although Dürer could certainly appreciate the conventional symbols of beauty and grandeur, nothing seemed to capture his interest more than his nature studies. Dürer was a sympathizer of Martin Luther, who embraced the idea of the universal priesthood of believers spoken of by Saint Peter. This is another manifestation of the greater light and the sanctification of common things.

The Medici family was a catalyst to the Renaissance. Lorenzo de Medici collected geniuses as a hobby. He was a patron to Leonardo da Vinci, Galileo Galilei, Sandro Botticelli, Domenico Ghirlandaio, and Michelangelo Buonarroti. The Medici family produced three popes, yet the Reformation visited even this enclave of papal culture. Lorenzo was enamored with the writings of Erasmus, a great influence on many Protestants. Michelangelo was introduced to the doctrines of the Reformation late in life through his close friendship with Vittoria Colonna. Vittoria came under the influence of the reform-minded monk Bernardino Ochino. Through Vittoria, Michelangelo gained a new circle of friends. Their spiritual leader was the Spaniard Juan de Valdés, who was influenced by Erasmus. Valdés taught justification through faith alone (*sola fide*).

The soul of Europe was a heap of dry tender when the Reformation began, and the spark of the renewed gospel began a fire that burned bright and hot. The flames of this new culture of the universal priesthood were fanned by the timeliest invention in history—Guttenberg's movable type press. Guttenberg's press spread Luther's Reformation message like wildfire. It made the Bible accessible to the common man, giving authority to the universal priesthood of believers. Its translation into the common tongues facilitated a massive wave of spiritual liberation that is still being felt today. The effect of the noontide sun on the newly enlightened minds of God's people was truly remarkable. They shook off their ancient slumber and beheld a whole new world of truth.

It was no wonder that the Divines of the Reformation were a little cautious about visual art because it had been used so effectively as a means of creating an illusion of spiritual authority to the simple laymen of the church. Saint Peter's Basilica represents an astonishing legacy of artistic achievement. Yet it is also a legacy that was funded by the shameful selling of indulgences. Understandably, many of the reformers had little use for this dark legacy of art that accompanied such avarice and debauchery.

But most of the reformers were never contemptuous of visual art itself. They simply rejected idols and insults to the gospel of grace. They had no particular regard for jewel-encrusted artifacts or for grand edifices like Saint Peter's Basilica. With increased access to the Bible, the lavish art of the church and the demagoguery of corrupt church divines were no longer an effective façade for those who conspired to suppress the light of the gospel. Widespread literacy exposed the pretenders to apostolic authority and provided moral clarity for meaningful reform.

Similarly, the artists who were inspired by this greater light were less interested in gilded halos and skies of angels than the natural effects of light and perspective. They were not just interested in saints and nobility but also were fascinated by common things in nature such as animals, plants, and faithfully rendered human anatomy. This reflected their deliverance from a world of mere dogma into the clean noontide light of biblical wisdom and the shadow ministry of natural revelation.

The children of the Reformation achieved a brighter legacy as lovers of an enduring beauty. They saw the laws of nature as laws established by God and were assured of their constancy by a sacred covenant. They studied those laws with as much reverence and due diligence as any moral law uttered from the mouth of God at Mount Sinai. They gave the world modern science, constitutional law, systematic theology, logic, jurisprudence, and a wealth of literature. The persecutions they suffered made them what they were. Western democracies may have become a different culture but for the short lifespan of many churchmen of that era. The reformed church became an urgent kingdom in progress, faced with the constant daunting task of pushing back the legions of spiritual darkness. Many had to fight for their survival. Our spiritual ancestors were zealous kingdom builders. But if all that they could leave us were a splendid set of blueprints and a kingdom in abstract, it is far more than we could have expected. As it was, they gave us more than they themselves imagined.

The reformers made a genuine separation between the duties of minister and magistrate. They were world makers, not king makers, and every field of human endeavor prospered under this new paradigm, each as a sacred trust and ministry by itself, including the arts. Through them, God breathed a divine unction into common endeavors and trades became vocations. This worldview produced men of many talents. When the Puritans came to the New World, they brought with them a pearl of great price—the pure gospel and the compelling vision of a peaceful, free society. It was a treasure they held closely and consciously, and they guarded it with utmost zeal. The Puritans, more than any other peoples, were keenly aware of corruptibility of any human enterprise and took unprecedented measures to resist it.

The Puritans saw their enterprise as an opportunity to form a just and free society that could serve as a model for other nations. They believed that the effectiveness of such a model depended heavily on maintaining the moral and religious purity of the citizens. They tried to keep their Christian society pure and have been called intolerant as a result. We can find fault with this or any historical group of people. But those who harshly judge the New England Puritans ignore historical context. Puritan society was one that was established as an exclusive domain, like a church or private residence. The early New England Puritans had no obligation to accommodate any form of pluralism. In fact, they saw themselves contractually bound to maintain its purity. The Puritans were champions of the greater light, and they were determined to keep it burning white-hot in the new world. Puritan society was a meritocracy. There was to be no permanent serf class, no vainglorious leader or elite blood line of rulers. Here, men of humble beginnings could become wise and industrious and do great things.

It is this legacy of the greater light that came to distinguish America as the Land of Opportunity. The life and work of Charles Willson Peale represents this legacy well. Painting was widely considered a seedy occupation by Peale's time, and most prodigious young minds would have been led into other occupations. Peale was a rare exception, providing a good example of what an American patriot looks like as an artist. He shattered the seedy counterculture stereotype of artists and became a pillar of society. Charles was a man much like his good friends Thomas Jefferson and Benjamin Franklin. Like the reformers of previous centuries, such men were world makers. Yet their calling was not to reform the church, but to defang tyranny. Peale's art serves a valuable narrative role that completes our understanding of the times. But he is an interesting study for other reasons.

Peale embodies the full scope of the greatness of this era and of the land of opportunity. He was a man of meager beginnings as the son of a convicted criminal, rose to a high place of leadership in his society, and achieved great things. Peale, like many of his contemporaries, excelled in everything he tried. He was an artist, conservator, statesman, inventor, naturalist, and museum curator. Some people have compared him to Leonardo da Vinci. That is because there is a common bright thread of natural reverence that runs though the intellect of both of these men. Like Leonardo, Charles was fascinated with God's works of creation, and it is this that drove him to become a naturalist. This is a manifestation of the greater light and of God's continued sanctification of common things. Consider the obsession of a naturalist in the context of Saint Paul's teaching regarding God's works of creation. Paul wrote, "For since the creation of the world his invisible attributes are clearly seen, being understood by the things that are made" (Romans 1:20). The spiritual light of God's creation fascinated Peale. He possessed the power and spirit of Leonardo da Vinci, whose sense of divine revelation through nature was clearly central to his tireless spirit of investigation. Peale was the product of a culture born of the Reformation, and he knew it.

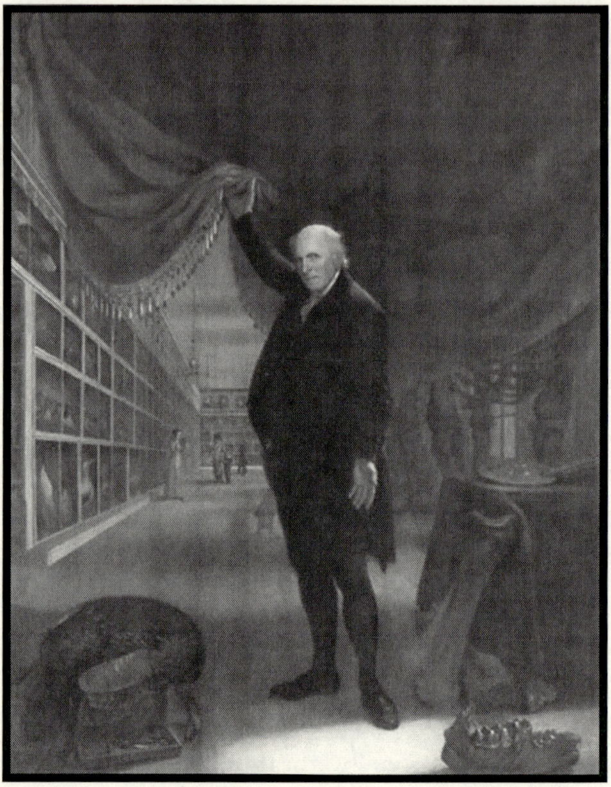

Fig. 12, Charles Willson Peale, *Self-portrait*, 1822

In his self-portrait, Peale depicts himself in a gesture of invitation, lifting a curtain to reveal his prized museum of natural history. As an ultimate gesture of his love of fine art, he named his children after great master painters. Some of them continued their father's artistic legacy and improved on it.

Our spiritual ancestors could have never guessed what God would do through them. But their stunning success as world builders had also created a haven for the enemies of enlightenment through a free marketplace of ideas that is protected by law. Our generation has come perilously close to allowing the destruction of the very epistemological foundation that our promising new world was built upon. Arrogant and godless men have rewritten history. They have contrived an illusion. They have proliferated a lie. The historical debauchery and anti-Christian thinking that has characterized so much of postmodernist art and literature has preserved an illusion of a secularist America in the mind of modern man. It is a great irony that the academic and creative liberty of the cynic thrives on a moral and intellectual vigor that is only possible in historically God-centered cultures.

It is characteristic of God's lavish grace to provide the needs of his people in unexpected ways. God gives to his people in overabundant supply, pressed down, shaken together, and overflowing. God's grace pours forth in abundance, exuding through every corner and crevice of our lives. Any extemporaneous encounter between God's people at the communal hearth of fellowship is a potential means of grace. The art and the ceremonies of the Mosaic Law are described in Holy Scripture as types and shadows of heavenly things, and the church's ceremonies are her holy sacraments.

The sacraments, like the sacrifices of the Law, have a pedagogical and empathetic role like that of the sacred art of the tabernacle. Unlike the Old Testament ceremonial law, the sacraments are more than types and shadows. The sacraments celebrate the substance of the covenant promises fulfilled as present reality, not just things for which God's people hope. A sacrament is a formal institution and a normal means of grace for God's people. Yet God's grace is certainly not limited to sacramental means. Art, like the general fellowship of the saints, has a conspicuous if less formal value as a means of grace, and it is used in that way throughout the Holy Scriptures. Art is the illumination of divinity. Art can serve as an assurance of healing, a monument of remembrance, or a visual token of devotion and resolve.

Why else would God have Moses erect a bronze serpent? Was it not enough for Moses to simply write about the serpents? Why did he not sing about them? Why Did God command Moses two place two cherubim on the mercy seat? Why not something inscribed in words instead? Here is the reason: God has taught us, unambiguously, that some spiritual truths are most effectively expressed in visual artistic form.

God's enduring world of visual beauty is ever present, speaking continuously to the mind and heart in the context of our everyday existence. Beauty is its own form of sacredness, and it sanctifies all of life for the people of God. God's sanctifying grace permeates every little mundane aspect of the lives of God's people. Zechariah wrote of a golden spiritual age, "In that day "*Holiness to the Lord*" shall be engraved on the bells of the horses. The pots in the LORD's house shall be like the bowls before the altar. Yes, every pot in Jerusalem and Judah shall be holiness to the LORD of hosts" (Zechariah 14:20–21).

True to this vision of spiritual enlightenment, the Northern Reformation brought a conspicuous change to the subject matter of art. At this point, artists no longer considered saints and nobility as the only worthy candidates for their subject matter. Post-Reformation artists rediscovered that celebrating the beauty of the common elements of our existence in art had the potential effect of transforming the entire visual world into a meditation of beauty with all due reverence to its Creator. The common and small things of our visual world represent a sort of quiet and unpretentious beauty that has existed from the dawn of time and whose testament to the divine nature speaks continuously. This still small voice of natural revelation is powerful and enduring, representing the full dress of beauty itself.

There was a golden age of art in the reign of King Solomon, whose extravagance is described in elaborate detail (see 1 Kings 6:18–35).

Solomon also commissioned extravagant artwork for his own house (see 2 Chronicles 9:15–20).

When our holy warfare is over and death itself has died, perhaps then we will begin paving our streets with gold. The greater light has not made gold less beautiful. It has simply made common things more precious. This new earthly paradigm calls for art of a different form. In the days of our sojourn in this world we have no particular need of gold-embellished holy places. God's presence, our mercy seat, is manifested in the redemption of God's people and the world that they shall create for God's glory. This is the substance that has replaced the shadow of things yet unseen by our pre-advent ancestors. The veil of partition has been torn asunder. All of life is sanctified. Certainly, the world in which we live is still corrupt. But in the life of God's people, there is no holy and profane, but only sanctity in all of life and being. We are a holy nation and a royal priesthood. If the creative gift was important in the Old Testament, it is even more important in the New Testament.

Because the Bible has so much to say regarding sacred art, it is easy to think that God intended all art to be reserved for religious use. In truth, it may be argued that all art is religious in its very nature. But we can surmise from things the Bible says that God never intended his people to sing only hymns or to create art only for use in formal worship. God's people also had love songs and instrumental music. God's people also created jewelry, embroidered works, and made sculptures and carvings for the sake of beauty and in context with things having nothing to do with formal worship. God seems to approve of all of Solomon's art collection. It was God who gave Solomon his wealth as a reward for seeking God's wisdom.

The Old Testament sacrifices were a ratification of a holy promise, and the art of the tabernacle was given to be a facilitator of worship. The ceremonial law provided a bombardment of all the senses: the sound of harps and the choir, the sights of the tabernacle and its lavish art, the smell of perfume and incense, the feel of the ceremonial cleansing with hyssop, and the tastes of the Passover feast. The early Christians were expelled from the temple and the synagogues, but because of the Jewish rejection of the Messiah, the covenant promise was extended to Gentiles. Thus the early church was largely stripped of the artistic conventions of Old Testament worship both by New Testament design and by practical circumstances. But the kingdom Saint John envisioned was extremely lavish:

John describes the new Jerusalem as an enormous cube of jasper, and pure gold, like clear glass with foundations of precious gems, twelve gates, each of one pearl. The street of the city is described as pure gold, like transparent glass. Most significantly, John sees no temple in it and says, "The Lord God Almighty and the Lamb are its temple" (see Revelation 21:12–22).

The point of having streets of gold in heaven is not just to describe heaven as opulent. The streets of cities have always been considered dirty—a place used as a metaphor for the common and unclean. French residential architecture of eighteenth-century New Orleans was designed to have the front entrance *away* from the street. In the Old Testament, gold was used for sacred things. But in the New Jerusalem, even the streets are sacred. Streets of gold represent the ultimate sanctification of the commonplace, just as every pot and the horses bells shall be "*holiness to the Lord,*" according to the Prophet Zachariah.

Old Testament saints looked for a heavenly kingdom, as do we. Although the patriarchs were sojourners, God made their posterity trustees of a great artistic legacy. God has made us the trustees of the greater light. The essential relationship of art and the means of grace have not changed in New Testament times. Art remains a powerful force in the hands of God's people, yet the form of artistic expression appropriate for the New Testament age of grace has changed. All is now holy. There is no more temple. There is now no need for a gilded focal point of worship, but we continue to need art. Indeed, we need a higher and more pure expression of art as children of the greater light who live in an age of a greater light. The inscription of "Holiness to the Lord" has passed from the crown of the high priest to the things of everyday life.

# THE MYTH AND **MAJESTY OF ART**

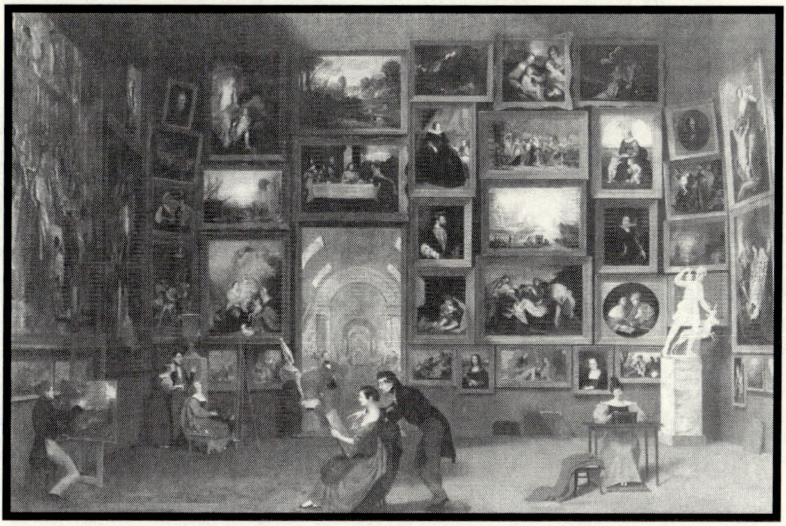

Fig. 13, Samuel F.B. Morse, *Gallery of the Louvre,* c. 1832

In the above painting entitled *Gallery of the Louvre,* Samuel F.B. Morse depicts some rather small images of people in a large gallery. The paintings on the wall depict great and holy things—portraits of saints and nobility, sacred and momentous events. The people are not passive viewers. They are there to study the works at the museum and to copy them. In those days, copying was considered a good and legitimate way of learning from the masters. Learning how to paint was considered a noble pursuit, even if one had no intention of being a professional artist. Morse himself wanted to make a career of painting. But when his wife died, he stopped painting, and he went on to invent the telegraph and Morse code.

This chapter contains a few concepts familiar to the readers who have art degrees. Non-artists need this for orientation. If you are an artist, enjoy the review, but look for ideas that may have never been mentioned during your numerous lectures and critiques.

A visit to the art museum was a religious experience for me as a youth. In the museum, it was common to hear people whispering, as if speaking in a normal tone of voice was a sacrilege. A small boy who would profane this temple by speaking too loudly might cause his mother to softly whisper an admonition into his ear that he was not to raise his voice in the art museum. Sound carried well in the museum, echoing off its marble floor and walls. This encouraged whispering all the more. What creates this intuitive sense of the sanctity of art?

Art has a deeply spiritual aspect. And yet much has been done in the name of art that is offensive to Christian sensibilities. This irony has created a deep ambivalence among people of good conscience toward art as a profession. Christian artists have to accept a heightened scrutiny because the modern stereotypes of artists are not always flattering. Stereotypes can be unfair and prejudicial, but they exist for a reason. A disproportionate number of artists fit the stereotype. The people of God appreciate responsible professionals who respect family, community, common values, and good morals, and far too few historical examples of sound Christian character are present among artists. Yet the biblical models prove that art can be an honorable and divinely approved vocation.

The children of light are responsible for redeeming culture. An important part of that task is to redeem the arts. To do this, it is important to understand the proper role of the arts in culture. Think of culture as man. His legs are tradition, his heart is faith, his arms are his industry, his mind is the law, and his face is art. As a man's face is bound to his identity, so art is bound to the identity of a culture. It communicates the morals of civilized culture to the common man. Scholars may discover civilized culture in books. Civil magistrates may find it in the law. The theologian may discover it in the Holy Scriptures. But without the arts, civil wisdom will not be learned or long preserved among the majority of people. Both the power of art and the problems of art are the intangible values that it is intended to enshrine.

Practical trades are naturally self-regulated by universal standards rooted in practical and tangible results. Every man wants precisely the same thing from a plumber—fixed pipes. Giving customers good service is good business, and the tangible rewards of good business can keep even godless men devoted to certain good standards in plumbing. But what universal desire keeps artists committed to good standards of aesthetics? Some people see beauty in perverse things and see ugliness where others see beauty. It is to be expected that the unregenerate mind will indulge corrupt spiritual desires.

All of this gives weight to the proposition that art should be considered a spiritual ministry to be studied, nurtured, and influenced by the church. Art must be held to a system of diligent spiritual accountability, or it will degenerate. Yet church leaders are often reluctant stewards of such a seemingly convoluted and confusing field. But understanding art is not really so difficult. The goal of this chapter is to provide clarity and validation for the church's rightful authority as a basis to establish her own doctrine of aesthetics.

A sound cosmology makes good aesthetic judgment obtainable. Perhaps the average layman has better judgment than he thinks but is intimidated and confused by the presumably informed opinions of experts. Yet if art is a spiritual ministry, why would anyone trust the opinions of so-called "experts" who have no particular insight regarding the things of God? There is both beauty and nonsense in the work of today's artists. With a good ideological foundation, it is not so difficult to separate the wheat from the chaff and to distinguish between the true majesty of art as a spiritual ministry and the mythology of art as a playground of pedantic elitists. The field of visual art has bestowed the mantle of expertise on far too many people who are not all of one mind. This invites a just challenge to any who would presume to speak with authority on the subject of visual art.

It might serve us well to ignore formal credentials when determining what sort of expert should guide us in judging matters of aesthetics. Imagine that you are lost in a great forest and come upon a kind, uneducated woodsman who was born in those woods and had hunted there since childhood. He says he can lead you back to the city. Even an educated man with a degree in forestry would trust the woodsman's guidance over his own in such a circumstance. Similarly, an art guide must stand on spiritual truth. Those who have faithfully sought out the things of God have come to know a great forest of spiritual truth. For understanding art, spiritual truth is a more valuable body of knowledge than the opinions of a spiritually illiterate expert in art. Christians should have more confidence about art. The honest seeker who asks enough honest questions about art will eventually find greater clarity and greater appreciation for the creative gift.

Such terms as *abstract art, modern art,* and *realism* are useful in common parlance, yet in the study of aesthetics, these words do not always serve us well. Abstract art has been around in one form or another throughout history, and abstract concepts and relationships are interwoven throughout much of what is commonly called realism. Those who speak of realism usually refer to art that contains some representational image rendered with a high degree of academic sensitivity to light, shadow, space, proportion, and form. There is plenty of pre-Renaissance art that is not realism in this sense. Many people think of modern art as unrealistic, but any painting created in modern times is modern art, and some modern artists paint with a high degree of realism. Those who speak derisively of modern art usually dislike the kind of art that ignores traditional academic skills, but many modern artists still respect the value of fine craftsmanship.

Fine craftsmanship is certainly not antithetical to abstraction. Consider how well crafted most musical instruments are. A violin represents nothing other than itself. It is basically a non-objective and abstract form, yet it is the epitome of fine craftsmanship. Also, realism judiciously employs elements of abstraction. The representation of three-dimensional forms on a two-dimensional format is itself an element of abstraction. A painting may consist of brush strokes and daubs of paint used to describe the subject matter in a way that differs somewhat from the appearance of the object itself. These are added elements of abstraction. The daubs of paint become simplified interpretations of the effects of light, shadow, color, and form, but the paint still has the appearance of a pasty substance applied to canvas. That is an element of abstraction. The artist finds pleasure in feeling paint and mixing colors. One who looks at the painting can imagine how the paint was applied and experiences a vicarious pleasure. In a drawing, the artist may use a gracefully curving line to symbolize the edge of an object catching the light, contrasted with the darker space behind it where he creates a sense of negative space with a few simple strokes. These too are abstractions. The lines are clearly trails of carbon on paper, but the abstract language of the lines—used correctly—can create an elegant sense of form and space.

There are elements of abstraction that even make the art of photography what it is. The very process of making a photograph introduces abstractions. A flat, two-dimensional image in a rectangular format alters the overall experience of the depth of field and creates compositional relationships to the format.

Much of contemporary art exploits the inherent beauty of the medium. Making a quality pigment is an art in itself. It is not uncommon for a painter to unpack a costly pigment with some degree of reverence, treating the pigment itself as a work of art much in the same way a musician regards his instrument as a work of art.

There is abstraction in the old masters. There is realism in much of modern art. There is fine craftsmanship in much of what is abstract. This is why common parlance and generalities can be misleading. Any useful system of logic requires a way of speaking precisely as a way of avoiding generalities and exceptions. Only then can we begin to discover unwavering principles we may elevate to the status of a logical discipline. To that end, it is helpful to assign some precise meanings to words.

- Academic skills: Art skills taught in traditional academies, such as the sciences of materials and techniques and the use of color, light, shadow, contrast, proportion, perspective, dimension, and form.

- Representational image: An image of a recognizable object or a real or imagined form

- Symbol: Any mark, object, or image intended to evoke specific associations with things or concepts

- Icon: A symbol of exceptional importance or focal attention

- Craftsmanship: The skillful and precise use of material to create something

- Exquisite: Exceptionally well crafted

- Non-objective: An image that contains no representational likeness of any object

- Abstract: A symbolic or simplified way of describing a thing or an idea

- Abstract quality: The quality of line, shape, texture, or pigment valued for its own visual effect or symbolic language and not solely intended to serve the illusion of form

- Illusionistic: An image that uses light and shadow in a way that effectively creates a sense of form

- Beauty: The sense of pleasure, gratification, or meaning derived from forms, ideas, or sensations

This last term, *beauty,* is especially challenging with regard to precise meaning because beauty has so many forms. We may speak of beauty as something that delights us, but many things can delight us and for many different reasons. This is why it is helpful to specify the forms of beauty individually. In doing so, we may begin to identify principles that make the nature of beauty far more understandable. Here are the forms of beauty:

- Sublime beauty: Found in the majesty of God's works of creation. This is the beauty of creation's whole and pleasant forms, the fragrance of flowers, the grandeur of a mountain, the vastness of space, or the colors of the sky.

- Enigmatic beauty: The allure of the mysterious, the cryptic, and the intangible. This beauty can be found in the hidden plot of a novel, a dissonant musical chord, the lyrics of a hymn, the visions of prophets, or the dreams of dreamers.

- Interpretive beauty: Beauty that is interpreted in a more comprehensible form, such as showing the beauty of light shining through a flower petal with a simple field of color or a single stroke of paint. This form of beauty is reductive in nature. To look at the glory of the midday sun, one must look through a dark glass. Similarly, interpretive beauty makes us more conscious of God's sublime beauty by introducing a filter of abstraction so that our minds can absorb the experience. But the sublime beauty is overwhelming. It is more than we mere mortals can absorb. It is God's gift of art that aids our perception of his sublime beauty. Perhaps many people have never truly seen a sunset until they have seen a painting of a sunset. Interpretive beauty enables their vision of such things.

- Exquisite beauty: This is the beauty of something crafted with great skill. Something can be ugly in every other way, but if well crafted, it has its own intriguing form of beauty. Something of exquisite beauty affirms, typologically, that we as God's creatures are fearfully and wonderfully made.
- Explicative beauty: This is the tangible beauty of holiness or the beauty of God's moral order and his typological revelation of himself, such as the faithful union of a husband and wife, a mother's love for her child, or a moral leader's altruistic sacrifices for a just cause. Such things reveal the attributes of God and bring order and hope to life.
- Associative beauty: This is anything that evokes pleasurable associations with other forms of beauty. Some things we might not otherwise find beautiful will seem beautiful to us if they awaken memories of something else that is beautiful to us. A boy might enjoy the smell of livestock because it evokes memories of his grandfather's farm and of horseback rides in the country. An outdoorsman may enjoy the smell of a skunk because it reminds him of his vacation times in the wilderness.
- Vain beauty: This form of beauty is connected in some way with perverted desires or delusions. An object of vain beauty may posses some honorable forms of beauty although it is coveted in ways that are offensive to the ideals of God's enduring forms of beauty.

- Pedagogical beauty: This is the beauty of instruction. A work of art can be seen as beautiful when it effectively teaches and idea or concept that we want to see disseminated.

Beauty is expressed on numerous levels, and it comes in various proportions and combinations. But if we begin to consider the nature of beauty's various specific forms, we will begin to see a useful system of aesthetic logic emerge.

To understand beauty is our essential first step in understanding the guardian and minister of beauty. What is the measure of an artist? All human worth is inherent, based on the declaration that we are all created in God's image. How will we assay the ultimate value of something so intangible as beauty? It is not the greatness of our talents that God values, but the soundness of our stewardship over everything God has given. To whom much is given, much is required. But the true value of our stewardship is sometimes hard to see. The Apostle Paul tells us that God will test every man's work, whether made of "gold, silver, precious stones, wood, hay, straw" (1 Corinthians 3:12). Ultimately, the value of art and everything else will be measured by its effectiveness as an instrument of enduring good. In life, this value can be inscrutable, so we must allow for the fact that the meaning of some things will not always be knowable. We must accept by faith that God will ultimately give meaning to the service of his people, even if the fruits of our labors are not apparent. Beauty is perceptible only when we perceive a portion of God's eternal purpose irrevocably fulfilled in our labors. Any consensus regarding what is beautiful is ultimately a consensus of what is enduring and desirable. Such things will always be beautiful to God's people.

With so much imbued in the creative gift, it is fair to ask whether there really is any principal difference between sacred art and other art. For me, it is a distinction that the theology of Cornelius Van Til has almost eradicated. I once heard Casey give a lecture on the significance of the symbols of priestly service in the Old Testament ceremonial law. He described the priestly garments and the temple furnishings in great detail and explained the spiritual truths reflected in every small part. He made clear that absolutely nothing about the ceremonial law was arbitrary. Indeed, the writer of Hebrews emphasizes that every detail was to be considered important according to God's instruction: "See to it that you make all things according to the pattern given to you on the mountain." Like most art students, I was taught to value individual creativity, spontaneity, and imagination. But here was something much greater—patterns for the tabernacle specified and commissioned by God himself through Moses. But what could a Christian artist of the twentieth century possibly learn from Old Testament ceremonial law?

I asked Casey if a Christian artist should see everything he creates as a reflection of a divine truth. "Yes!" he responded quickly and emphatically. Was Casey really saying that everything an artist makes must have a spiritual lesson imbedded into it? In his own home, Casey had art on the wall that was neither of biblical subject matter nor captioned with any Scripture text. So what did he mean by saying that all art must reflect some divine truth?

I began to make a connection between Casey's famous ontological view of truth and his corresponding view of beauty. All enduring beauty was from God and must reflect God. Perhaps it is missing the point to say that an artist who seeks God must be careful to reflect divine truth. It may be more accurate to say that if an artist seeks God he is utterly unable to suppress divine truth in his art. This one idea was worth a great deal to me as an artist. It seemed like the ultimate irony that Casey was utterly inept as a visual artist, yet his theology helped me answer some of the greatest doubts I had as an artist.

I began to look at my own art as a form of prayer and meditation, and I discovered that many other artists saw their art in the same way. Leonardo da Vinci explained it well:

> The deity that resides in the science of the painter causes the mind of the painter to transform itself into a similitude of the divine mind, since it proceeds with free power to generate the diverse essences of various animals, plants, fruits, landscapes, plains."[8]

Leonardo believed that his artistic interpretations of nature gave him a deeper knowledge of God's creation and thus a deeper love for God.

Drawing from a live subject, nature or still life has always produced in me such a connection. My etchings, which are filled with symbols and narrative, have appealed to my instructors and to other artists. However, I have found that my simple portraits and studies are what appeal to most other people. The power of simple, interpretive beauty should not be undersold, for all the reasons Leonardo stated. On the following page is a portrait of Dr. John Skilton. This is the kind of image that would not appear in my portfolio review as a master's candidate for a degree in printmaking. Nevertheless, I have come to value this kind of simple drawing for its own aesthetic rewards.

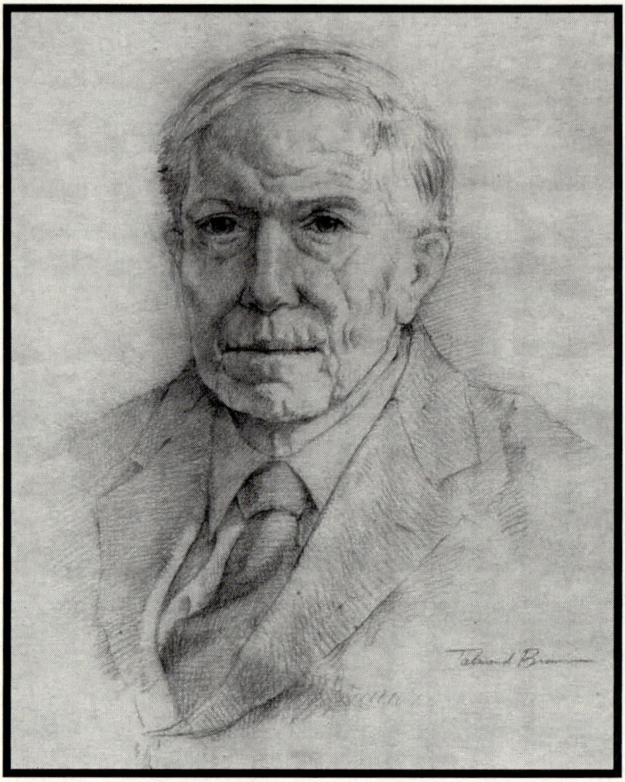

Fig. 3, S. Talmond Brown, *Portrait of Dr. John Skilton,* 1980]

Casey Van Til's comments regarding art's reflections of divine attributes eventually completed a circle with regard to my developing views of the nature of symbols. This has to do with a concept that my graduate advisor, Lee Davis, tried to pound into me. The concept is essentially this: The greatest power of symbols is not found in a symbol's meaning according to tradition, custom, or legend. It is found in personal symbols derived from life experience. Symbols may be derived from mundane and innocuous experiences of day-to-day life, but they obtain meaning as a part of God's web of natural revelation. We may never be conscious of the knowledge that such things impart to us, and yet they affect us.

Lee gave me this example: If you open your window and see

the dried remains of a grasshopper in the windowsill, it becomes a part of your visual world. It may seem innocuous and insignificant, but it becomes a personal symbol with various associations. Indeed, I associate dead grasshoppers with hot summer days and the smell of grassy fields where grasshoppers swarm. When such symbols appear in the mind's eye, it is a story trying to come out. Lee encouraged me to find those symbols with something he called reflex imagery. That is, to draw whatever comes to mind or whatever your mind sees on the blank page or in random markings. As you draw, those personal symbols begin to emerge. Pursuing this method drove me insane, but it was worth it. It taught me a great deal.

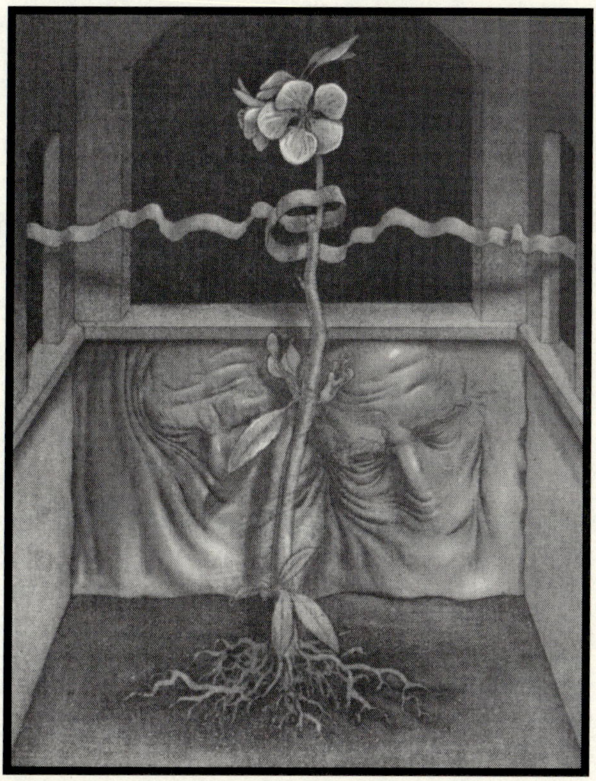

Fig. 15, S. Talmond Brown, *Veiled Faces*, 1994]

Sometimes this method of working actually resulted in something I liked. On the previous page is such an image. The images came spontaneously, except for a flower I plucked from outside the studio. I soon associated the flower in the center of the room with the life of Christ. A ribbon enters the room, encircles the flower, and passes out of sight through an opposite window. Christ is from everlasting to everlasting and has become visible to us in his incarnation into our finite world. A curtain takes the shape of veiled faces in the background, and the eyes are closed. I did not immediately associate the image with anything specific, but when I showed it to my sister, Cathy, she quoted to me a portion of Isaiah 53:

> Who has believed our report? And to whom has the arm of the LORD been revealed? For he shall grow up before him as a tender plant, And as a root out of dry ground. He has no form or comeliness; And when we see him, *There is* no beauty that we should desire him. He is despised and rejected by men, A man of sorrows and acquainted with grief. And we hid, as it were, *our* faces from him; he was despised, and we did not esteem him.
>
> Isaiah 53:1–3

As an artist, achieving a good likeness of a face, a still life, or a landscape has always been the easy part of my art education. Learning to retrieve personal symbols was much harder, but the skill paid great dividends. The art of the Bible is replete with symbols throughout its sacred text. Learning how to retrieve personal symbols has made me more sensitive to the symbols that appear in the Scriptures. Over time, sometimes unconsciously, images and events described in the Scriptures have become part of my own reservoir of personal symbols. That, I am convinced, is part of God's design for art.

An artist explicates an awareness of beauty that is ultimately based on his knowledge of God. The essential truths of God are revealed to us through the light of nature to all people. Art celebrates the beauty of God's holiness, and it is often the only point of spiritual commonality that lost souls have with God's people. I believe God uses art to draw spiritually dead people into hearing the call to redemption.

The artist, like any preacher of truth, must overcome the corrupt desires of humanity to fulfill true spiritual needs. How does a minister of truth teach a form of truth that is offensive to the hearer? It is an old problem, one well summarized in the warning of the Apostle Paul: "For the time will come when they will not endure sound doctrine, but according to their own desires, because they have itching ears, they will heap up for themselves teachers; and they will turn their ears away from the truth, and be turned aside to fables" (2 Timothy 4:3–4).

The artist must provide something that appeals to his audience, but not indiscriminately. Good artists, like good pastors, can use the allure of one kind of beauty to reject vain beauty and to help sinners cultivate a taste for an underappreciated enduring beauty that sinful flesh is slow to receive. This is how both artist and pastors may train people to love enduring beauty and reject vain beauty. As purveyors of truth, artists must use skill and discernment. Like pastors, Christian artists have a spiritual ministry and should be accountable to the church.

The ministry of the Christian artist is to obviate the beauty of holiness and God's eternal purpose. It is the sacred vocational trust of every one of God's people to take inventory of his gifts and assess the faithfulness of his stewardship for the kingdom. We cannot ultimately judge the entire worth of art, but we must measure what we can. God requires accountability. It is the mark of good stewardship to embrace accountability and seek it out. Most professions benefit from tangible universal desirables by which one may apply some human measure of success: Engineers, lawyers, and doctors are judged by clear standards. The bridge withstands an earthquake, the client gets a favorable ruling in court, or the patient's health improves. The nature of the artist's ministry is significantly different in that its success relates to many intangible and differing standards.

Accountability for an artist is fraught with danger. What can the artist measure? Certainly we may speak of the rules of perspective, proportion, materials, and techniques, but the focus of art is beauty itself, and beauty comes in different forms. Our perception of beauty will inevitably differ on various levels and can be affected by uniquely individual experiences. Associative beauty, exquisite beauty, and explicative beauty can create wide differences in aesthetic perceptions. For the people of God, the perception of all beauty is ultimately bound to the substance of our faith, for God makes all things beautiful in his season. This is why art is a distinctly spiritual ministry. It cannot be a viable discipline apart from faith.

Fine art seeks to be valued for beauty's sake. Art confronts us with the reality of God's beauty and thus the reality of God's eternal purpose. This aspect of the artist's ministry invites introspection. But it is fruitless to ponder intangible and inscrutable things with no objective point of reference. Purely subjective art allows pretenders to dawn the mantel of erudition, as if they have risen to an elite class of cultural enlightenment. It is impossible to measure the worth of purely subjective things or assign merit to it in a scholastically honest way. The same work of art that appeals to one person may leave another person cold. This is why Georgia O'Keeffe can dislike the work of Jackson Pollock, who is loved by Peggy Guggenheim, who hates the work of Andy Warhol. It is all opinion, and who can argue objectively for or against any of it? Apart from art's spiritual ministry, the artist has only the exacting disciplines of craft and logic as a universal point of reference.

Some contemporary artists have formed an unofficial priesthood, shrouded in subjectivism. These are cultural elitists who don't see their work simply as art but as "high art." The Bible speaks clearly of the virtue of craftsmanship, but we cannot find in the Bible any such concept as high art. The concept of high art reflects a desire of some artists for cultural beatification. Elitists want to be thought of as prophets, philosophers, luminaries, and vanguards of social change but without the immense weight of accountability that should go with it. Such pretense rejects accountability as a means of keeping the fantasy of self-importance alive. Craft is a natural threat to those who have reason to fear being exposed by objectified standards. In the Bible, craft is the only objectified standard of beauty that is repeatedly mentioned. By objective biblical standards of craftsmanship, your grandmother's splendid quilt is full of artistic merit. Why should a painting or sculpture be considered any higher expression of creativity than a well-crafted quilt? The Bible gives us no clear evidence of any genre, media, or category of creative expression that is elevated above another. The Bible extols craft in rather broad terms: "Do you see a man who excels in the work of his hands? He shall stand before kings" (Proverbs 22:29). And again, "Whatever you hands find to do, do it with all your might" (Ecclesiastes 9:10).

The layman should not put too much weight in the aesthetic judgment of an artist, nor should the artist be too dismissive of the sensibilities of the layman. We must shun the arrogance of the elitist and insist that the artist is not always entitled to any special deference as a judge of beauty, as if he were a prophet or philosopher. A few artists in history may be described in such lofty terms, but any honorable calling may be an instrument of social progress at some particular point in history. God uses all kinds of people to advance his kingdom, including artists. Fine art is neither frivolous, nor is it everything.

As Christians, we are called to be a people of faith. But our faith in God sometimes requires becoming doubters with regard to ways of the world. But departing from the ways of the world can be a long sojourn with the hand of God leading us through incremental changes in our progression toward enlightenment. At certain times in the life of a faithful doubter, the seeds of doubt are planted and watered. There are other periods when the vines of doubt simply take in the sunlight and slowly grow unnoticed. Then there are days of epiphany when doubts suddenly come to full bloom and the faithful doubter finds himself cured forever of some worldly illusion. All who seek the will of God will experience such times.

Such an epiphany came to me during a local art exhibition in Houston. The piece I entered had previously won an award at a national exhibit, but it was rejected from a local show. When I picked up my entry, I saw much of the other work that was rejected, and it was quite good, showing excellent drawing skills with great craft and composition and color, so I was anticipating a good show. But the body of work that was accepted seemed much inferior to the body of work that was rejected. The work that was accepted was dark, crude, and primitive and showed little regard for craftsmanship. Some pieces had cynical and edgy themes, and some could be described as left-winged, political propaganda. The judge of the show was a local artist who had chosen all of the art that looked like his own work. The judge rejected many pieces that exhibited superior craftsmanship, skill, and sensitivity—apparently useless criteria for judging great art in the mind of this judge. His cosmology affected his perception of beauty on the deepest level.

I decided that I would never again enter an art show that was juried by someone whose own work left me cold. This was an attitude adjustment that has been in progress for a while, like a slowly growing vine. After college, I felt that I should know more about art than I did. Worse still, I could find nobody to fill the gap for me, even among renowned, living artists I had met at the two prestigious art institutions I had attended. It almost drove me insane. There was something about the prevailing, local art trends that I found oppressively boring. I was eager to believe that there is something of commonly recognized aesthetic value in everything that educated artists might call "art." But in all my years in school, I had found no rational methodology for judging the brightest and best in fine art.

I came to believe that there was no consensus regarding normative standards of beauty and no consensus among reputable artists regarding the difference between good art and bad art. Art today is simply validated by social pressure on artists to give homage and affirmation to certain trends and prevailing opinions. I began to resent the intellectual and aesthetic suicide that this seemed to entail. With the vines of faithful doubts in full bloom, I decided that I should not be bothered if some art left me cold. If the work of a famous artist seemed unremarkable to me, I would no longer assume I was missing something. I would listen to anyone who could show himself wise, cogent, and reasonable in his views of art, but I would no longer have great confidence in anyone else's aesthetic judgment, regardless of his expertise.

I continued to perceive enough beauty in some primitive and nonrepresentational art to prevent a complete slide into cynicism. I occasionally found art students who shared my frustrations with inverted aesthetic values and who were not shy to express them.

I recall a day trip when one of my art professors took us graduate students on a lecture tour of the Dallas Museum of Fine Art. We came to a painting titled *The Shepherd Faustulus Bringing Romulus and Remus to His Wife* by Nicholas Mignard. It was painted in a lovely classical style in 1654. The lighting, form, proportions, and colors were masterful, yet our professor had something mildly disparaging to say about it. He had nothing but praise for some contemporary paintings that demonstrated far less skill and craftsmanship. One of the female graduate students expressed some frustration over how the professor could dismiss such a beautiful painting and began to argue with him. The conversation went something like this:

> Student: How can you put down this painting after saying all those good things about that boring abstract painting you just praised? Look at the colors! They are still vibrant after four centuries! Look at the beauty of the figures—the warmth and softness of the flesh tones! How can you think that contemporary painting is a better work of art than this!
>
> Professor: Certainly there is beauty in this painting, but there is more to artistic merit than academic skill. You should do more reading about contemporary art.
>
> Student: What I have read thus far has not given me any clue! (She responded with some frustration.)
>
> Professor: Perhaps if you were to read—
>
> Student: Reading doesn't help me with this. Why can't you just tell me what is so wrong with a beautiful classical painting style?
>
> Professor: Just read. I can suggest some titles you can check out from the library.
>
> Student: Why am I supposed to see modernism as some kind of great advancement in art? Seeing this painting makes me feel like art has greatly regressed!

And so the argument continued. I sympathized with what she was saying, but I said nothing. And then, as I stood there listening to her argue with the professor, a sudden realization came to me: I was craving a cup of coffee. The tour ended, and the rest of the class headed for the museum café, so I left my professor arguing with the contentious coed and headed off to join the other students. When I turned a corner, I saw a large Jackson Pollock painting displayed on a brick wall near the cafe. It looked good to me there. In fact, I imagined that in that particular place and context, while enjoying a cup of coffee, that abstract expressionist painting was a welcomed sight. I continued to sympathize with the views of that bold, young art student who loved the Mignard painting that showcased objective and demonstrable skills. But there are also styles of painting that have a level of appeal that has nothing to do with advanced artistic skill, but of the raw aesthetic appeal of color and contrast, texture, and activation of space. This sort of art has legitimate aesthetic value too. Nevertheless, I have come to believe that some painting, however legitimate as artistic expression, cannot be taught or judged as an academic discipline. Anything that can be criticized, rewarded, graded, certified, or rejected in academia should be taught or judged by some objective standard. Otherwise, how does an institution show justice in its cause for denying or awarding an academic degree in art. Not all artists need an education, and not all art needs to be certifiable by academic standards. This is an important distinction since trying to look at all art through the same aesthetic value structure can lead to much confusion.

I was confused during most of my years as an art student, but in all those years I can remember a few moments of lucidity when some priceless truth came into focus.

One such moment came when my graduate advisor was extolling the greatness of a particular piece of primitive art only to explain emphatically, "If you want to be a good primitive artist, don't go to school!"

Primitive art is not about highbrow pretensions of genius. It is about an honest and childlike view of the world. Some forms of art, while having a certain beauty, cannot be taught and should not be represented as an academic discipline. Picasso believed that children are artists by nature, but most don't remain that way once they grow up. Picasso loved abstraction, and in this context he was right. Children are abstractionists by nature. Abstraction does not have to be taught. It is how God made us. Abstraction is a good thing because it is a way of simplifying our perceptions of the world. Children naturally begin drawing stick pictures. A child must be trained in the skill of non-abstraction in order to describe light and shadow in a way that conveys a plausible visual experience of form, space, proportion, and color. To apply this academic skill is a discipline of the mind by which the artist learns to control the powerful innate instinct to abstract. This academic discipline does not renounce abstraction entirely but empowers the artist to resist abstraction when it suits his purpose. Yet abstraction remains a valuable instrument of creative expression. In fact, some forms of art find their best expressions through the unexceptional or untrained mind. This principle applies not just to primitive art, but to other genres as well. It is incongruous to speak of such forms of art as reflective of artistic genius. That misses the point. Its beauty is that it reflects humanity. It is a window into the soul.

Some forms of art do reflect intellect, but this is beauty in a very different form. Intellect is exhibited mostly in craftsmanship. Some forms of art depend on craftsmanship more heavily than others do. It is easy to see why the craft of the potter is used so often in the Bible as a metaphor of the Creator/creature relationship. There are numerous theological lessons contained in the creation of a vessel of clay on the wheel. The potter begins his work by kneading a lump of clay. The clay must be consistent and free of lumps and air pockets. As the potter places the clay on the wheel, the first thing he must achieve is a centered lump of clay. He turns the wheel as he baptizes the lump with water. A beginner will put his hands around the lump and attempt to center it by pressing from both sides, but this never works. The lump wobbles around in his hands as it turns on the wheel. The master potter sets his hand firmly at one position in space and does not allow it to move. This forces the clay to conform to the master's hand. Once the clay is centered in the potter's hands, the potter can begin to form the clay by pressing into the center of the clay and raising the side. After the pot is removed from the wheel and allowed to dry, it is then fired, glazed, and fired again with intense heat. The heat vitrifies the clay to make it a strong and useful vessel.

To become honorable vessels of God's creation, we must also be consistent, free of hard spots and voids. Our unmoved, immutable Creator centers us. He conforms us to his hand. We are born of water; then we go through the fire and we are changed. We have no more capacity than a lump of clay to form ourselves into honorable vessels. We are the work of our Maker's hands.

A clay vessel is a good metaphor for humanity in other ways. It is made to contain something, and what it contains defines its character. A good clay vessel has a resonance that indicates it is free of cracks. It can be useful and beautiful, but the inherent worth of its substance is low. It is made of the dust of the earth. Saint Augustine said that the word *dust* in the Genesis description of Adam's creation is more properly understood as "slime" because God caused a mist to rise up and water the earth. By implication, the earth was wet like clay. We are the slime of the earth, yet we are wonderfully and fearfully made because we are made in the image of God.

The artist, like the theologian, does not add to the basic

knowledge of God. God's revelation of himself is already communicated to all people through his works of creation. It is sometimes the job of the artist to pierce the conscience and inspire obedience to God's law and to destroy speculations and false teachings that would suppress the knowledge of God, who makes all things beautiful in his season. To know God is to know the essence of enduring beauty, and all people are without excuse with regard to the knowledge of God or of his beauty.

Just as the theologian has no secret gnosis of God and his attributes, so the artist has no secret gnosis of aesthetics. Like the doctor of the law, his role is to bring to the light of consciousness the common knowledge that God has revealed to all of mankind. Just as the theologian brings to light the knowledge of God and his attributes, so the artist brings to light the enduring beauty that is founded on God's efficacious providence. Both the theologian and the artist are equipped to do battle against the vain beauty that would beguile and suppress the knowledge of enduring beauty that God has placed inside the heart of every person. As in every discipline, there is a cryptic body of knowledge for the theologian and for the artist. But these are peripheral to the core of either ministry. The theologian may have an uncommon knowledge of church history, Greek, Hebrew, and biblical studies. But in the basic knowledge of God and his attributes, the theologian has no advantage over any other person. The artist may know principles of drawing, design, perspective, color, and pigment, but he has no distinct advantage with regard to his ability to appreciate a thing of beauty. When an artist renders on canvas the effects of light through leaves or captures in stone the suppleness of flesh, he has drawn attention to the beauty of God's creation and has thereby magnified the attributes of God.

It is not necessarily a sign of sophistication to see beauty where others do not, nor is it always uncouth to dislike what others proclaim as beautiful. Those who fear being labeled as simple or unsophisticated will often strain to see artistic merit in mediocrity or fail to see excellence in what is not fashionable. It is one thing to remain open-minded and to explore new horizons and new ways of seeing the world. It is another thing to refuse to acknowledge the truth when an emperor truly has no clothes.

Art can be a means of instruction or inspiration, but the greatest majesty of art is its power to affirm humanity. Art is to be cherished as a celebration of God's creation. Art can be a form of spiritual meditation, sharpening powers of observation and inspiring greater reverence for our Creator. Those who create art need not pursue it as a profession in order to excel at it. Art is not just a skill; it is a primary skill, essential for exploring the secrets of the mind and soul. It is something that affects various important aspects of our humanity and our human potential. That is the majesty of art.

Not every style of art should be judged by the same standard, as if every work of art were intended to showcase artistic genius. Everyone has heard the complaint, "My four-year-old nephew could do that." Of course he could! In fact, that is often the point. It may even be possible that some styles of artistic expression are actually improved by lesser intelligence or lack of formal education. A child's mind is less tainted by the social groupthink and semi-sophistication of society. This can yield a pure and visceral creative expression. Art has plenty of good uses not requiring intellectual sophistication, yet art should be billed honestly for whatever it is. A backyard puppet show is a wonderful thing for children to be involved in, but nobody will confuse it with La Scala. Writing, music, and visual art can be good for anybody's spiritual and intellectual development, but few artists will ever be like Shakespeare, Mozart, or Rembrandt. Some artists strive to discover the threshold of art rather than its pinnacle. Their work is a game of aesthetic limbo, an experiment in how to make something as non-exquisite as possible while achieving something that can be called art. Some artists remove themselves entirely from the process of making art and create accidents on canvas, which are represented as finished paintings. Some experts will pretend that they are able to detect some sign of artistic prowess in such works, but again, they miss the point. It is possible to take the painting of an ape or elephant and trick experts into believing that it is the work of an astute artist.

In 1917, Marcel Duchamp entered a urinal into an art exhibit as a prank and signed it *Mutt.* Many considered this a wordless commentary on art judges who could no longer perceive a qualitative difference between a real masterpiece and a ready-made, industrial product. Duchamp's artistic contribution to the aesthetic value of the urinal was, according to him, its simple presentation in a different context. Perhaps Marcel's explanation of his urinal was just an attempt to keep the joke alive. That said, his explanation actually does make sense. Duchamp's urinal does have a trace of artistic merit in its ironic pedagogical value. There is even more merit that may be claimed by the designer of the urinal, the industrial engineers who worked out the technical problems of mass reproduction, and the technicians who operated the molds and the kilns. The urinal has symmetry and a fine, white-porcelain finish. It has aesthetic qualities. It is not, however, like Michelangelo's *David.* A lesser and greater glory should be easy for all to distinguish, and it is not exclusively about the form. Nearly anyone can perceive the difference of aesthetic value between Michelangelo's *David* and a plaster reproduction of the same. Why should the lesser glory of a urinal be any harder to distinguish? In 1961, an Italian artist named Piero Manzoni went even further. He supposedly canned his own excrement, labeled it in several languages, displayed it as art, and priced it by weight equal to the price of gold. It has been reported since then that the cans are actually filled with plaster. Should an art buyer feel defrauded if he buys a can of *Merda d'Artiste* only to discover that it contains no authentic excrement? In the end, we may assess the elegance of such pranks as having their own form of artistic merit. Yet if the design of either Marcel Duchamp or Piero Manzoni is to expose the emperor's nakedness, it is not with the intent of persuading him to get some real clothes. Marcel was a major figure of Dada, a cultural movement that advanced ideas of absurdity, anti-art, and anarchy. Piero Manzoni was also widely considered an anarchist. Perhaps the emperor's new art has done more for the greater cause of truth than we can imagine. This is conceivable but also very hard to know. We may believe that there is beauty in it, but we cannot generally assert it as if we knew.

Beauty itself may be defined by ephemeral and subjective criteria that are useless to discuss if there is no commonality of values or epistemology. Most of today's anointed, fine-art priesthood judge artistic merit in terms of creativity and the notoriously imprecise criteria associated with it, such as imagination and originality. Creativity is important, but assessing it can be wildly subjective. To speak of artistic merit implies an objective, qualitative value, which may be recognized by others. That is why a classical art education will focus on objective standards that distinguish the greater skills of a master craftsman from the lesser skills of an apprentice. The secular art demagogues may scoff at this approach, thinking that it smothers the higher and more ephemeral attributes of creativity. However, a biblical epistemology will inevitably lead the student of fine art to value the relatively mundane disciplines of craftsmanship as the best path to aesthetic enlightenment.

The craftsman is a type of his Creator, and the work of his hands is a type of himself. It is the inherent, instructive power of the artist's typological relationship with his craft that gives the artist access to the more ephemeral elements of artistry. It is why wisdom and craftsmanship are so closely related in the Bible. Craftsmanship awakens wisdom and creativity. Creativity is an immeasurable attribute that does not come directly though instruction. By definition, it cannot be learned from another person, just as a seminal idea cannot be learned from another person. The pursuit of creativity absent the hard disciplines of craftsmanship is likely to result in boring contrivances that may pass for art but reflect nothing noteworthy of creativity. Exceptions may be found, but they are few.

Beauty is not one thing. A carving of the face of Medusa may be hideous and yet created with such great skill that it may be called beautiful. Beauty itself is sometimes spoken of in qualitative terms as in the Song of Solomon: "Oh most beautiful among women" (Song of Solomon 6:1). This implies a set of criteria by which beauty is assessed, even though this kind of beauty can be subjective. However, when speaking of artifacts as beautiful, the Bible commonly speaks of its craftsmanship. All manner of objective measure can be applied to craftsmanship: symmetry, brightness of color, accuracy in proportion and form, etc. God clearly distinguishes skilled craftsmen, and he also expected his people to be able to distinguish them.

Certain universal things are attractive to all people of a morally viable society. They will prefer life over death, truth over falsehood, order over chaos, clarity over ambiguity, and wholeness over deformity. That is the human connection to the divine order of creation, and it is how God speaks to us. God's order is sacred and beautiful beyond words. Any desire that turns God's order on its head reflects a move toward reprobation. The Apostle Paul spoke of God giving idolaters over to degrading passions (Romans 1:21–29). Every idol is a lie against the divine nature, and every perversion of natural beauty is a lie against God's created order. That is why beauty is a moral imperative that can be deduced from Scripture. This is why Paul explicitly said:

> Finally, brethren, whatever things are true, whatever things are noble, whatever things are just, whatever things are pure, whatever things are lovely, whatever things are of good report, if there is any virtue and if there is anything praiseworthy—meditate on these things.
>
> Philippians 4:8

There is a theological sense in which we assert that God makes everything beautiful. There is a kind of beauty that is known only by faith in God's providence. God provides everything for a purpose, even the wicked for the day of destruction. All that God has created is good according to God's secret counsel, but we must look to God's revealed counsel with regard to our earthly stewardship of beauty. We cannot judge artistic merit in terms of discovering some path to enlightenment through creative expression. We do not need artists to discover some profound truth regarding the human condition. These are all intangible things of which only a prophet of God may speak with real authority. In the world of God's inscrutable providence, a child's casual scribble can be more consequential to humanity than the seven ancient wonders, but we will never know. We can only judge what we can measure. Everything else we call truth must be taken by faith. To assess God's secret counsel is not in the scope of anyone's competence or of any art instructor's responsibility.

We are to value some things over others in keeping with the revealed counsel of God. We value the temple over the gold of the temple. We value humanity over beasts. We value mercy, love, and justice over tithes of spices. Yet we may speak of things, persons, or places as having greater and lesser beauty. We may distinguish a skilled craftsman as distinct from someone of lesser competence, for even among good things there is a greater and lesser good. In every day of creation, God saw that what he created was good. Yet the creation of man was described as *very* good. There is the glory of stars, the moon, and the sun, and these are not equal. God expects us to make choices and judgments with regard to beauty, and for everything we do there is a season. If everything is beautiful in its season, what does this say about things out of season? There is timeliness to some forms of beauty, and what is beautiful today may not seem so tomorrow. If you could have any famous work of art in the world, you would choose what most captivates you or pleases you or inspires you. The choice itself is a judgment of your distinct aesthetic values.

Some people will look at contemporary art and ask, "Is it art?" as if the term *art* is a sacred designation not to be wasted on the unworthy. Practically speaking, art is whatever most people understand it to be. Logically speaking, any effort of creative expression may be called art. There is a form of wholesome beauty in most of what is done in the name of art, and it is almost impossible for anyone to create something totally void of artistic merit. Nevertheless, not all art is good, and not all art that is good should be judged alike. There is a certain value structure of artistic merit that may be taken from the Bible, which speaks clearly against forms of idolatry and provides examples of what God approves. The Bible extols the virtue of fine craftsmanship and diligent industry. These are standards by which art may be measured as an objective discipline, but there is more to it than this. The Christian artist should be mindful of his pedagogical role as a type of the Creator and should take care to represent God's attributes in the work of his hands. This is the essence of artistry, and it may be applied to any honorable profession that is done well. True artistic genius is rare, and it is made obvious by objective standards of achievement. The work of the artist can be as noble as the holy ideals he embraces or as morally offensive as the false gods he serves. Art can be a powerful instrument of either good or evil.

The subjective opinions of an expert regarding beauty will

reflect that expert's personal cosmology. The opinions and beliefs of art experts are not always consistent with what the people of God should acknowledge as beautiful or good. The Bible supplies that cosmological foundation. God has regulated art and has distinguished its ministry with both blessings and curses. Anything that serves as such a lightning rod for good or evil should be a ministry of the church, which is uniquely equipped to understand the myth of art, as well as its undeniable majesty.

# GOD'S MYSTERIES—OUR **TREASURES**

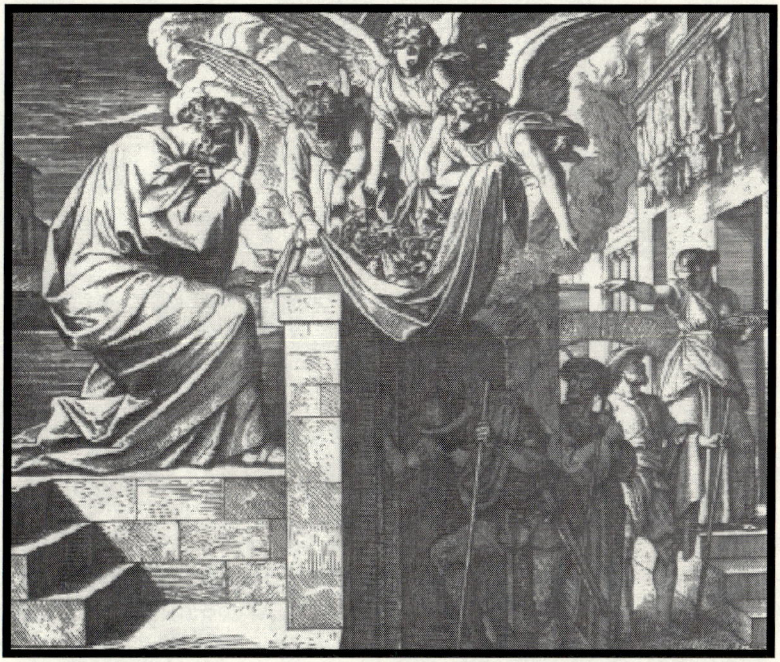

Fig. 16, Julius Schnor von Carolsfeld, *Peter's Vision,* c. 1855]

Julius Schnor von Carolsfeld has created an image that—absent explanation or context—would seem to be a puzzling scenario. Peter is depicted sleeping on a rooftop, having a vision as surreal as anything from the mind of Salvador Dali. He sees a sheet full of unclean creatures being lowered down from heaven. In Acts 10, Luke gives us the account of this vision that came to the Apostle Peter that evening at the city of Jopa:

> [H]e fell into a trance and saw heaven opened and an object like a great sheet bound at the four corners, descending to him and let down to the earth. In it were all kinds of four-footed animals of the earth, wild beasts, creeping things, and birds of the air. And a voice came to him, "Rise, Peter; kill and eat." But Peter said, "Not so, Lord! For I have never eaten anything common or unclean." And a voice *spoke* to him again the second time, "What God has cleansed you must not call common." This was done three times. And the object was taken up into heaven again.
>
> Acts 10:10–15

What do you suppose Peter was pondering after such a vision? The sheet may have reminded Peter of his fishnet and the days of culling through its contents, rejecting those fish that the Jewish dietary laws identified as unclean creatures unfit for God's people. The crustaceans, parasites, and bottom-feeders that live in the muck and filth of the sea bottom were symbolic of unclean lifestyles. The dietary laws reminded the Jews that they must reject impurity and be separate as a people. Now, as a fisher of men, Peter was about to learn that God was gathering Gentiles and declaring them clean. God presents the unclean creatures in a sheet, as if harvested from the earth like so much grain already winnowed from the chaff and gathered neatly together. Peter wondered what this vision could mean, but soon God made the meaning of this vision clear. He said to Cornelius the centurion, "You know how unlawful it is for a Jewish man to keep company with or go to one of another nation. But God has shown me that I should not call any man common or unclean" (Acts 10:28).

Have you ever wondered why God gives us such riddles and puzzles? Why didn't God simply say, "Peter! I am going to start calling the Gentiles to faith in the gospel. I am sending a Roman solder named Cornelius to you. Receive him and his companions into the church as brothers in Christ." Instead, this message was cloaked in such an enigma that the Apostle Peter was left pondering its meaning. When we have something important to say to our children, we speak as clearly to them as we can. Yet God often does the opposite. This calling of the Gentiles was an important milepost in the history of the church, but there was something about the enigmatic nature of Peter's vision, which served an important purpose. Even though human nature craves clarity, God usually chooses enigmatic ways to communicate to prophets. He made a rare exception with Moses and explained the distinction when he spoke to Aaron and Miriam in a pillar of cloud saying,

> [H]ear now my words: If there is a prophet among you, I, the LORD, make myself known to him in a vision; I speak to him in a dream. Not so with my servant Moses; he *is* faithful in all my house. I speak with him face to face, Even plainly, and not in dark sayings; And he sees the form of the LORD. Why then were you not afraid to speak against my servant Moses?
>
> Numbers 12:6–8

Enigmatic beauty is a principle of revelation as much as it is a principle of aesthetics. Certainly, the church has embraced the Holy Trinity, the incarnation, and the resurrection as mysteries upheld fervently by ancient councils. This chapter examines the nature and the importance of enigmatic beauty as a means of revelation.

There are two realms of truth by which revelation may come. One realm of truth is objective, abstract, reductive, clear, and full of contrast. It is a ministry of abstraction. This is the way of expositors, assayers, and miracle workers. Their ministry is one of proof, law, doctrine, and dogma. We may refer to it broadly as the ministry of light. Abstraction is a focal observation of an essential truth, object, or idea. Creating an abstraction makes a concept easier to understand because it is stripped down to its raw, essential objective and presented without dimension, context, or detail.

The other realm is the way of the artist. This realm of truth is experiential, figurative, expansive, and full of nuance and mystery. It is a ministry of dreams, symbols, sacraments, ceremonies, parables, and songs. It is a ministry that uses enigmas to lead us into a deeper understanding of spiritual truth by forcing us to construct a more complete foundation of understanding. Simple abstract clarity cannot offer such understanding. It is a level of understanding we would never receive if answers came to us too easily. We may refer to this broadly as the ministry of shadows. God's ministry of shadows makes us work. If the work is done faithfully, God's shadows lead us to discover multiple layers of meaning.

While the power of abstract truth is achieved by its stripping the essence of truth of context and detail, the key to understanding an enigma is precisely its context and its detail. Enigmatic beauty is the allure of the unexplained and the mother of intrigue. It captivates the mind and provokes investigation. Enigmatic beauty is the promise of discovery and the hope of understanding. In a painting, enigmatic beauty may manifest itself in the form of an image presented in a manner that is mysterious or cryptic. In a novel or a drama, it is the essence of a plot. In music, it may be found in a dissonant chord or in the lyrics of a hymn. Such things introduce an element of mystery that fires the imagination and sends it on a quest for discovery. The desire to unlock mysteries is basic to human nature. God has placed that desire in us. Many aspects of the Bible are enigmatic by design. This is what makes enigmatic beauty a principle of revelation as well as a principle of aesthetics. A student of the Bible may immediately find wisdom and understanding in its pages, but there are those passages that are elusive to our understanding. These enigmas can yield a great treasure of understanding when understanding finally comes. We may find enigmas used in all of the Bible's art forms—its proverbs, visions, prophecies, and ceremonies. The Bible's enigmas lead us to forms of wisdom that are not generally obtained through rote doctrine.

The clarity of doctrine gives us satisfaction and finality. But God would not have us close our Bibles and stop there. God gives us shadows and mysteries that challenge our understanding and lead us through various layers of revelation for answers. It is the way that God more often than not chooses to speak his Word. In the words of Solomon, "It is the glory of God to conceal a matter, but the glory of kings *is* to search out a matter" (Proverbs 25:2). Solomon described his search for wisdom in this way: "I, the Preacher, was king over Israel in Jerusalem. And I set my heart to seek and search out by wisdom concerning all that is done under heaven; this burdensome task God has given to the sons of man, by which they may be exercised" (Ecclesiastes 1:12–13).

We as a people are to be exercised by the task of seeking wisdom, and aspects of biblical culture are profoundly shaped by this collective search for wisdom to which God has called us. In this journey, we may find principles of enigmatic beauty that energize the Bible's spiritual witness to the world. God has put eternity in our hearts, along with an enduring sense of mystery, which will never be completely exhausted. We lose much by overlooking the importance of God's mysteries in biblical teaching. There is a contrary thread of historical Platonic cosmology, which has not served the church well. It has led to an obsession and beatification of abstract clarity. It has also led to the loss of historical reverence for the sacred mysteries of our faith and has undermined the effective witness of the church. The result is a watered-down view of religion characterized by legalism, methodology, pietism, and pragmatism.

I remember what the Bible meant to me as a new Christian. I knew little of God's Word then, but my affection for God's Word in those days is something I can only aspire to regain as a more knowledgeable Christian. While I have grown in my faith, in some respects I feel I have shrunk a bit since the day I first laid my sins at the foot of the cross. As a new believer, the Bible was a great mystery to me. Its message pierced my flesh to the bone. It was not just the concept of God's Word that I loved, but the book itself was an object of sentimental value to me—somewhat like a child's comfort blanket. In retrospect, I perceive that it was the great sense of mystery in God's Word that supplied my reverence and affection for it. In those days I could not look at the Bible as simply a user's manual for that cosmic appliance called man. The Bible was a hidden treasure, full of mystery and promise. Knowing so little of the gift of God's Word, I could have only known the giver.

When did I lose this sense of reverence that came with knowing the giver of God's Word? Perhaps the excessive process of systematizing my beliefs took my eyes off the mysteries of my faith. My new shepherds gave me spiritual truth in plain English and explained the Bible to me with great abstract clarity. This was much needed in my spiritual life, yet I came to distrust any form of religious practice that did not focus on the clearly spoken words of the Scriptures. Anything that reminded me of liturgical worship was suspect. I even became a little uncomfortable with some of the musical worship of Protestant churches I would visit. I remember occasions when the pastor called the congregation to silent prayer and the organist would begin background music to set the mood. I thought that was gimmickry at the time. By then I had become a purist for abstract expressions of biblical truth. I wanted stark, unvarnished words of doctrine, and I was determined to expunge all the symbols in my religious life and be led by the pure light of ideas. I wanted a world of substance without symbols. I did not know it at the time, but I was becoming Platonized.

As a teenager, I was in a Bible study group that met at a local park close to my home where we sometimes sat on the basketball court. Sitting with my legs crossed on the concrete was not a comfortable position for me, and I found that if I sat on my large study Bible while not using it my legs would not go to sleep. The reaction of a young Jewish-Christian girl in the group was memorable. The sight of me in my cutoffs sitting on the Holy Scriptures on the pavement seemed like the ultimate sacrilege to her. This seemed silly to me since my Bible was no longer an object of sentimental value to me. It was more like a textbook about faith, salvation, and morality. It was only the substance of the biblical ideas that were important to me. Sitting on my Bible might scuff the already worn cover, but it would never alter the text. In retrospect, I have come to believe that the Jewish girl had a good point. Reverence and symbolism can be taken to an extreme, becoming a form of superstition, but there is significance in symbols. And how we treat something that should be important to us can affect how we think of it.

True reverence need not require elaborate measures. When Jesus gave up his Spirit, the veil of the temple was rent from top to bottom. God himself has removed the veil that separates us from his presence, and things reserved for holy use should be presented with more simplicity in this age of greater light. And yet reverence remains important and reverence is largely based on mystery. Who is more mysterious than our God, the one whose ways are inscrutable, whose face no man can behold, and whose name is ineffable? It is he who demands utmost reverence, and a shroud of mystery remains over all that is holy. Should knowledge of biblical truth drive out all sense of mystery? On the contrary! The Bible, rightly studied, should give us clarity in some things and yet utterly engulf us in its mystery. The full counsel of God's Word provides us with mystery and clarity, shadow and light. Having benefited in my life from good teachers who have led me to much clarity with regard to the light, I have in later years perceived the need to ponder the shadows of God's Word with renewed appreciation. To know ourselves rightly is to know how little we will ever understand the depth of God's wisdom and the mystery of his ways.

Much of the dynamic strength of a biblical culture is derived from the proper respect for certain principles that are ultimately taken on faith and utterly shrouded in mystery. We believe, for instance, in the inherent dignity of man as a creature made in God's image. This is the foundation of our reverence for social justice and human rights. But what does it really mean to be made in God's image? We may achieve some rudimentary understanding of this concept, yet there will always be a large element of mystery to it. As long as our social order maintains reverence for such mysteries, our civil liberties will have advocates. Yet to secure the mystery of God's image and reverence for human dignity, we must overthrow an old pagan cultural bias that seeks to reduce everything to some form of absolute logical clarity.

We take great comfort in what is logical, clear, familiar, and conventional. By contrast, we have cultural distrust of the strange and the weird. This is somewhat aggravated by the legacy of common abuses that are associated with enigmatic things. It is the legacy of false religions, which have led people astray with some new wind of doctrine. It is the legacy of "experts" that turn out to be charlatans. It is the legacy of crooked lawyers who use legal jargon as the language of legalized theft. It is also the legacy of erudite-sounding art critics who perceive an independent genius behind a work of art never intended to be more than a joke or casual doodle. Those who would deceive us may exploit the natural allure of enigmas, but deceivers do not use the Bible's kind of enigmas. They will incorporate a bit of nonsense disguised as astute reasoning. Yet so great is our desire to perceive order that nonsense can sometimes present itself unveiled and undisguised, only to have our minds assign it the dignity of form and meaning. Such was the case of the Dada and the theatre of the absurd. These were avowed anarchists, openly devoted to nonsense, anti-art, and chaos. Yet in spite of this, many people have been reluctant to accept what this genre was about. Sometimes human nature compels us to find meaning even in naked, unabashed nonsense. But the Bible does not give us nonsense, but purposeful enigmas to embrace. God's many enigmas are designed to serve a constructive end.

It is not God's will to restrict us to some stark, abstract version of the truth. True wisdom must be woven from the fiber of creation itself through life experience. Enlightenment must come through the typological revelation of sacraments, culture, art, and the full gamut of interpersonal relationships, which makes up the image of God in man. The exercise of searching our way through these shadows is crucial to our spiritual development, and the Bible sanctifies all of creation as a divinely appointed means of revelation. Plato's children have historically eschewed the shadows of earthy existence in search of stark abstractions. In Plato's allegory of the cave, he describes prisoners in a cave who are bound so that they can only see one wall of the cave. A fire behind them burns, and puppeteers behind the prisoners create shadows on the wall of the cave. The prisoners do not perceive the real objects; only their shadows. To them, the shadows are the reality. If such a prisoner were allowed to turn and look behind, he would be blinded by the firelight and the puppets would appear less real than their shadows. If he were brought to the sunlight, he would be so blinded that he could see nothing. Gradually, his eyes would adjust and he would be able to see objects in daylight and eventually the sun itself. In Platonic parlance, the shadows represent a mere perception of reality that is removed from the true reality of the pure idea.

This allegory describes a way of thinking that is deeply imbedded into western culture because we are all Plato's children to some extent. But it is a way of thinking that we must escape in order to understand the biblical language of shadows as our path to the greater light. The Epistle to the Hebrews describes the new covenant in terms of shadows replaced by substance (see Hebrews 10:1–7). Plato's allegory seems to echo this biblical concept on some level. In important ways, however, the shadows of Scripture and the shadows of Plato's cave are very different. The world is not our prison-cave. God made it, and it is good. Plato's dichotomy of substance and shadows is not found in the Bible. The substance that replaces the shadows of the Old Testament law is not some abstract idea, but the flesh and blood of Christ—a concept that the Gnostic could not accept because Gnostics were Neo-Platonic and, to them, all flesh is a mere shadow of reality.

To Plato, all truth was stark abstraction, which is why Plato's academy in Athens venerated the exchange of abstract ideas, rational debate, and verbal discourse. Plato would have approved of a syllabus and lecture as teaching tools because these things are consistent with his style and ideology in that they reduce the principles of truth to logical abstractions.

Yet, most of what we recognize as God-inspired Scripture is not written in this abstract genre. There is little in the Bible that reads like a page from Plato's *Republic.* Most of the Bible is song, poetry, visions, prophecy, art, ceremony, and lots of stories and history. Throughout all of these, God's enigmas are planted like so many thought-provoking seeds of wisdom. When we find a curious use of words in a psalm, a strange symbol in a vision, or a story of peculiar circumstances, it is all for a reason. God has embedded a special kind of spiritual wisdom into all of these things. He has shrouded his Word in layers of mystery and enigma that their meaning may be mined like jewels.

Like the prisoners in Plato's cave, we are indeed blinded by a greater light. But to us, the greater light is the light of God's glory, and it is the "shadows" of our world that give us access to his light. So we do not eschew the earthly shadows of creation. On the contrary, we sanctify these shadows and give thanks for them. Enlightenment comes through "things that are seen" in God's works of creation, together with whatever quickening the Spirit of God gives us through eyes of faith. The search for ultimate truth cannot be reduced to the dry logic of the abstract, the verbal, and the conceptual. Ultimate truth is rooted in God's ubiquitous works of creation and is revealed through the prism of his Word. It is manifested as God's likeness in man and is bound up in our very existence. If some of God's truth seems veiled to us, perhaps it is because we are in the shadow of God's protection so that the pure light of glory does not blind us.

But what we may perceive of God's glory is not the same for all. The Apostle Paul spoke of a level of spiritual knowledge that not every disciple is able to receive and yet every Christian is expected to obtain eventually: "And I, brethren, could not speak to you as to spiritual people but as to carnal, as to babes in Christ. I fed you with milk and not with solid food; for until now you were not able to receive it, and even now you are still not able; for you are still carnal" (1 Corinthians 3:1–3).

Similarly, when Jesus spoke of his ascension to the Father, he said to his disciples, "I still have many things to say to you, but you cannot bear them now" (John 16:12). Various stages of moral strength allow our built-in knowledge of God to push its way to the light of consciousness as one matures. The most important spiritual truths are not those things about God we come to discover, but things we already know and simply come to accept.

Christian discipleship is not a process of learning something new, but of unlearning an old lie by which the knowledge and revelation of God is suppressed. There are degrees of spiritual understanding, and God's ultimate design moves us from lesser to greater understanding. The Apostle Paul wrote to the saints in Corinth,

> For we know in part and we prophesy in part, but when perfection comes, the imperfect disappears. When I was a child, I talked like a child, I thought like a child, I reasoned like a child. When I became a man, I put childish ways behind me. Now we see but a poor reflection as in a mirror; then we shall see face to face. Now I know in part; then I shall know fully, even as I am fully known.
>
> 1 Corinthians 13:9–12

As Paul described his own advancement to manhood as an analogy of spiritual knowledge, he spoke as one who now sees a poor reflection of what we shall all see more clearly later. It is easy to gloss over Paul's analogy as something pertaining only of the hereafter—and heaven will no doubt bring unimaginable clarity—but the context of this passage relates, in part, to seeking understanding in this life in a way that helps us to apply the gifts of the Spirit. Paul wrote, 'Brethren, do not be children in understanding; however, in malice be babes, but in understanding be mature. In the law it is written: "With men of other tongues and other lips I will speak to this people; And yet, for all that, they will not hear me"' (1 Corinthians 14:20).

Paul's quote here is a paraphrase of Isaiah 28:9–12. To understand the mind of Paul, it is instructive to read words of Isaiah:

> Who is it he is trying to teach? To whom is he explaining his message? To children weaned from their milk, to those just taken from the breast? For it is: "Do and do, do and do,

> rule on rule, rule on rule; a little here, a little there." Very well then, with foreign lips and strange tongues God will speak to this people, to whom he said, "This is the resting place, let the weary rest"; and, "This is the place of repose"—but they would not listen."
>
> Isaiah 28:9–12

Isaiah denounces the religiosity of apostate Judah as an immature and banal legalism. He compares them to children "just taken from the breast" and characterizes their understanding of the Word of God as "do and do, rule on rule." Why does the legalist seek comfort in the abstract clarity of "do and do" rote traditions? Perhaps it is precisely to avoid the tortuous soul searching that brings sinners in touch with the Spirit of the law. Perhaps that is why those who truncate God's Word with a legalistic rule-on-rule approach to spiritual knowledge may well become the targets of God's more enigmatic means of instruction—his severe chastening. There is mystery in God's Word, and those who seek the full counsel of God will continuously ponder enigmas. True discipleship leaves no room for legalism. Those who seek to avoid the hard conflicts of discipleship through the idolatry of legalism and convention will have enigmas thrust upon them one way or another.

For the ultimate legalist, God prescribes the ultimate enigma. He chooses to speak to him through foreign and strange tongues and predicts, "They will not listen." But notice how Saint Paul paraphrases Isaiah: "And yet, *for all that,* they will not hear me." Paul seems to say that God's people have even less excuse for not understanding the word of God after having heard it in a foreign language. What irony! We use foreign language as a metaphor for things we *don't* understand. We say, "That's Greek to me!" or "Can you repeat that in plain English?" God confused the tongues of men to scatter them from Babel. Yet here God chooses a foreign language to communicate something. This confirms that truth is sometimes best communicated through enigma rather than clear articulation. This is especially true if the religiosity of the people has been reduced to a dry and banal legalism. When the *Word* of God is substituted for mere words of God, intelligible speech is sometimes useless. Perhaps God's Word spoken through the lips of foreigners speaks more clearly than any message heard in one's native tongue. The strange language the Judeans soon heard was that of their Babylonian captors. At first, they did not listen. But this bit of divine therapy finally worked for some of the captives of Judah. Here are the words of Jeremiah: "It *is* good for a man to bear the yoke in his youth. Let him sit alone and keep silent, because *God* has laid *it* on him; Let him put his mouth in the dust—There may yet be hope." (Lamentation 3:27–29).

Putting a young man's mouth in the dust and forcing him to bear the yoke of his captors is God's own special way of communicating to such a people. It delivers a message that is doubtlessly memorable. Something about the process of mortification helps us assimilate truth. The unveiled truth that is not processed through mortification can be poisonous to the unregenerate soul, even spiritually fatal. Like Simon the Magician, some that seek spontaneous enlightenment may desire gifts with no regard for the giver. God will sometimes deny spiritual enlightenment as an act of mercy or grant it as an act of judgment. God banished our first parents from Eden in order to protect them.

God would not have our first parents live forever in their state of death and despair. The tree of life would be offered to them and us, but only in due season, for those who come to the tree of life without an adequate sense of their own depravity or of the holiness of God will bring condemnation to themselves. The writer of the Epistle to the Hebrews wrote:

> For *it is* impossible for those who were once enlightened, and have tasted the heavenly gift, and have become partakers of

> the Holy Spirit, and have tasted the good word of God and the powers of the age to come, if they fall away, to renew them again to repentance, since they crucify again for themselves the Son of God, and put *him* to an open shame. For the earth which drinks in the rain that often comes upon it, and bears herbs useful for those by whom it is cultivated, receives blessing from God; but if it bears thorns and briers, *it is* rejected and near to being cursed, whose end *is* to be burned.
>
> Hebrews 6:4–8

Jesus gave a similar analogy in the parable of the sower:

> But he who received the seed on stony places, this is he who hears the word and immediately receives it with joy; yet he has no root in himself, but endures only for a while. For when tribulation or persecution arises because of the word, immediately he stumbles.
>
> Matthew 13:20–21

Note the paradox of the seed that takes root too quickly. It germinates quickly but soon dies by the sun's intense rays. It is God's desire for us to send out deep roots into the sublime knowledge of his attributes as well as our own inadequacies. It is God's natural and typological revelation that provides this, not intellect. To survive the burning light of truth, one must be well rooted in the soul-changing revelations of the attributes of God.

This is the universal knowledge of God spoken of by the Apostle Paul in Romans 1. It is this witness of truth that makes all mankind without excuse. The forsaking of the clear light of revelation leads to reprobation. For the reprobate, greater revelation becomes a greater judgment, a more severe indictment for having seen the clear revelation of God only to reject it in spite of everything. God spoke to Isaiah saying:

> Go, and tell this people: "Keep on hearing, but do not understand; Keep on seeing, but do not perceive." Make the heart of this people dull, and their ears heavy, and shut their eyes; Lest they see with their eyes, and hear with their ears, and understand with their heart, and return and be healed.
>
> Isaiah 6:9–10

In this case, God used his clear revelation as an instrument of greater condemnation. This is much like Saint Paul's description of the heart of Pharaoh in his Epistle to the Romans: "For the Scripture says to the Pharaoh, 'For this very purpose I have raised you up, that I may show my power in you, and that my name may be declared in all the earth.' Therefore he has mercy on whom he wills, and whom he wills he hardens" (Romans 9:17–18).

These subjects of revelation and judgment appear similarly in Luke 10 where Luke describes how Jesus rebuked the disbelievers who had seen his miracles:

> Woe to you, Chorazin! Woe to you, Bethsaida! For if the mighty works which were done in you had been done in Tyre and Sidon, they would have repented long ago, sitting in sackcloth and ashes. But it will be more tolerable for Tyre and Sidon at the judgment than for you. And you, Capernaum, who are exalted to heaven, will be brought down to Hades. He who hears you hears me, he who rejects you rejects me, and he who rejects me rejects him who sent me.
>
> Then the seventy returned with joy, saying, "Lord, even the demons are subject to us in your name."
>
> And he said to them, "I saw Satan fall like lightning from heaven. Behold, I give you the authority to trample on serpents and scorpions, and over all the power of the enemy, and nothing shall by any means hurt you. Nevertheless do not

> rejoice in this, that the spirits are subject to you, but rather rejoice because your names are written in heaven.
>
> Luke 10:13–20

Jesus had finally given the skeptics what they had wanted—signs and wonders. They finally had the objective and unambiguous confirmation that Jesus was indeed acting with divine authority. Yet they still rejected him.

Abstract clarity is a wonderful thing in God's season. But in our impatience for it, we sometimes bypass forms of truth that God would have us learn first through normal and intuitive forms of revelation. Those who seek inexplicable proofs of the most basic divine truths are already without excuse for disbelieving them. Jesus gave us many signs, but he also told us, "It is a wicked and perverse generation that seeks a sign." When the disciples of Jesus said to him, "Show us the Father," Jesus responded saying, "Whoever has seen me has seen the Father." The very Son of God had lived among them for some time, teaching them, yet for all of this they asked of him, "Show us the Father." Did they know what they were asking?

The Apostle Paul speaks of seeing God face-to-face in heaven when he says, "For now we see in a mirror, dimly, but then face to face. Now I know in part, but then I shall know just as I also am known" (1 Corinthians 13:12).

Many take Paul's analogy of the mirror as a reference to the darkening influence of sin. This may be part of it, but I believe there is something more to this. The dim mirror is a provision of God's mercy. We must, by necessity, look through a dim mirror to behold God's glory at all. We would die if we looked upon God's glory with naked eyes. God shrouds his truth with a certain degree of enigma in order to enable us to grow in spiritual wisdom and to assimilate by degrees what is already known to us in the inner recesses of our souls. The unveiled truth is death to disbelievers; it seals their condemnation. Yet to those who can receive the truth well, it is life. Paul described it this way: "For we are to God the fragrance of Christ among those who are being saved and among those who are perishing. To the one *we are* the aroma of death *leading* to death, and to the other the aroma of life *leading* to life" (2 Corinthians 2:15–16). While the gospel "is veiled to those who are perishing" (2 Corinthians 4:3), God's enigmas serve a different purpose for his people. God rewards those who diligently seek him, and in his darkest mysteries are seeds of revelation. It is human nature to desire clear answers to everything, but great treasures are to be found in God's mysteries, which force us to send our roots deeper into the rich soil of revelation. They conceal a lesser light in order to reveal the greater light of God's wisdom and attributes. God gives us both shadow and light. As the Shekinah glory gave light by night and shade by day, so the shadow of the Almighty reveals the light of his glory in ways that we would never see otherwise. The proverbs, the enigmas, and the sacred arts of Scripture are provisions of mercy. As long as we wear this sinful flesh, God's shroud of mystery must protect us from things we are not ready to believe.

The light of creation leaves us sinners without excuse before God while we look to the Holy Spirit to convict and change our hearts. God's mysteries are often his appointed means of grace to speak to the heart. We should be thankful for the best and brightest theologians, but we should not consult them too quickly. Perhaps it is better to struggle directly with God's Word for a while and only afterward read commentaries. When we do read the worthy insights of such luminaries as John Calvin, John Owen, or Mathew Henry, perhaps we should presume that the better part of their wisdom came to them through shadows. God's shadows, rightly regarded, are our best commentaries. These are the sacraments, the parables, the sacred arts, and all of God's typological means of natural revelation. They are all God's appointed means of grace. The greatest light that God gives to us is not what is obtained through the eyes of sinful flesh but through the redeemed eyes of faith. We have been warned of the idolatry of convention—the abstract knowledge of dogma divorced from the knowledge of the lawgiver. Redeeming light is not the light of dogma. Redeeming light is the sort of ineffable wisdom that is written upon the heart through a life lived by faith. Our treasure comes through the shadows and mysteries of our faith and through the persistent leading of the Holy Spirit.

# A SEASON FOR **PARABLES**

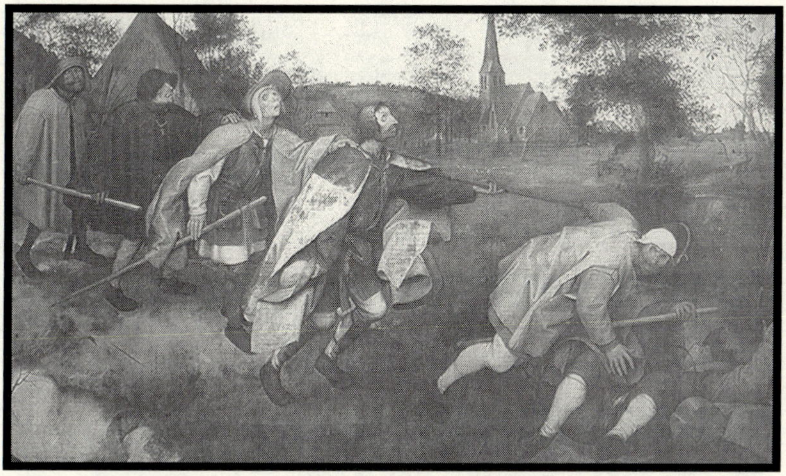

Fig. 17, Pieter Bruegel, *The Parable of the Blind Leading the Blind*, 1568

Bruegel has depicted a parable found in the Gospel of Luke, where it is written, "And he spoke a parable to them: 'Can the blind lead the blind? Will they not both fall into the ditch? A disciple is not above his teacher, but everyone who is perfectly trained will be like his teacher'" (Luke 6:39–40).

Bruegel enlarges the point. Jesus mentions only two men, but Bruegel shows six—one blind leader and a train of five blind followers. Bruegel was known for his depiction of peasants, but the men in this painting are not wearing peasant's attire. Are we to believe that these were men deemed worthy of leadership? Notice that they have all forsaken the rightful use of their canes, that instrument of independent judgment that blind men may use to guide themselves on their path. Why use independent judgment if you have someone who will lead you? These men would not inspire confidence in any but for the blindness of those who follow.

The walk of faith is not like the path of blind fools. The faithful will ultimately look to God and not man for guidance. A disciple is not above his teacher, and if we hope to rise above our teachers, no mere man can be our ultimate guide. It is possible to surpass our earthly teachers and declare with the psalmist, "I have more understanding than all my teachers, for your testimonies *are* my meditation" (Psalm 119:99). However, those who excel beyond their teachers must look to a higher authority, who is God, and he speaks to us mostly in the language of shadows.

This chapter explores more fully the nature of the ministry of shadows as it may be studied in the form of parables. Parables offer a unique window of insight into the ministry of shadows. A good student of parables finds a form of guidance in them that no mere academic discipline can offer. This is typical of shadow ministries in general. A parable is unlike dogma. It states only the obvious and leaves it to the mind of the hearer to see the truth it intends to convey. A parable is designed to awaken the conscience from within and to inspire a willing obedience that is born of inward awareness. Those who are so taught may recognize truth from the mouth of an ass as easily as that which comes from the mouth of a wise man.

The ministry of light is objective, abstract, reductive, clear, and full of contrast. The ministry of shadows is experiential, figurative, expansive, and full of nuance and mystery. The first realm, the ministry of light, is the way of the expositor. The second realm, the ministry of shadows, is essentially the way of the artist. These are not mutually exclusive ministries. In fact, they are interdependent. Most abstract forms of instruction contain some cognitive reference. Words are abstract, but they cannot communicate truth if they do not create mental images and associations from real life. Conversely, a painting may seem realistic, but its beauty as a painting may depend on its judicious use of abstract clarity. Even if a painting is created in the most illusionistic style, an artist may choose an interpretive line, a brush stroke, a color, or contrast where none would be so clearly defined in the actual object represented. God's Word is both light and shadow. There is in God's Word a ministry of light that shines forth in points of epiphany, revelations, miracles, and milestones of sacred history. Yet the Bible is written mostly in the style of a ministry of shadows. This balance of light and shadow makes the Holy Scriptures neither too subdued to be effective nor too intense to look upon.

It is the design of parables to make us think and to acquire the sort of understanding that can only come through some degree of struggle. Perhaps it is for this reason that Jesus leaves us only a small window through which to look. The parables of Jesus pierce the conscience and evoke emotional responses. The parable teaches us in the way of an artist, using experiential, subjective, and cryptic methods to draw hearers to the truth that is suppressed within.

There were times in the earthly ministry of Jesus that he took on the role of the expositor. As a minister of light, Jesus' revelations were often incendiary. When he said, "Before Abraham was, I AM," it filled his enemies with rage and they resolved to kill him. The same effect was achieved when Jesus gave sight to the blind, healed the lame, declared that he had authority to forgive sins and raise the dead, and finally raised himself from the dead. Such things bring out the worst behavior in God haters. That is the nature of objective truth. Our God is a consuming fire. But Jesus was merciful, and he selectively wielded his ministry of light. His light was merciful for those he sought to save. When Jesus preached to the multitude, he forsook the way of the expositor, chose the way of the artist, tempered his light within the ministry of shadows, and his words fell upon the multitudes like a gentle rain. After his resurrection, Jesus also spoke as an expositor to two disciples on the road to Emmaus. Luke records that "beginning at Moses and all the Prophets, he expounded to them in all the Scriptures the things concerning himself" (Luke 24:27). There was a compelling order of logic in this expository teaching that left the hearts of these disciples burning (see Luke 24:30–31). After a while, Jesus forsook the role of expositor and gave them something that looked like a sacrament, which, like a parable, is an allegory designed to convey a spiritual truth.

To understand why Jesus used parables, consider the nature of objective truth. Abstract clarity is the ambrosia of the redeemed. It is for those who can endure the light. The first Epistle of John gives assurance of the truth of the gospel based on the clarity of revelations that Jesus provided to his apostles (see 1 John 1:1). Clarity is a wonderful thing, and there is a body of revelation in which God has given us great clarity. Objective truth becomes our confessions of faith. Yet it is not for any of us to demand instant clarity in all matters of truth. Clarity must sometimes come at the end of a journey, or we may never be fit to receive it. Doubting Thomas demanded absolute clarity, and for this Jesus had a mild rebuke: "Thomas, because you have seen me, you have believed. Blessed are those who have not seen and yet have believed" (John 20:29).

Thomas did at last believe. Jesus had a harsher rebuke for those who sought a sign and yet remained unbelieving in spite of the resurrection: "An evil and adulterous generation seeks after a sign, and no sign will be given to it except the sign of the prophet Jonah" (Matthew 12:39). Much of the revelation God—in his own inscrutable design—is shrouded in various degrees of mystery. The hard sayings of Scripture are as much God's word as the fundamentals of our faith. The people of God are the guardians of great mysteries, which ought to be celebrated not forsaken.

Let us own God's mysteries in all of God's Word, even those much-neglected portions of Scripture that seem to push the envelope of our spiritual comfort zone. Embrace the genealogies, the antediluvian histories, the imprecatory psalms, the edgy satires, and the seemingly anthropocentric musings of Ecclesiastes, Song of Solomon, and Job. It is all God's Word, and it is there for a purpose.

Likewise, the parables of the Bible serve an important purpose. When Nathan confronted David with his sin against Uriah, he used his parable of the ewe lamb to access David's inward sense of justice. Nathan could have taken the role of expositor. He could have simply explained the law to David and pointed out how he had broken the law of God. But Nathan did not want to give David a mere intellectual and abstract awareness that he had sinned. It was important for David to experience the outrage of that sin in his heart. If Nathan had given David a lecture and a syllabus to explain his sins against God's laws, true repentance for David may have been long in coming. Intellect without passion allows sinners to throw up barriers of denial and self-justification. Nathan would not give David that form of light to sear his conscience. He wanted David to see his sin objectively by representing his offense as that of another man. He wanted to raise David's ire against the unvarnished ugliness of sin without alerting those self-justifying mental defenses that would have kept him from seeing the truth. Nathan turned the accusation on David only after achieving that sense of moral outrage. Nathan may well have had a lecture for David later, but Nathan's first tactic was the way of an artist and a storyteller to accomplish God's purpose.

A parable is a narrative or allegory designed to convey an obscured message. There is something about the veiled message of a parable that short circuits our resistance to God's revelation. Jesus painted word pictures of persons and circumstances, which reveal divine attributes and principles of spiritual truth in a veiled fashion. Like Nathan the prophet, Jesus chose the way of an artist, knowing the common desires of men and the universal spiritual struggles of Adam's race. The earthly ministry of Jesus was a season for parables, and Jesus produced parables like ripe apples falling from a tree and used them to speak to the hearts and consciences of sinners.

The disciples preferred plain talk, but Jesus knew they needed more than that. Jesus spoke plainly when he said, "The Father has given all things to me." This important declaration required nothing but belief from his listeners; it did not require an individual experience or judgment. Yet beyond belief—for even demons believe—we need eyes that see and ears that hear. This is why Jesus gave parables: to reconstruct our eyes and ears. Whenever he said, "The kingdom of heaven is like," Jesus drew upon earthly examples of common human experiences and forced his listeners to access the divine light of natural revelation. This is what parables supply, and it is what makes parables such an effective and memorable way of communicating spiritual truth. In fact, a good example of this "belief-in-abstract" principle comes, appropriately, in the form of the parable of the Two Debtors. The context of this parable, recorded by Luke, is important:

> Then one of the Pharisees asked him to eat with him. And he went to the Pharisee's house, and sat down to eat. And behold, a woman in the city who was a sinner, when she knew that *Jesus* sat at the table in the Pharisee's house, brought an alabaster flask of fragrant oil, and stood at his feet behind *him* weeping; and she began to wash his feet with her tears, and wiped *them* with the hair of her head; and she kissed his feet and anointed *them* with the fragrant oil. Now when the Pharisee who had invited him saw *this,* he spoke to himself, saying, "This man, if he were a prophet, would know who

> and what manner of woman *this is* who is touching him, for she is a sinner."
>
> And Jesus answered and said to him, "Simon, I have something to say to you."
>
> So he said, "Teacher, say it."
>
> "There was a certain creditor who had two debtors. One owed five hundred denarii, and the other fifty. And when they had nothing with which to repay, he freely forgave them both. Tell me, therefore, which of them will love him more?"
>
> Simon answered and said, "I suppose the *one* whom he forgave more."
>
> And he said to him, "You have rightly judged."
>
> Then he turned to the woman and said to Simon, "Do you see this woman? I entered your house; you gave me no water for my feet, but she has washed my feet with her tears and wiped *them* with the hair of her head. You gave me no kiss, but this woman has not ceased to kiss my feet since the time I came in. You did not anoint my head with oil, but this woman has anointed my feet with fragrant oil. Therefore I say to you, her sins, *which are* many, are forgiven, for she loved much. But to whom little is forgiven, *the same* loves little."
>
> Luke 7:36–47

It is one thing to know abstractly that all people are sinners and that God hates sin. But those who have seen the true darkness of sin will hate sin and love God all the more once they are redeemed. These people are not necessarily greater sinners. Their sin is simply less concealed. The woman who washed the feet of Jesus with her tears was of ill repute. She was contemptible to the Pharisees, but Jesus spoke more severely against the Pharisees than her. Although the Pharisees had ostensibly pure lifestyles, Jesus knew their hearts and called them whitewashed tombs, a brood of vipers, and sons of the devil. Jesus never spoke this way to a sinner forced to wear the shame of sin like a scarlet letter. It is the scarlet-letter sinner who is most likely to repent and who will love God most when the sinner repents. The penitent woman knew the substance and the reality of her sinfulness and understood the darkness from which she had been delivered.

The parables communicated this sort of substance and reality of spiritual truth to those who had ears to hear among the lost sheep of Israel. Jesus used parables with such consistency that it became a hallmark characteristic of his ministry. Matthew identifies the telling of parables as a messianic trait, fulfilling an Old Testament prophecy paraphrased in the Gospel of Matthew with these words: "I will open my mouth in parables; I will utter things kept secret from the foundation of the world" (Matthew 13:35). Mathew is referring to Psalm 78, where David said,

> Give ear, O my people, *to* my law; Incline your ears to the words of my mouth. I will open my mouth in a parable; I will utter dark sayings of old, which we have heard and known, and our fathers have told us. We will not hide *them* from their children, Telling to the generation to come the praises of the LORD, And his strength and his wonderful works that he has done.
>
> Matthew 13:35

The parable is designed to restrict us to a vital way of seeing and hearing before we can be served by other means of revelation. In Matthew 12, Jesus played the role of expositor when he put the Pharisees soundly in their place. Perhaps the disciples of Jesus were expecting more of the same show of logical prowess when he proceeded to speak to the multitudes. But instead, Jesus spoke to the multitudes through parables.

When the disciples asked him why he spoke in parables, Jesus said:

> Because it has been given to you to know the mysteries of the kingdom of heaven but to them it has not been given. For whoever has, to him more will be given, and he will have abundance; but whoever does not have, even what he has will be taken away from him. Therefore I speak to them in parables, because seeing they do not see, and hearing they do not hear, nor do they understand. And in them the prophecy of Isaiah is fulfilled, which says: "Hearing you will hear and shall not understand, and seeing you will see and not perceive; For the hearts of this people have grown dull. Their ears are hard of hearing, And their eyes they have closed, Lest they should see with their eyes and hear with their ears, Lest they should understand with their hearts and turn, So that I should heal them." But blessed are your eyes for they see, and your ears for they hear; for assuredly, I say to you that many prophets and righteous men desired to see what you see, and did not see it, and to hear what you hear, and did not hear it.
>
> Matthew 13:11–17

Jesus opens a glorious theological can of worms in this explanation. If it raises more questions than it answers, that is by design. We must all spend time pondering God's enigmas if we are to understand God's explanations in full. Although the parables of Jesus are enigmatic by design, our Lord's intent was not to keep the multitudes in the dark indefinitely. There was and is much to be found in the parables for those who will eventually acquire "ears to hear." Although Jesus spoke explicitly to his disciples, they too needed help in understanding the parables, for they still sought an explanation of the parables. This can only mean that they understood the parables on some level, yet there was more to be learned in them.

When we seek the explanations faithfully, we will find them. As Jesus said, "Whoever has, to him more will be given, and he will have abundance." Who are those who hear but do not understand and who see and yet do not perceive? Perhaps all of us are included to some degree because there is much that even the greatest among us will not understand. But the regenerate mind is the one who progresses in understanding, moving from darkness to light and then to greater light, becoming more and more like Jesus Christ. The seed of the Word is planted in the hearts of men, but it is the Spirit that quickens it to life.

The disciples of Jesus must have come to understand that it was important for the multitude to receive God's Word through a veil of symbolism and figurative language. Perhaps the parables were beginning to make sense to the disciples, when once again Jesus spoke to the multitude with more parables. This time he gave them the parable of the Wheat and the Tares, the parable of the Mustard Seed, and the parable of the Leaven. (Matthew 13:24–33). After Jesus sent the multitudes away again, the disciples were no doubt looking forward to getting an explanation of all this. Once again, Jesus explained it, but part of his explanation included something unexpected—more parables! A short time ago, Jesus had said that parables were for those "to whom it has not been given to know the mysteries of the kingdom of heaven." Conversely, Jesus had said to them, "Blessed are your eyes for they see, and your ears for they hear." Yet Jesus proceeded to speak to them in parables. He told them the parable of the Hidden Treasure, the parable of the Pearl of Great Price, and the parable of the Dragnet. His disciples came to understand, no doubt, that even as those who have eyes to see and ears to hear, they were still in need of parables rather than pure abstractions.

By the time of the Last Supper, the disciples seemed tired of the veiled lessons. They wanted open declarations from their Lord. Jesus was about to go to the cross for them, and they were still looking for an earthly kingdom. In the Gospel of John, Jesus explained to them,

> These things I have spoken to you in figurative language; but the time is coming when I will no longer speak to you in figurative language, but I will tell you plainly about the Father. In that day you will ask in my name, and I do not say to you that I shall pray the Father for you; for the Father himself loves you, because you have loved me, and have believed that I came forth from God. I came forth from the Father and have come into the world. Again, I leave the world and go to the Father."
>
> His disciples said to him, "See, now you are speaking plainly, and using no figure of speech! Now we are sure that you know all things, and have no need that anyone should question you. By this we believe that you came forth from God."
>
> John 16:25–30

Like those disciples, we prefer clear and concise explanations. But God, in his infinite wisdom, continues to give us enigmas. We must be patient for the days of abstract clarity, when truth at last comes into focus. There are many such days. As Christians, we do not see enlightenment as something that can be marked with a single rite of passage. It is an ongoing and largely inscrutable process. We may mark the day of our redemption, but our sanctification is an ongoing journey. We are simultaneously wise and foolish, and our wisdom is only as sure as our love for God at any given moment. Having heard the parables of Jesus, we may indeed be enabled to receive the plain expository teachings of Scripture, but we never outgrow the parables. Like the sacraments, they remain essential for the continued sanctification of our hearts. God does not leave us with mere abstractions. The arts, the parables, the sacraments, and the communion of the saints are like a dark glass through which we may look upon God's abundant revelations so that we are not blinded by the light of glory revealed through them. Our entire life experience has become a body of enigmas, which God has given us to search out. God has put eternity in our hearts.

The effectiveness of parables proves that we know more spiritual truth than we realize. To bring this inward spiritual knowledge to the light of consciousness is a good thing, but we are not expected to understand everything at once. Jesus gave us a perfect example when he washed the feet of his disciples. When Peter expressed some apprehensions over this, Jesus said, "What I am doing you do not understand now, but you will know after this" (John 13:7). Jesus was planting the seeds of a future harvest of understanding. He became an example, and only later did his disciples learn the spiritual meaning in this. Jesus made use of an element of typological revelation that has a way of breaking down a sinner's resistance to spiritual truth. This was an enigma that must have sent their minds racing. Once understood, it was a lesson they would not soon forget. The disciples' former way of thinking was rooted in the way of the world. Jesus turned it on its head and overthrew it. The disciples were confronted with the emotional conflict of having their dirty feet washed by their Lord, who would soon afterward die on a cross for them. Jesus immersed the disciples in his own typological witness of truth so that he could eventually lead them into a conscious quickening of spiritual enlightenment and of moral resolve.

God's typological means of grace plays a different role than literary expressions of the Word. God's ministry of light is vital, but he chooses to preserve his redemptive legacy in the sacred dramas of Communion and Baptism. Consider how God used art to revive a legacy and begin a reformation during Hezekiah's reign. Hezekiah's reforms began with the restoration of the temple. This restoration led to the rediscovery of the book of the law and prophets (2 Kings 22:3–13). God's written law had been so utterly forgotten that the reading of it provoked Josiah to rend his garments in fear of God's judgment for having forsaken God's ways. This illustrates an important relationship of the ministry of light and the ministry of shadows. The conspicuous presence of Solomon's glorious temple, a ministry of shadows standing in disrepair, led to the revival of God's written Word, the ministry of light, in the hearts of men. This is analogous to the ministry of art to individuals.

Art *is* the legacy that draws the truth seeker into the written Word. God will even use it to draw people to the truth who were never particularly interested in the truth before—people who may never be exposed to the gospel any other way. Art that celebrates the beauty of God's holiness is often the only point of spiritual commonality that those outside the covenant have with God's people. Art that is pregnant with religious meaning is enigmatic to the unconverted. Human nature wants enigmas explained just like children at Passover who ask, "What do these things mean?" These people might run away from you if you share the gospel in the form of a sermon.

The beauty of holiness is expressed in the things of beauty that reveal to all humanity the attributes of God. Art is the colorful bloom and lovely fragrance of the flower of enduring beauty, which draws the truth seeker into the pollen of God's Word. But Plato's children—in their craving for abstraction—have bred a flower without color or fragrance, which ultimately leads to fruitlessness. Art is divinely approved. It cannot be rejected as human gimmickry. It is the artless flower of Plato that we must reject as gimmickry. The ascetic's kingdom in abstract is contrary to God's design. Art, for the people of God, is a natural and healthy expression of reverence. God expects us to adorn what we value, and we value all of life. There is a time for stark abstractions, but there is also a time for parables. Jesus uses parables in a way that illustrates our need for the shadow ministries that God has given us. We are creatures that require nuance and mystery in order that we may be taught by the still, small voice of God's presence and grow ever stronger in our ability to look upon the searing light of God's plain spoke word without being blinded.

# A TIME FOR **ACTIVISM**

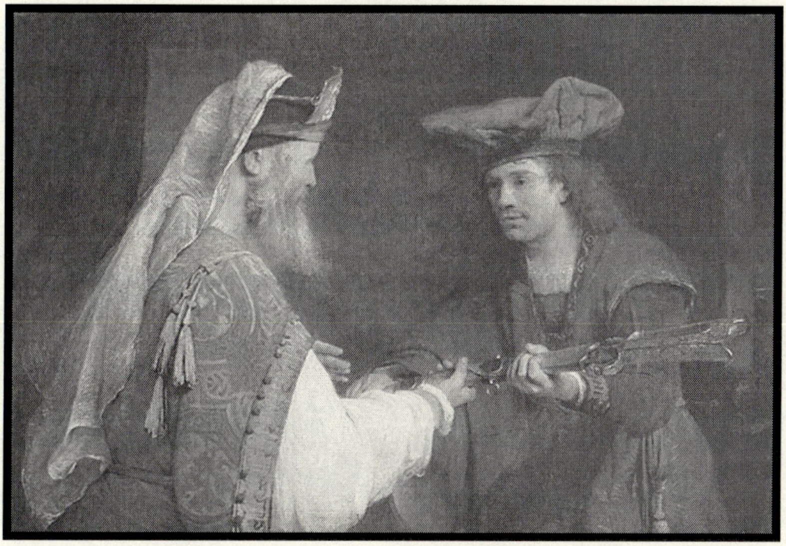

Fig. 18, Aert de Gelder, *Ahimelech Giving to David the Sword of Goliath,* c. 1680

The above painting by Aert de Gelder depicts the priest Ahimelech giving David the sword of Goliath (1 Samuel 21:4–9). He helped David escape the wrath of Saul. Jesus recounts how Ahimelech gave David the showbread, which the ceremonial law forbids to anyone but the priest, saying that this act served a higher moral necessity—the preservation of the lives of David and his men (Matthew 12:2–4). This was the same time that Ahimelech gave the weapon to David. The sword of Goliath was wrapped in a cloth behind the priest's ephod. How did it end up there? Did David give the sword to Ahimelech in recognition that it was God who gave him victory over Goliath? Saul murdered Ahimelech and his fellow priests for enabling David and his men to escape Saul's wrath. Later, when David brought the ark of the covenant to Jerusalem, David wore the same priestly ephod that concealed the sword of Goliath and he danced in joyous procession before the ark. David was loyal to king Saul, even when Saul tried to kill him, but he was also fiercely loyal to the covenant and the priestly order, even to the point of acting as a proxy for the priests that Saul had slain. And there should be such camaraderie between the civil magistrate and the ministers of the Word, who both have different domains of influence but the same general goal of bringing God's light and order to a fallen world. On occasion, the ministry of the church overlaps the broader interests of justice and of civilized society. That is the time for activism.

Biblical activism is our righteous duty. It is our fulfillment of a cultural mandate given by God: "Be fruitful and multiply; fill the earth and subdue it; have dominion over the fish of the sea, over the birds of the air, and over every living thing that moves on the earth" (Genesis 1:28). This order is reiterated after the flood to Noah's family (see Genesis 9:1). This is significant because it shows that the fall did not abrogate the mandate of dominion. The writer of the Epistle to the Hebrews speaks of the Noetic covenant as an archetype of redemption. The plan of redemption and the mandate of dominion are one in the same. God sends his people to transform the world and bend it to his will. The gospel incorporates the cultural mandate to fill the earth and subdue it, but does not supplant it. Every expression of the covenant features a mandate in one form or another. The Noetic, Abrahamic, Mosaic, Davidic, and new covenants have distinctions but also share uniting features. Each covenant unfolds God's plan of redemption in progressive fashion, revealing with increasing specificity and clarity what the mandate of dominion means for the redeemed people of God. Here is the covenant communicated by God to Abraham:

> I *am* Almighty God; walk before me and be blameless. And I will make my covenant between me and you, and will multiply you exceedingly. Then Abram fell on his face, and God talked with him, saying: "As for me, behold, my covenant is with you, and you shall be a father of many nations. No longer shall your name be called Abram, but your name shall be Abraham; for I have made you a father of many nations. I will make you exceedingly fruitful; and I will make nations of you, and kings shall come from you."
>
> Genesis 17:1–6

Yet God planned more than a great physical posterity for Abraham, for God gave him this promise: "In your seed all the nations of the earth shall be blessed, because you have obeyed my voice" (Genesis 22:18). The promise to Abraham was spiritual in nature, and the promises made to Abraham apply to a spiritual posterity. The Apostle Paul teaches us that "[T]hose who are the children of the flesh, these are not the children of God, but the children of the promise are counted as the seed" (Romans 9:8). Through Abraham, God established not only a message of redemption but also an entire culture of redemption. This culture was to be a light to the world, as described by Isaiah: "For behold, the darkness shall cover the earth, and deep darkness the people; but the LORD will arise over you, And his glory will be seen upon you. The Gentiles shall come to your light, And kings to the brightness of your rising" (Isaiah 60:2–4). Jesus describes the culture of redemption this way:

> You are the salt of the earth; but if the salt loses its flavor, how shall it be seasoned? It is then good for nothing but to be thrown out and trampled underfoot by men. You are the light of the world. A city that is set on a hill cannot be hidden. Nor

> do they light a lamp and put it under a basket, but on a lamp stand, and it gives light to all *who are* in the house.
>
> Matthew 5:13–15

Through all of this, the culture of redemption remains a mandate of dominion, and Jesus gives it to the church in the form of the Great Commission:

> All authority has been given to me in heaven and on earth. Go therefore and make disciples of all the nations, baptizing them in the name of the Father and of the Son and of the Holy Spirit, teaching them to observe all things that I have commanded you; and lo, I am with you always, *even* to the end of the age.
>
> Mathew 28:18–20

Wide overlaps exist among the Great Commission, the message of personal salvation and the kingship and dominion of Jesus Christ. The church cannot separate personal salvation from the cultural mandate and the Great Commission; it is all one vision. This is why Jesus taught us to pray, "Thy kingdom come, thy will be done *on earth* as it is in heaven." Has not the church declared Jesus Christ to be King of kings and Lord of lords? Why then did Jesus say to Pilate, "My kingdom is not of this world?" (John 18:36). Jesus came not to be an earthly king, but to rule over earthly kings from heaven. He came to make earthly kings his servants. The kings of that world ruled by the sword and by political intrigue. Christ did not come to achieve a cheap conquest in this crass and trivial arena. Instead, he would change the world. This is why the kingdom of Jesus is not of this world. Many Jews were looking for a conquering Messiah who would remove the Romans by force of arms, but Jesus came with a different plan. He transformed the world by transforming the mind, restoring the conscience, and redeeming the soul. The kings of the earth ruled by bloody conquest, but Christ rules from heaven through the transformation of earthly potentates. Christ did not come to depose all earthly rulers, but to make them his servants. Jesus establishes rulers who uphold not the arbitrary laws of man, but the perfect and just law of God. It is God's law and Christ's kingdom that we seek to establish in order to be liberated from the oppressive laws of men. As God's people, we are called to action to defend that vision. To that end, the cultural mandate applies now more than ever. God has given us clear and specific mandates to respond to injustice, falsehood, impiety, and immorality. We are commanded to retrieve a brother who has fallen into sin, to defend the rights of others, to keep ourselves apart from the impure ways of the world, and to cast out false brethren from the communion of God's people. If we are serious about obeying God in such things, we will inevitably be drawn into political conflict.

The complete gospel contains both abstract and activist aspects of God's mandate to advance his kingdom. The abstract ministry of the church includes preaching the good news of salvation, discipleship, and doctrine. Notwithstanding the importance of these duties, the church cannot obey the Great Commission by attending exclusively to these aspects of it. She must also attend to good works, prayer, the sacraments, and art. Human nature craves abstraction, and it is tempting to view the shadow ministries as mere distractions to the direct message of the gospel simply because the message is so important. But believing the message of salvation is just as important as hearing it. The biblical model of a spiritual ministry involves ministering to the whole man.

But if the church continues to forsake her broader cultural mandate, she will likely witness even greater degeneration of culture and even fewer converts to the faith. Some evangelists speak of changing the world by bringing lost souls to saving faith in Christ. But in practice, God brings most of his people to faith through a change in culture—a new circle of friends, a better home life, or sudden changes in life that encourage introspection. In fact, this seems to be the biblical model—change of culture first, harvest of souls thereafter. John the Baptist came to change the culture to prepare the way for the Messiah. John's purpose was "'*to turn the hearts of the fathers to the children,*' and the disobedient to the wisdom of the just, to make ready a people prepared for the Lord" (Luke 1:17).

When the Messiah did arrive, there was still more preparation to be done. Jesus spoke in parables and would not disclose that he was the Messiah until late in his ministry. John and Jesus were preparing the culture for the great advance of the gospel. It was only after the resurrection and ascension of Jesus that large numbers of people finally began to understand the gospel, beginning at Pentecost. The light of the gospel shines best through a culture that has some semblance of a godly order.

Justice, mercy, and faith—according to Jesus—are the weightier matters of the law of God (see Matthew 23:23). Respect for justice inseparably includes justice as a function of civil government (see Exodus 23:1–5, Jeremiah 21:12, and Amos 5:15). Our Savior's call for justice forcefully implies that the church must have an activist role in society to change civil government for the better. The Westminster Divines cite Leviticus 5:1, which says, "If a person sins in hearing the utterance of an oath, and *is* a witness, whether he has seen or known *of the matter*—if he does not tell *it,* he bears guilt" (Leviticus 5:1). The Westminster Divines also site the complaint of Isaiah, who declared, "No one calls for justice, nor does *any* plead for truth" (Isaiah 59:4). We are morally bound to call for justice and to plead for truth. Biblical morality does not always leave us the option to mind our own business or to "live and let live."

A commitment to obey God's law may someday require us to thrust ourselves into political controversies. Jesus tells his disciples that they will be brought before kings. Joseph, Daniel, and Paul all stood before kings by God's providence. Their obedience to God directed their destinies. Biblical activism can be a messy and hazardous business, and it is tempting leave such matters to civic leaders working independently of the church. But the church does not have the option of washing her hands of civic and social responsibilities. She cannot simply accept the continuing corruption of culture, as if there is nothing that can be done about it. Jesus does not allow his church to defer all hope of a better world to the hereafter. We are expected to offer ourselves in obedience to God's call to establish his will on earth as in heaven.

Activism can certainly be taken to an extreme. The church's clear message of salvation must never be smothered with inverted priorities in the name of being faithful to kingdom duties. But she should also be wary of the succumbing to the half-gospel of abstraction. The church can create a certain comfort zone for herself by avoiding earthly entanglements and confining her ministry to a world of purely spiritual and abstract ideals, but this is not God's way. God, in his mercy, may choose to use it, but the spiritual fruit of man's way is usually sparse and worm eaten. There is no dichotomy between the ministry of the word and our kingdom responsibilities. We must reject the false dichotomy between the spiritual and physical concerns for our broken world. The gospel requires us to care for both. To properly fulfill her spiritual responsibilities, the church must attend to her earthly and mundane duties as well.

But what *should* the church claim as her rightful sphere of influence? A sharply drawn line can be followed. Ministers of the Word are called by God to speak the truth of God's Word entirely and uncompromisingly. No part of God's Word is too small or too great to be declared in due season. He should encourage activism whenever the gifts and passions of other individuals lead them into it with an appropriate attitude and a desire to serve God.

The heart of the church's ministry belongs not to the minister of the Word but to the *people* who are directed by the Word to pursue justice, mercy, and righteousness. It is each individual's calling to fulfill whatever ministry God has placed on each servant's heart. That said, there is no biblical rule that absolutely limits pastors to such a middle-management role. Faithfulness to God's Word sometimes requires activism. Jesus said to his disciples, "[H]e who has no sword, let him sell his garment and buy one" (Luke 22:36). Jesus calls for vigilance in dark times and expects his disciples to defend themselves from assassins. If a time comes when evil men are breaking down sanctuary doors to kill the worshipers inside, a pastor could appropriately fetch guns from behind the pulpit and distribute them to the men of the church to defend the flock. Such extreme circumstances do happen in parts of the world. We do not ordinarily look to ministers to organize an armed force, but a good shepherd defends his sheep. The disciples of Jesus were ready to take up arms for their Messiah when they said to him, "Lord, look, here *are* two swords." And he said to them, "It is enough" (Luke 22:38). Why did Jesus say that two swords are enough? Peter only used one sword that evening, and for this Jesus chided him. Jesus was speaking of a later day when his disciples should have a weapon for self-defense. Two swords are not enough for an army or militia. The church is not called to armed resistance as a rule, and there is a time to step out in faith and carry no sword or purse at all. But there are also times of extreme danger when the shepherds of God's people must buy a weapon and protect their family and flock. We can sometimes provoke the anger of assassins just by speaking the truth. Silence before evil men is not a morally acceptable option because we are ambassadors for Christ and our duty is to glorify the Lord's name. While we must respect the normal institutions of justice, there may be times when those institutions become completely corrupt and we, like so many of our fathers, must take up arms.

The acts of patriarchs, prophets, apostles, and church fathers provide models of activism that cut through all epochs and dispensations of sacred history. The gospel was never intended to be a mere peaceful, abstract revolution of religious enlightenment. The gospel is inherently offensive to tyrants. It has been the catalyst for political intrigue, persecution, war, and revolution. Although our weapons are spiritual, the weapons used by Christ's enemies often kill the body. Wherever the gospel has prospered, the insatiable gorge of hell has responded by spewing out violence like a boiling caldron against the just and innocent. When this happens, Christians who find themselves in a position to seek justice through normal means are bound to do so. But sometimes the people of God will be compelled by conscience into armed revolt.

During the American War for Independence, the Tories charged that churchmen were inspiring the revolution. There is some truth to this. These were Congregationalist and Presbyterian ministers. These black-robed ministers helped sow the seeds of the revolution, and they were called the Black Regiment. Like other ministers, the weapons of the Black Regiment were spiritual. They fought with sermons.

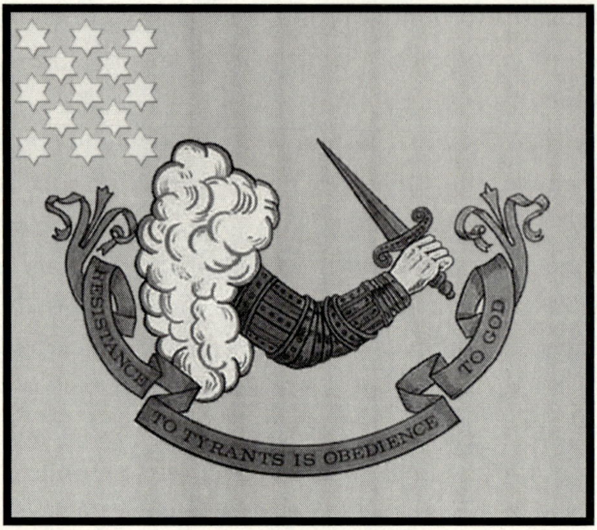


Fig. 19, Battle Flag of the American Revolution
*Gostelowe Standard No. 10*, c. 1776

One of the battle flags of the revolution, shown above, featured the saying "Resistance to Tyrants Is Obedience to God." This is a quote of Jefferson that he borrowed from an earlier historical figure of the English Civil War, John Bradshaw. Bradshaw led the prosecution of Britain's King Charles I. The prosecution of the king established—in Britain—that monarchs could not rule without the consent of the parliament. American colonists saw this as a historical precedent to challenge the right of King George to rule the colonists without *their* consent. To some Christians, the motto "Resistance to Tyrants Is Obedience to God" may seem overstated. However, much of sacred history is the epic struggle of God's people against tyranny, such as, Moses against Pharaoh, Elijah against Ahab, Sampson against Moab, and Deborah against Sisera. These are all parts of a humanity's broader epic struggle against the ultimate tyranny of sin. Every conquered tyrant foreshadows the fulfillment of God's promise that the seed of the woman would crush the head of the serpent.

This precedent of resistance continues unbroken through the New Testament and the age of the early church fathers. John the Baptist was martyred for speaking out against Herod's unlawful marriage to Herodias (see Mathew 14:3–5). Jesus told Pilate that his authority came from above (John 19:11). Jesus purposefully made of himself the ultimate political dilemma. Pilate's act of succumbing to mob rule became a historical archetype of magisterial dereliction of duty. The Apostle Paul was not shy about claiming his rights as a Roman citizen before Felix. Paul could have left himself under the jurisdiction of Felix and looked to providence to direct his destiny. Instead, Paul validated an activist approach when he shrewdly used Roman civil law to his advantage. By appealing to Caesar, he escaped assassins who had vowed to kill him and obtained a journey to Rome, earning numerous evangelistic opportunities while awaiting an audience with Caesar.

Early church history follows this activist precedent when Justin Martyr, in his "Apology," addressed the Roman Senate to vindicate the faith and practices of Christians who had been the target of persecution and slander. The historical and biblical model for the church is not to avoid political redress and shrug off anti-Christian sentiments as something to be expected or to avoid indictments against public figures. The Bible validates the idea of churchmen speaking out in their own defense as well as ecclesiastical indictments against political wrongdoers.

The reformers were not at all shy about offending cultural conventions and political interests. John Knox, in particular, was notoriously acerbic. One of his better-known works was a criticism of the regimes of Bloody Mary and Mary Queen of Scots, entitled "First Blast of the Trumpet against the Monstrous Regiment of Women." Knox was never one to make any effort at political neutrality or to speak to royalty with any deference with regard to the sins they committed against their subjects. The father of the Eastern church, Chrysostom, continually criticized

Eudoxia, the wife of Emperor Arcadius, for her decadent and extravagant lifestyle. Chrysostom chided Eudoxia both indirectly and directly, and he was eventually exiled for this. Paul, Stephen, Justin Martyr, and Chrysostom may have all been accused today of being too confrontational or of making things too "political." Like these churchmen, many of our spiritual forefathers were outspoken at the risk of persecution and martyrdom. By contrast, we who have a right to free speech protected by law are reluctant to speak boldly or to offend anyone with the truth about the public sins of civil magistrates.

The church must speak with the apostolic boldness that works as salt and light in the world. Its potential effect on the world is reflected in the words of Lactantius: "God has risen up princes to rescind the impious and sanguinary edicts of the tyrants and provide for the welfare of mankind; so that now the cloud of past times is dispelled, and peace and serenity gladden all hearts."[9] Doing the will of God will inevitably make us enemies of the world, yet we declare with the Apostle Paul:

> Though we walk in the flesh, we do not war according to the flesh. For the weapons of our warfare are not carnal but mighty in God for pulling down strongholds, casting down arguments and every high thing that exalts itself against the knowledge of God, bringing every thought into captivity to the obedience of Christ, and being ready to punish all disobedience when your obedience is fulfilled.
>
> 2 Corinthians 10:3–6

Although Paul speaks of a war "not according to the flesh," an element of action is required for all of this. There is nothing abstract about true church discipline, and we are commanded to fulfill it (see Mathew 18).

Simple acts of obedience to God's Word have the potential of transforming any Christian into a defender of the faith, a revolutionary force, an iconoclast, a rebel for a good cause, or a political activist. God has not given us a kingdom only in abstract. We are salt and light. When the church becomes sequestered and withdrawn from the culture war, she cedes control to men of darkness and violence. When people of faith fight for the things they believe, they create free and just societies. We do not fight for our culture because we trust in our own strength to redeem it, but because God has commanded us to fight for it. To those who see this as a radicalization of the faith, I assert that precisely the converse is true. We seek to redeem our culture while it may be redeemed peacefully with weapons that are spiritual in nature—reason, persuasion, mercy, compassion, art, and beauty. The alternative is to allow the God haters to eventually take full control of our culture, renounce our God-centered foundation of civil rights, and set the stage for a bloody conflict in the future. We seek to redeem our culture *before* the enemies of Christ's church begin to enslave and murder God's people, *before* any disciple of Christ must sell his coat to buy a weapon, and *before* the Black Regiment of tomorrow is compelled to rise up and call those who cherish freedom to armed revolt. Biblical Christianity creates a potential for peaceful reform. But to pursue this way of peace, we can accept no passive vision—no kingdom in abstract—but one of active cultural conquest and of our Lord's ultimate dominion in the hearts of a free people.

# REDEEMING THE **CULTURE**

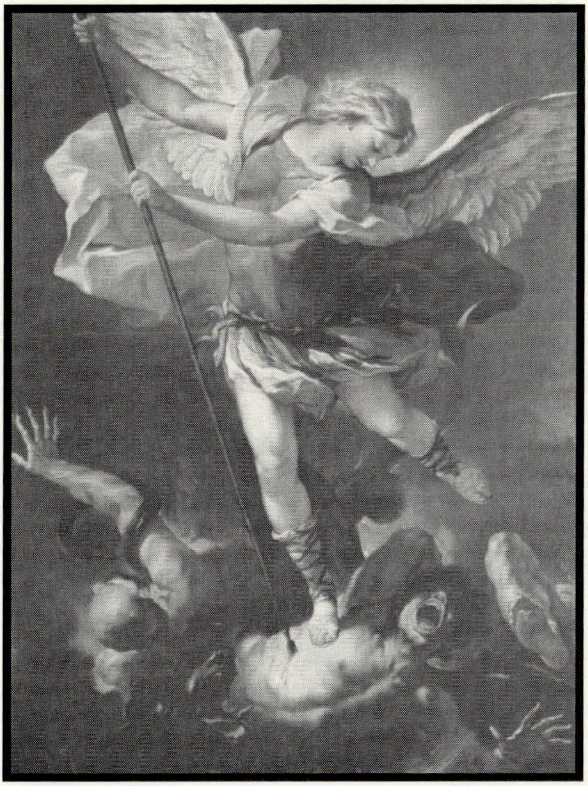

Fig. 20, Luca Giordano, *St. Michael Vanquishing the Devil,* 1663

In the above painting, Luca Giordano depicts Michael the Archangel subduing Lucifer. There are many depictions of Michael fighting the devil. Sometimes, as in Saint John's description in Revelation, Lucifer is a dragon:

> And war broke out in heaven: Michael and his angels fought with the dragon; and the dragon and his angels fought, but they did not prevail, nor was a place found for them in heaven any longer. So the great dragon was cast out, that serpent of old, called the Devil and Satan, who deceives the whole world; he was cast to the earth, and his angels were cast out with him.
>
> Revelation 12:7–9

Since the Renaissance, painters have often created anthropomorphic depictions of Lucifer, as in Giordano's portrayal of him as a brutish pagan. This battle between Michael and Satan epitomizes an epoch struggle between good and evil that continues to this day. Jesus said to his disciples, "I saw Satan fall like lightning from heaven" (Luke 10:18). He had just sent his apostles to heal the sick and cast out demons. It was not an entirely invisible battle that Jesus perceived. Sometimes our invisible war against the darkness seems quite visible and it is always very real.

Real, transformative Christianity is nothing like Gnosticism. The portion of our struggle that we can sense is important to us (see 1 John 1:1). In Christ, the war became visible in the form of fulfilled prophecy, miracles, and wonders. The ultimate visible victory in Christ's war against death was, of course, the resurrection. What is wrong with the church today? Perhaps, in the name of piety, we have forsaken our earthy duties and should heed the angel's admonition given to the apostles at the beginning of the book of Acts: "Why do you stand gazing up into heaven?" (Acts 1:11). We have work to do. It is good to speak of positive cultural reform. But without a visible dimension to our battle, we will find ourselves waging a timid war with a real aggressor who will continue to inflict enormous spiritual casualties. Yes, there can be too much gazing into heaven. We must stop thinking like Gnostics and pull our minds out of the clouds. It's time to blow our master's trumpet, form ranks, and join the real battle for the souls of our fellow citizens. If we tarry, the children of darkness will eventually cause bloodshed.

What is the church's role in a visible culture war? Perhaps the heart of the culture war is the shadow ministry of art. Art has not always served orthodoxy well, nor has the church always served artistic expression well. Yet it is this relationship between art and the faith of God's people that has elevated art to its highest expressions. While God has prescribed art to glorify himself, man has also used it as an instrument of rebellion. This is because art is simultaneously an indispensable means of inspiration and a great spiritual danger, and this is why art is the business of the church. If the church does not manage the ministry of art for good, the children of darkness will manage it for evil. Whoever controls art shapes culture—humanity's sense of beauty and order, of good and evil, and of law and justice. These are the things that must be guarded by our institutions—churches, academia, conservatories, and magistrates—all serving in specific spheres of influence. These institutions shape and inform our world's values, and they must be won over.

The culture war has many fronts. The Apostle Paul taught that no spiritual gift is unimportant to the work of the church (see 1 Corinthians 12:14–26). Perhaps true reform and true gospel prosperity will begin when the church begins to act upon what the Bible teaches regarding the spiritual gifts of God's people. We heed God's call to service out of obedience and not because God has any need of our frail and clumsy efforts to change the world. After all, with the mere symbol of his presence God conquered the Philistines. God does not need us. If there is such a thing as a spiritual gift, it can only mean that God desires to use his people as instruments of his will. Instead of doing everything for us, God awaits the church's faithful obedience to the cultural mandate and to the Great Commission.

As long as a few people of the covenant remain faithful, our culture is redeemable. Every man or woman whose heart is stirred to action should be encouraged to make a contribution to advance the ways of God's kingdom over the ways of the world. This is basic to our Christian witness to the world and is the essence of cultural reform. The arts are inevitably an important part of the ideological battleground between godliness and worldliness. The church should encourage gifted artists to value their spiritual gifts and to exercise them. The church, as a matter of good stewardship, should give all diligence to discover all the gifts of God's people and to advise them spiritually on how to use them. Scripture encourages creative gifts in broad terms. The writer of Ecclesiastes says, "Whatever your hands find to do, do it with all your might" (Ecclesiastes 9:10). Proverbs says, "Do you see a man *who* excels in his work? He will stand before kings; he will not stand before unknown *men*" (Proverbs 22:29).

The Apostle Paul makes no distinction between creative gifts or other spiritual gifts. He writes, "*Whatever* you do in word or deed, *do* all in the name of the Lord Jesus, giving thanks to God the Father through him" (Colossians 3:17). Sometimes God will give us someone with a familiar gift—a visual artist, a musician, or a writer. Yet every now and then the Bible gives us someone gifted in a peculiar way. Only two people are named in Scripture as having a gift of interpreting dreams, Joseph and Daniel. Only one person in Scripture was given miraculous physical strength, and that was Sampson. A person's individual ministry forms itself as he discovers his own unique way of serving the church. We cannot presume to fit every individual into an off-the-shelf ministry complete with syllabus and textbook.

What if a church could set up a committee of key helpers with expert knowledge to direct a mission into the cultural life of the local community? They could work under the auspices of the church leadership to organize, direct, and encourage local talent through musical performances, art exhibits, or literature symposiums. What if we looked to the retired people among us—those with a wealth of experience and wisdom as well as time—to mentor young students? Some congregations have a goldmine of human resources, having retired teachers of history, law, literature, music, and fine arts. Some church music directors may have expertise in other art forms like creative writing, debate, or visual art. The church could expand this person's ministry from a minister of music to a minister of culture directing a number of cultural ministries. Some forms of cultural expression, such as the Eucharist, are for God's confessing people. Good artistic direction, like good theology, helps to maintain worship in an atmosphere of utmost reverence. This is the highest calling of art. Yet our ministry of culture must not be isolated. Our light should be placed on a lamp stand. The church's ministry of culture should include elements designed to lovingly draw the local community into the light of the church's influence.

Anyone can have a role in the Reformation of our culture whether artistic, scholastic, administrative, financial, or pastoral. In the cause of our precious culture of freedom, every spiritual gift serves an important role. Art plays an important role in the life and worship of God's people. If we do not believe this, we should disband our choirs and sell our choir robes and hymnals. We should also sell our beautiful edifices with stained-glass windows. We should move our congregations into cheaper warehouse-like structures and apply the savings to a form of mission work that reduces the gospel to the pure abstract messages of the spoken and written Word. Many Christians would see such artlessness as a monstrous form of irreverence, and they would be right. Scripture itself has produced and ordained art for God's glory. Art is embedded in our sacraments, which are essentially sacred art. Scripture, by its validation of the sacraments, affirms that creatures made in God's image need art. For we are told that by taking the Lord's table, we proclaim the Lord's death until he comes (see 1 Corinthians 11:25–27) and that baptism is an appeal for a clean conscience (see 1 Peter 3:21).

The broader culture war entails retaking much of the institutional authority that the church has ceded to secular influences over the centuries. There is such a backwash of cultural decay that advocates of biblical morality have trouble maintaining a moral cultural environment in their own domains. The church has made her domain too small. She is now being ghettoized, having her influence confined to a few precious scraps of ground where she may build her sanctuaries and seminaries. Good stewardship requires a different strategy. We will see revival in the church when we see a cultural revival in the general population. We will see a cultural revival when people of faith once again exercise a crucial influence over academia, conservatories, media, and civil magistrates.

The church should take steps to protect the institutional assets she still controls. Enemies of the gospel don't care to build their own great institutions but prefer to steal those institutions built by Christians. That trend must be reversed. We must protect that which God has entrusted to us. Christian churches and institutions should hire lawyers to create an airtight legal instrument to effectively keep the church's assets in the hands of faithful, Bible-believing Christians forever. Why not appoint a standing panel of trustees who, by the terms of the trust, derive their authority from their individual sworn adherence to biblical doctrine? Perhaps a slate of specific beliefs should be established for trustees and rigorously maintained. With a good team of lawyers in the past and with enough foresight, perhaps Harvard, Princeton, Yale, and a few church denominations would still be in the hands of true, believing Christians.

Many Christians today donate money to institutions that have become ideologically and scholastically corrupt. Through their graduates, secularists have begun injecting a poisonous and hostile cosmology into academia, government, churches, and culture. What would happen if the church set up independent accreditation boards for colleges and universities? What if these boards had the power to discredit corrupt institutions and advise contributors to those institutions to end all support? What if these accreditation boards constantly reviewed departments of liberal and fine arts? These accreditation boards could also review the so-called soft sciences or social sciences, which would include history, philosophy, sociology, psychology, counseling, education, journalism, and political science. Perhaps the church could develop its own course curricula, which could be offered to colleges. Perhaps the church could host lectures and debates and coordinate these with local colleges.

If a wealthy benefactor wants to set up a trust fund for a worthy institution, that person should arm the trustees with clear instructions and legal authority to redirect all contributions to a better cause if the institution loses its moral character. The church should use her influence to discourage all donations to educational institutions that hire faculty hostile to Christian interests or that fail to advance deserving Christian scholars while awarding scholarships, professorships, and honorariums to those of lesser achievement. Contributors should be encouraged to target their giving to specific deserving academic departments or individual Christian students.

The church should encourage Christians to establish new trust funds and scholarships for exceptional students and make funds payable only to church-accredited institutions. The church could organize a matching-funds program to encourage existing scholarships to be awarded to qualified Christian scholars. This would effectively leverage the scholarship funds from Christian contributors to Christian students and would reduce the scholarships available to those who would work against the interests of

Christians. The church, acting in an organized effort, could provide heavy financial incentives for academic institutions to avoid the appearance anti-Christian prejudice or secularist favoritism.

You artists, craftsmen, musicians, writers, and performers have a weighty responsibility. You whose hearts are stirred within should organize yourselves into guilds and study the elements of artistic beauty, which is the sacred trust of every artist. You should start friendly, constructive arguments among yourselves regarding the biblical elements of beauty and how you may best reflect your Creator in the work of your hands. Draw your pastors and elders into this conversation. Let them help you find guidance from Scripture and expose your views to peer review and theological debate. The Bible is a goldmine of wisdom in the study of aesthetics. Remember that you are the type of our Creator in a profound and unique way. People of your calling have been used by God to provide a vital means to spiritual enlightenment, conviction of sin, and true reform. Uphold the hand of the Lord's anointed and know that God may use you to end the long spiritual drought of our era. The secularists who have long styled themselves as the guardians of reason are being exposed as impostors in the eyes of God's people. The people of God are beginning to realize the spiritual and intellectual fraud perpetrated against them. You are the guardians of the cloud of witnesses, the shadow languages of divine grace, the communal hearth, and the greater light. Maintain these, and the gates of hell will not withstand the cultural juggernaut that the people of God will eventually become.

Shepherds, let the church teach, direct, and encourage gifted visual artists. Find those among you who are well trained and knowledgeable about the visual arts. Set up a committee of artists and consult them regarding how to make the sanctuary and the service more aesthetically conducive to worship and spiritual instruction—whatever inspires reverence and prayer and whatever gives focus on the preaching of the Word and the sacraments. The art that Christians should choose for the sanctuary may be completely different from what they would put in a hallway, foyer, office, or classroom. Hallways and classrooms should be galleries of Christian legacies. Gather your cloud of witnesses—your visible legacy of martyrs and heroes of the faith. A legacy of great original art can take generations to develop. However, God has blessed us with modern imaging technology that gives us access to quality reproductions of great historical artworks that already exist. These things are important for us and for our children, that we may be reminded of the deadly seriousness of the saints' epic struggles for the gospel. We have not been given a kingdom in abstract—a kingdom of mere theory and concept. Our battle is real. An original work of art is preferable, but there is nothing wrong with a good reproduction. Have your art ministers go through every room of the church property and install good quality reproductions of artworks that depict historical events, such as Anton von Werner's painting "*Luther before the Diet of Worms*" or "*One morning at the gates of the Louvre,* by Édouard Debat-Ponsan (depicting the aftermath of St. Bartholomew s Day Massacre). Sunday-school material for children is typically full of cartoon illustrations of Abraham, Noah, and David, among others. Whatever their value as instructional tools, our children should have more than this to visually represent their faith. Cartoons do not properly convey the reverence and utmost seriousness of our faith. Our children should also behold the sufferings of the martyrs. Our children should be raised with a deep sense that our spiritual warfare is serious and real.

Find the Bezaleels among God's people, give them special theological training, and call them to organize cultural missions that operate under the auspices of the church government as an official ministry. Have your committee of art experts find an artist who is well gifted and commission some art for the church, such as a painting, a carving, a vessel, a stained-glass window, a sculpture, a musical composition, a drama, a hymn, or a work of literature. An artist who receives a commission from the church should be a person of rare and undeniable accomplishment. You may not find such a person in your congregation or even in your town. Remember that art is potentially dangerous, having a potential for serving idolatry, avarice, lust or vanity, but it is also a powerful influence for good. The artistic decisions you make should not be made capriciously. The design of an edifice or selection of hymns should be given as much thought as the Sunday morning sermon. Guide your committee of art experts and let them advise you and present their recommendations to the congregation for approval. Think of what a positive spiritual exercise such a collaborative endeavor can become.

Be warned, however, that mediocre art can do more to damage the aesthetic integrity of a sanctuary than to improve it. Better is a freshly painted wall than a bad painting. A well-executed representational work of art is a wonderful thing, but not all artists do it well. Perhaps a colorful, nonrepresentational work of art would be a better choice. Whatever your decision, let your art experts guide you and give them guidance according to what the church leadership and congregation deems appropriate.

Some areas of creative expression have been trivialized by the postmodernist tradition of art. Cultural demagogues of our day have formed a kind of secular priesthood of artists, which elevate one form of art above another, according to its propensity to affirm a particular set of postmodernist ideas. This form of elitism is inconsistent with biblical aesthetics. In the Bible, the sculptor's art is not elevated above the art of perfumers, jewelers, choirs, or orators. In this context, art generally supports a religious service of worship. This principle should be considered when a congregation chooses an architect for a new sanctuary. A good architect will design the building to support the theology and mission of the church. If the skill and artistry of a good architect is fully used, the church will be more conducive to worship and more useful in general. Architecture is a comfortable art form for the church because there is a built-in orthodoxy of function and engineering science that dominates architecture as a form of art.

How would you apply such a principle to the sartorial arts? Certainly, universal standards may be found to distinguish a quality garment, but no overriding orthodoxy of function influences the style of a garment more than the caprice of the clothes designer. The utilitarian function of a garment requires very little artfulness, but a fine garment is as much a work of art as a painting. It reveals a beauty that transcends form and function. Numerous biblical references indicate that the sartorial arts were of great importance in biblical culture. In Exodus, God commanded the priestly garments to be made for beauty and for glory. Isaiah describes the Lord himself as clothed in glory with the train of his robe filling the temple (see Isaiah 6:1). Clothing is an expression of caring. Jesus poetically describes the lilies of the field as clothed by God in raiment better than King Solomon's clothing (see Matthew 6:29). The book of Proverbs describes the household of a righteous woman as one that is clothed in scarlet (Proverbs 31:21). In Isaiah, Israel is personified as a woman favored of God and clothed with the finest attire. The book of Revelation similarly describes the church of Christ as a bride attired in fine white linen (Revelation 19:8).

Think of how much attention is given to Hollywood and home entertainment today. For good or ill, electronic home entertainment media will be a big cultural influence for a long time. But cinema can be elevated to a respectable art form. The church should make some effort to tame the home entertainment beast by advancing what is intellectually and spiritually profitable. Good cinema, musical, and documentary productions can promote thought and introspection.

Before the days of home video, I was involved with a small group of Christians that would meet once a week to watch films. Our host used his father's workshop and film projector. We would watch science and history documentaries and art films. The best part of the night was when we discussed the films afterward. A good film should enhance the thought life and can produce a lasting treasury of common experience in critical thinking, good fellowship, and edifying conversation. That is perhaps why most people prefer to see movies with someone. The church should organize its own community of experts to review major cinematic productions. Our experts should have something to say about their decency, cosmology, and overall artistic merit. Much can be said about the potential corrupting influences of Hollywood. There is more to it than sex and violence. Much of the corruption is in the form of crassness and superficiality, which reflects the general environment of Tinsel Town. What if the church could defang the entertainment industry? Perhaps the church's own community of experts could exercise some friendly and positive consumer influence over the kind of movies that are shown in the local theater. What if a church could reach out to the local theater management and issue some friendly encouragement to avoid Hollywood productions that promote anti-Christian bigotry or morally offensive behavior? It is not unheard of for a businessman to change his business for purely altruistic reasons, but the church could leverage a profit incentive as well. Local church leaders could encourage aesthetically and morally sound cinematic features and could reward such choices with the frequent and loyal patronage of church members. Some theaters have found an off-Hollywood film niche on their own and are able to make it work. If the church could draw the industry into these kinds of conversations, perhaps it could be a commercial grassroots force for change. A similar arrangement could be made for your local live-performance companies. A good live performance has an aesthetic dimension that is impossible to match with cinematography. If live-performance groups perceived that half their patrons were active church members, do you think they would give much attention to playwrights that write theatrical scripts offensive to Christians?

Why should the church trust secularists to provide reviews on literature, cinema, drama, music, and fine art? There is a higher authority than the opinions of secularists. Christians must be informed by God's Word and become the *greater* experts. Do secularists have a logical and moral foundation for judging what has enduring truth and beauty? No, but the church does. Her logical and moral foundation for aesthetics is in the Holy Scriptures. All bad taste is rooted in some form of moral affront, validating vice, promoting falsehood, appealing to lust, hatred, prejudice, etc. There are countless forms of artistic malpractice that exploit or indulge the dark side of human nature. We sinners typically desire to coddle and excuse rather than confront such things, but great artistry is distinguished by its ability to elevate and inspire us toward better things. That is precisely the ministry God has given to the church, to whom God has given unction, ordination, spiritual authority and the wisdom of God's Word.

What if the church's own cultural watchdogs could have intelligent and insightful critical reviews published regularly? With enough persistence, the church could become a *de facto* moral and intellectual compass of the entertainment industry. If Christian critics were more influential, perhaps Hollywood producers would have less incentive to push indecent and offensive products. For the church to fulfill a ministry of artistic criticism she must educate herself from God's Word. She must know that God has not only made his people the witness of the gospel but of every good and beautiful thing that gives glory to him.

With artistic authority comes a *de facto* power of censorship. Censorship is a good thing when used responsibly, but how to censor a film is not always an easy judgment. Even works of high moral and aesthetic value can be appropriate for some audiences and inappropriate for others. There are passages even in the Bible that I will not read to small children, but censoring any part of the Bible from the canon is an idea that was rejected by the church fathers and explicitly forbidden in the Bible itself. Similarly, great documentaries like those that record the historical conflicts against evil dictators serve a valuable purpose. Such things serve to warn us of the reality of evil and the darkness of the unregenerate heart. Yet one must obviously show these things with some discretion. Some harsh realities are not for young children. Some morally valuable movies provide good viewing but for one or two objectionable scenes. What if Christians could convince movie producers to reedit and rerelease such movies in a special edition? Old cinematic productions represent potential free money for the producers. If shown a residual profit potential by removing a few scenes, film producers might gladly accommodate.

The church's imprint on culture will never be effective if she is limited to the pulpit, Sunday school, and theology books. These are good things, but the church's cultural authority must not end there. The church needs novelists, playwrights, filmmakers, architects, musicians, painters, designers, actors, dancers, poets, orators, and craftsmen of all kinds in her ranks. She should organize artists into Christian guilds. This would provide a forum and support network for developing a biblical foundation for their crafts in a way that offers valuable direction for each discipline.

The church should not encourage someone to become a professional artist unless that person shows exceptional aptitude, but many people can profit greatly from amateur artistic endeavors.

The greater value of the creative gift is not its value as a profession, but its value as a catalyst for broad-based personal growth.

The church should watch for children with a special aptitude for music and should encourage their parents to give them formal lessons. Congregations could take special collections, if needed, and use the proceeds to offer scholarships to a highly gifted child. Both Chrysostom and Augustine were trained in the art of oratory. These were the fathers of the Eastern and Western church respectively. Would the Church be a good steward of such gifted minds today? Perhaps there are retired artists in the church who could volunteer some teaching or tutoring time for a gifted student or two with special aptitudes for visual art, drama, oratory, science, writing, or law.

The church should find good writers and put them to work writing reviews for cultural events, books, theatre, cinema, music, and debate. The church should get those reviews published in the church newsletters, local community and college papers, major newspapers, and Internet forums. These could be letters to the editor, editorials on political issues, or rebuttals to published articles. This is just the sort of modest beginning that has led many writers to eventually extend their influences far and wide. The church could establish an internship fund for gifted writers and aspiring journalists. What if the church could supply a steady stream of gifted writers to become good journalists who are not indoctrinated with the cognition-killing poison of secularism? Think of the difference that could eventually make regarding how the news is reported today. Whether consciously or unconsciously, the news media has become a massive coordinated effort to suppress or pervert the truth and to advance lies. A watchdog role against media indoctrination falls within the church's rightful domain, but it is a role that the government can never assume without encroaching dangerously on free-speech rights. Having the church as a powerful advocate for truth in a free market of ideas relieves government of the temptation to punish dangerous lies and propaganda.

Our forefathers, in their biblical wisdom, knew that the truth will always prevail against lies if allowed free and open expression. That is why our founders embraced the reformers' view of the liberty of conscience and forbade the government power to punish thoughts or beliefs. The government may only regulate the actions of people according to laws designed to protect the rights of all people. Only two places in Scripture specifically describe the purpose of civil government, and both passages say the same thing: the purpose of government is to praise good and punish evil (see Romans 13:3 and 1 Peter 2:14).

Can a church stay completely out of politics and still obey God? Keeping the church out of politics may seem preferable, but it is not always possible. In some cases it is completely unconscionable. If our gospel message has not created political conflict, perhaps it is because we have watered down the message for political expediency. In a republic, the *people* are responsible for the government. It is our right and duty to elect just magistrates to establish just laws. We cannot behold the filth and darkness of our culture and do nothing to fight it. Our constitutional values are informed by our faith historically and personally. God cannot be pleased with us if we abdicate our constitutional powers as citizens. It is the church's moral duty to speak out against political corruption and injustice, and the church is in sin if she fails to do so. Christ alone is our ultimate King. It is God who gives authority to magistrates. To hold civil magistrates accountable, the church must be an independent moral authority. For this reason, the church should not explicitly endorse political candidates. The Apostle Paul warned Timothy, "Do not lay hands on anyone hastily, nor share in other people's sins; keep yourself pure" (1 Timothy 5:22). We are indirectly responsible for the acts of bad spiritual leaders whom we place into positions of power. We are also responsible for bad civil magistrates whom we put into positions of power.

If political endorsements give even the appearance of compromising our moral objectivity, that is reason enough to avoid them altogether. However, the church should by no means be shy about praising or condemning specific acts of politicians. God appoints every ruler for his own purpose. Any magistrate is a potential force for good or evil. Our duty is to hold all magistrates accountable—without deference or prejudice. This role for the church is well established by biblical example and centuries of historical precedent. The church should pray for those in power and teach respect for those who govern as God's ministers. But she should also be an equal-opportunity tormenter for those who corrupt their office and do evil. The church should, in some cases, formally adjudicate the actions of a political leader. If he is found to have acted corruptly, the church court should draft a respectful statement of protest and call upon that political leader to reverse himself. The shepherds of God's people have been given moral authority. Even though the civil magistrate in our nation serves Christians and non-Christians alike, the Bible gave us constitutional principles of civil government. Biblical principles enshrined in the constitution give the civil magistrate the guidance and moral authority to serve the general public in a way that respects conscience and religious liberty.

The church cannot expect to be left alone by the world to practice her faith unhindered. The world will encroach upon all that belongs to the church and will even challenge her right to exist. The reformers hated the way of blind indoctrination. It is an impenetrable darkness if left unchallenged. They discovered that there is no lie as dangerous as a "truth" that is left unchallenged. So the children of the Reformation embraced accountability with peer review, scholastic discipline, and modern science. This is the culture that we should seek to reestablish. We value universal liberty of conscience, open and honest debate, and a fearless devotion to the light of truth. It is to preserve such ideals that we must seize the culture before it falls irreversibly into the worldly ways of blind indoctrination. Our counteroffensive is the cleansing light of truth itself because we believe that the doctrines of darkness cannot endure it. When the Reformation shook Europe into a new spiritual consciousness, no institution was left untouched. The reformers did not cede moral and intellectual authority to anyone. They trusted no worldly institution with any monopoly on truth, and they boldly challenged falsehood wherever it raised its ugly head. They trusted God's Word, and they followed his promises. Will we ever see such warriors of culture form ranks again? This generation must invoke the full unction of the Spirit and the bride of Christ. This generation must investigate every conceivable avenue of cultural influence and seize it. We must wage our cultural war with utmost resolve. It is more than justifiable. It is morally imperative.

# OUR CROWN— **GOD'S GLORY**

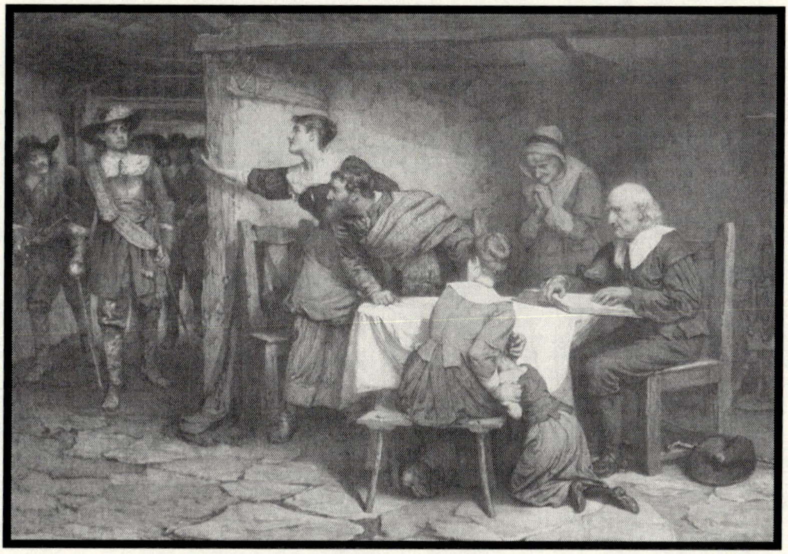

Fig. 21, William Harris, *The Covenanters,* 1887

## A HIDDEN LEGACY

In the above watercolor painting, William Harris depicts a Scottish Covenanter family at their evening devotionals, being interrupted by soldiers entering their home with swords drawn. A woman comforts a frightened child. A wife holds her husband back as he rises to his feet. An older man remains seated, still marking the place of his Scripture reading, as an older woman prays in the background. The Covenanters would have been loyal subjects but for the king's hostility to the Covenanters' beliefs and his determination to persecute those who held to them.

Scenes like this likely played through the minds of the American founding fathers as they deliberated the words of the first amendment of the Constitution. This is precisely what they sought to prevent. Such freedoms did not originate from the pens of erudite scholars but from the humble cottages of thousands of persecuted families. Those who came to the shores of the New World wanted to see the end of such things.

I was raised with a distorted view of history. I remember as an adolescent sitting in World History class and listening to a lecture on the Renaissance. I don't think my teacher intended to undermine my faith, yet the only people of faith ever mentioned in class were those who stood in the way of progress. Educators were being forced to kowtow to an asinine interpretation of separation of church and state. They could not explain to us the positive contributions of people of faith in the progress of civilization. Yet somehow, the negative history of the church *did* get on record. For example, I learned how Galileo got in trouble with the church for his scientific observations, and I also learned about Columbus proving to silly Christians that the earth was round. However, I was *not* told that Galileo himself was a devout Catholic who aspired to be a priest or that Columbus had missionary goals. I received selective historical information.

The effect of this myopic presentation of history was my indoctrination into a secularist view of the world. I was led to believe that the (Christian) Dark Ages were ended by the rediscovery of ancient pagan Greek and Roman cultures and that science and human reasoning led us into the glorious light of modern civilization. The apparent absence of faith from all that is positive in history and modern culture made religion appear irrelevant to me. The prevailing cultural attitude was that religion should never be taken too far or too seriously, for that would be fanaticism. Fanaticism creates conflicts with science and blocks progress. These impressions were consistent with the spirit of the times. The entire culture was filling me with doubts. By age fourteen, I was becoming an agnostic, although my mother raised me as a Roman Catholic. She had a higher view of religion. For me, however, religion became a private matter that played an irrelevant role in my life. Nobody was trying to tell me that my religion was useless, but the culture was telling me that its relevance pertained only to the hereafter—assuming that there really *is* a hereafter. If my faith was so irrelevant to the visible world, how could I trust it to be relevant to some spiritual world? Whose knowledge could I trust with regard to things unseen? I felt as though I was at the center of an elaborate hoax and was beginning to disbelieve. But then something happened.

My church built a beautiful new sanctuary, and I remember the first time I saw that church on the inside: the beautiful stained-glass windows, marble floors, and impressive organ. Behind the altar was a large mosaic of the ascension.

Notwithstanding my doubts, this reminded me that even in this age, many people smarter than me took their faith quite seriously—seriously enough to create a beautiful sanctuary. This is not what people do with fantasies. People adorn what they value, and this outpouring of creative expression made me believe that there was something of substance to the things of faith. I had listened to Scripture readings and sermons during masses, and I had listened to catechisms and stories of saints and martyrs, but these were not the things that kept me from losing my faith. In the end, the thing that blocked my slide into agnosticism was the art of the church.

At age sixteen, through the influence of Christian schoolmates, I came to understand the gospel. I learned that fanaticism had nothing to do with taking one's faith too seriously. Fanaticism is having an outward zeal for the faith while contemptuously violating some of its most important principles. My new friends were not fanatics. They were simply devout. They seemed like a sort of Christian counterculture. As I read the Bible and learned more about history, I began to realize how impossible it was to understand history without understanding the Bible. I was discovering a hidden legacy of faith. I came to understand that faith was far from being irrelevant to the progress of civilization. In fact, it is people of faith who have nearly always been the ones spearheading positive social progress.

Not any one group of men, by great might or intellect, has made freedom possible. Those who harbor such conceits can only be authors of tyranny. Freedom is the fruit of God's wisdom. It is advanced by God's grace through the faith of his many humble servants in spite of their faults. The children of the world seek a crown of glory. They crave the honor and praise of men. But Saint Paul was content to be reviled and rejected by men. Paul did not seek a worldly crown, but a crown of righteousness given by God. To the righteous, such a crown is its own reward, and to God alone goes the glory. God has called us to desire the righteousness of Christ, who has imputed his righteousness to us. On our own merits, we are nothing, but we may certainly change for the better. We seek the crown of righteousness both as individuals and as a free society. The book of Revelation speaks of the gospel as the tree of life with leaves that are for healing the nations. We know that the light of the gospel is mankind's only hope of achieving salvation for the soul and of achieving justice in the laws and governments of this world. All that we have has been given by grace. We have received a crown of righteousness that we do not deserve and must guard with utmost humility. We strive for God's glory.

The cultural indoctrination I received as an adolescent was a toxic challenge to my faith. No lie can undermine one's faith as effectively as being shielded from the whole truth. Those who try to undermine the veracity of the church by pointing to her many sins don't understand the substance of our faith. The sins of the church only prove the essential truths of the gospel—that mankind is prone to reject God's ways and can only hope in the grace of God for salvation.

## STRONG MEDICINE FOR A FREE PEOPLE

The accuser of the brethren will remind us of the Salem witch trials, the Spanish Inquisition, the burning of heretics, and the legacy of avarice and corruption that has infected the church for much of her history. Such carping is an exercise in irrelevancy to the true believer. The power of Christianity is rightly observed in the message of Christ and its power to transform those who follow Christ. It cannot be honestly judged by its most notorious pretenders. The message of Christianity is medicine to the soul. If doctors neglect to prescribe medicine that heals or if patients neglect to take it, is the medicine itself to be judged useless? No! It is illogical to judge the goodness of a medicine by the incompetence of a doctor or the negligence of a patient. Christians are weak sinners, and our spiritual medicine has proved effective wherever it has been properly applied.

Our Puritan forefathers had strong medicine for a free people. They were musically astute, and they loved literature, nature, and science. Artistic expression in Puritan New England came most impressively in the form of its literature. They were a people inspired by the works of Milton, Shakespeare, Bunyan, and Cicero. Puritan academics were well studied in classical literature, which they read critically. Overriding all of this was an unwavering devotion to the teachings of the Bible, which they studied with utmost reverence and attentiveness. The literary taste of the Puritans gives us a clear indication of the intense spiritual fervor that burned in their hearts. The epic poem "Day of Doom" by Michael Wigglesworth was published in 1662. It was basically a long, gut-wrenching sermon set to prose—pure Calvinistic theology. Its popularity was phenomenal, and it continued to be popular for the entire century, leading up to the generation that declared independence from Britain. This is good to keep in mind in light of secularist attempts to downplay the influence of Christianity on American culture.

Contemporary people may think that the Puritan lifestyle was boring, but Puritans lived inside their heads, and they liked it there. If Puritans lived today, *they* might find *us* a little boring. Puritan divines had a propensity for excruciating introspection and penance. If history sometimes judges them too harshly, it is probably fair to say that they, in part, invited it by their self-critical demeanor.

Critics of the Church typically engage in ironic absurdity when they denounce the church by standards that would not even exist but for the church. The story of the Salem witch trials is a perfect example of this. What made the Salem witch trials noteworthy was the fact that they were an aberration for Puritan New England—one of the few places on earth in that era where rational justice normally prevailed, and where compassion was practiced and where human rights for average people were defended. The Puritan vision was that of a just society ruled not by the arbitrary laws of men but by the immutable and just laws of God. This was foundational to the concept of unalienable human rights, and it was the Puritans who set the highest standard for this vision in the New World.

Perhaps the Salem atrocities against twenty people would have gone completely unnoticed by history if it had happened elsewhere. A great massacre of an entire settlement, called the Oyster River massacre, happened at about that that same time. How many people have heard the story of *that* travesty? Not many. Why is that? The perpetrators were not Puritans. When the children of the world commit atrocities, it is only local news that is soon forgotten. It is what the world expects of its own, as there is no sinless race, culture, or nation. This indicates that sins of the church would go unnoticed by history but for the humanitarian social standards that the church itself established. The church has provided the very light by which it is judged. It is a bit like criticizing Thomas Edison for his outdated light fixtures while having nothing to say about those who answered the darkness with candles and oil lamps or nothing at all.

The critics of our faith sometimes assign guilt to the entire church for historical crimes that may be more accurately described as sins committed *against* the church. Corrupt opportunists have often usurped ecclesiastical office simply to plunder the church and to persecute true Christians. Many other injustices that are often attributed to the church were actually the travesties of civil magistrates. For example, Joan of Arc was not burned at the stake by the church, but by the English regent John of Lancaster, first Duke of Bedford, who was strictly driven by politics. The church's traditional role at that time was to offer sanctuary to those accused by the state. Those deemed unworthy of sanctuary were remanded back to the state for prosecution. Certainly the church is not without sin, but her greatest and most common sin is her failure to resist her enemies.

Is it fair to associate all atheists with the atrocities of Stalin, Pol Pot, Mao, and Castro? These were all proud atheists who murdered millions. Do atheist atrocities inspire introspection among atheists? Perhaps for a few. Generally, however, non-Christians don't seem humbled about atrocities committed by those who share their ideological identity. But Christians behaving in an unchristian way becomes a talking point forever for anti-Christian bigots. Some will point a finger of accusation even as that finger drips with the blood of martyrs. But genuine Christians are quick to renounce the sins of their ancestors and to repent of their own transgressions. They cringe at the thought of the church's historical sins and resolve never to repeat them. Although the people of God are by no means sinless, they are a people of whom the world is not worthy. The people of God do not look to ethnic, religious, or cultural pride for their sense of worth, but to humility, self-examination, and repentance. It is a testimony to the greatness of the Christian religion that children of darkness expect much more of Christians than they expect of themselves. It is a double standard, but it is also a hapless validation of the church. Without the influence of the church, pagans would still be slaughtering the children of their enemies, treating women like chattel, and enslaving their fellow man. The law of God has given us civility, and the gospel of grace has taught the world the concept of tolerance. Christianity inspires moral outrage against corruption and social injustice. The church should not be criticized by a world that would never know the concept of justice or moral outrage without her.

The Puritans gave our nation its conscience. They sought to establish a just society, and they taught our nation to desire a national crown of righteousness. Their social structure was an experiment, and for the Puritan experiment to work, they thought they had to restrict their society like an exclusive club. In this context, those who were unqualified to be communing members of the church were also unqualified to be citizens. From the Puritan perspective, people of other faiths had no right to trespass the Puritan's exclusive and sacred domain, and dissenters should either respect the laws and culture or leave. But Puritan society would not simply be left alone and those who threatened its purity were prosecuted. This created a moral dilemma with their charter for a pure society. Puritans distrusted the "civil man," who had an outward form of righteousness but no heartfelt conviction of sin. They tried to keep the civil man from diluting the faith, but they could not forever keep those with evil conscience out of society or even out of public office. They eventually came to act like the persecutors of their ancestors. This cultural loss of innocence was the inevitable cost of trying to maintain a monolithic state. It was a travesty that Puritans of good conscience could not long endure and Puritans of good conscience began to force changes. Puritan leaders like Roger Williams chose the only logical alternative to a monolithic society—the path of tolerance.

## A LEGACY TRANSFORMED

Roger Williams was driven out of Massachusetts for his beliefs regarding religious liberty. Williams strongly believed in his own faith and was not shy about asserting that other religions were wrong. But he also believed in religious tolerance and that the church and state should function independently of each other. Williams also taught that encroaching settlers were wronging Indians. That same year, Williams' friend and prominent Puritan leader Thomas Hooker led one hundred of his congregation out of Massachusetts to found the new English settlement at Hartford, Connecticut. Hooker left Massachusetts largely because of his belief in extending voting rights to non-Christians but could never convince Governor John Winthrop. John Locke was a child of four years at this time. This is important for historical context because John Locke is considered such a big influence on our form of government. It is clear, however, that he stood on he shoulders of churchmen, Covenanters, and Puritans. Williams founded the state of Rhode Island as a haven of religious tolerance not just for Christians of different denominations but also for Jews and atheists. The early Constitution of Connecticut was established largely at the behest of Thomas Hooker and was called "The Fundamental Orders of Connecticut." This document contains principles that would later appear in the US Constitution.

This is the context in which the doctrine of religious freedom and tolerance gained currency in the seventeenth century. The First Amendment of the Constitution is first for good reason: faith and freedom of conscience are foundational to a free society. Its intent was never to insulate civil government from the influence of religion, but to protect Christians of differing faiths from religious persecution. The First Amendment forbade the civil government any power to interfere with the ministry of the church while effectively protecting the church's influence over civil government through her broad influence of the people. Religious liberty was first established *by* people of faith, *for* people of faith, and then graciously extended to those outside the faith. There is a concept of separation of church and state that can be found in the Bible on several levels. First, the Apostle Paul taught that civil authorities (non-Christians in Paul's day) were God's servants, established by God to punish wrongdoers (Romans 13:3–4). Second, the Scriptures set forth clear jurisdictions between civil and religious authorities (2 Chronicles 19:8). Third, God severely punished King Uzziah's usurpation of religious authority (2 Chronicles 26:18). But this biblical concept is very different from the ill-conceived notion that civil law can be morally neutral, and that the governing of civil and public affairs should not be informed by faith or moral convictions. The constitution was designed to achieve just the opposite.

We cannot ignore the sins of Puritan ancestors, but lesser societies have persecuted dissenters and religious minorities for centuries with no great dissent or protest of its leaders. But while lesser societies persist in darkness indefinitely, transformative Christian cultures revive the consciences of indigenous members of society to inspire positive social reforms. It is precisely this propensity for self-reform in society that distinguishes the

Puritans over all as an enlightened people, head and shoulders above most other societies of that age. An enlightened society is not one that never succumbs to evil, but one that has a seminal capacity to repent and correct itself without having change imposed upon it by outside pressures or a bloody revolution. The self-righteous chest beating of contemporary secularists over the sins of Puritans is an exercise in bigotry. The Puritans were giants with regard to their contributions to social enlightenment. Their critics will forever be dwarfed in their shadows.

Puritans were never exactly like the children of Israel, who were made to stand between Mount Ebal and Mount Gerazim and enjoined to enter into a holy covenant to keep God's law. The earliest Puritans achieved something similar to this with the Mayflower Compact, but they never had a divine mandate to establish a direct theocracy. Puritan leaders transformed it into something a little different. By the early eighteenth century, Presbyterians (Covenanters) who had fled the terrible persecutions of King James II had established a foothold in the New World. They, like the Puritans, believed strongly in providence. Both groups were resigned to what was apparently God's will according to providence—a pluralistic society. Then came the great awakening, circa 1730. The historian Joseph Tracy believed this was a precursor to the American Revolution. Leading up to this time, colonists seemed to start caring about visual art, so that by the age of revolution the colonists had some astute homegrown painters to supply the need for a national visual legacy. This was the era of John Singleton Copley, Benjamin West, John Trumbull, Gilbert Charles Stuart, and Charles Willson Peale. These were artists who brought to life the spirit of that age with images of revolution and great leaders burned deep into the nation's collective consciousness.

Although the descendents of Puritans were eventually compelled to embrace pluralism, the Puritans' quest for a national crown of righteousness did not die because of this. It simply changed. The larger vision of an enlightened free society endured among people of faith, and it spread to people of no particular faith. By the mid-1700s, there was a palpable desire among colonists of all stripes to build a shining city on the hill that could perhaps transform the entire world. It all rose to a crescendo in the age of Revolution.

## WHO GAVE US THE CONSTITUTION?

Our American forefathers sought to accommodate all who could be counted on as allies for the establishment of a free society for the common good. The United States Constitution created a society in which Christians were forever guaranteed their freedom of religion, but one in which Christians live peaceably alongside people of other faiths. What Christians and non-Christians achieved together was a kind of mediated theocracy in the form of a republic. Nobody calls our republic a theocracy today, but if we are indeed endowed by our Creator with certain unalienable rights and if civil magistrates are indeed God's ministers to protect those rights, we are indeed a mediated theocracy.

If there is a group that has truly earned distrust with regard to civil liberties, it is the secularist bigots—not all secularists, just those who are bigots. It is Christians who today find their rights under assault by a wolf that calls the lamb a predator. Secularist bigots expect others to act oppressively because they project their own motives and behavior onto others. Oppression is the path secularist bigots have taken when they have complete control. Granting liberty and tolerance from a position of strength is an enigma to most of them. Only *Christianized* cultures think that way.

Secularists see the severity of Old Testament law and presume that those who believe in God's law will seek to impose it on everyone. But this fear reflects a degree of ignorance regarding Christian theology and the church's relationship to the law. While Christians do see Old Testament law as God's Word, we do not see the entire law as representing God's plan for all time and for every circumstance. That was never the intent of the entire law. Moreover, Israel, as a theocracy, does not work well as a model for pluralistic societies of the New Covenant era. Israel was a special arrangement in sacred history that has never been duplicated. Even in the context of this theocracy, there were provisions of tolerance and mercy. Israelites were commanded in the law not to oppress foreigners and not to favor the native above the foreigner with regard to issues of civil justice. And foreigners were not compelled to become Jews or to practice Israel's religion. In fact, they were barred from the temple and its services unless they chose to convert on their own. Israelites were even commanded to leave the corners of their field so that strangers and sojourners could glean something to eat from them.

Although principles of tolerance and mercy toward covenant outsiders are found in the Old Testament theocracy of Israel, more appropriate biblical models exist for a pluralistic society than a direct theocracy, namely Joseph and Daniel. Joseph commanded all of Egypt, answering only to Pharaoh, and Daniel was a high official in the court of Nebuchadnezzar. Both served faithfully the national interests of pagan kings, and peoples, and both were uncompromising in their personal faith. Yet, interestingly, there is no record of either Joseph or Daniel interfering with the people's pagan religious practices. This style of government is consistent with the spirit of civic goodwill, which God has expressed through the Prophet Jeremiah, who said:

> Thus says the LORD of hosts, the God of Israel, to all who

> were carried away captive, whom I have caused to be carried away from Jerusalem to Babylon: Build houses and dwell *in them;* plant gardens and eat their fruit. Take wives and beget sons and daughters; and take wives for your sons and give your daughters to husbands, so that they may bear sons and daughters—that you may be increased there, and not diminished. And seek the peace of the city where I have caused you to be carried away captive, and pray to the LORD for it; for in its peace you will have peace.
>
> Jeremiah 29:4–7

This is God's expressed will for his people living in a pagan society. It is human nature to dominate one's enemies. But those who rise to power from among God's people have clear theological reasons to seek the temporal welfare of that society regardless of the religious belief of its people. The church, therefore, does not look to dominate her fellow man but to promote humility, self-examination, and repentance. This is what makes Christians the guardians of liberty and tolerance. Jesus and the New Testament writers made it clear that the church is not to expect a theocracy exactly like Israel to be established again in this world. Jesus said, "Believe me, the hour is coming when you will neither on this mountain, nor in Jerusalem, worship the Father" (John 4:21). Jesus also said, "Do you see these great buildings? Not *one* stone shall be left upon another, that shall not be thrown down" (Mark 13:2).

Secularists do not like to think of liberty as a product of a biblical cosmology. They want to be free of God. They want to validate their godlessness by taking credit for everything that looks like progress in modern society. They want to pretend that people of faith have never been more than dead weight on the road to human betterment and that getting rid of religion is the key to progress. Secularists want to expunge from public view every reminder of the faith that has made a free society possible, hoping that people will someday forget that Christianity ever existed. My early college experience seemed to suggest the existence of an outright plot to undermine my faith. I was exposed to a liberal arts curriculum that seemed designed to depress college students and lure them into a religion of cynicism. My twentieth-century literature class featured a reading list of books that got progressively more cynical. The authors were, of course, great writers, but could the world no longer produce artists that inspire and uphold a positive outlook on life? Does the Christian community simply never produce great writers, or do those writers get marginalized by mainstream publishers and critics? I was able to shake off the effects of my literature curriculum because I was well established in my faith and I had an alternate view of the world to hold to. My experience with the visual arts curriculum was a little broader. Some of my fine arts professors seemed to extol the weird, irreverent, grotesque, and obscene, but there were other art professors in that department who seemed more than willing to validate my view the world. I have come to believe over time that there are conscious secularist efforts in culture and academia to marginalize Christians.

Many secularists are convinced that Christians only get in the way of progress. But the true history of progress and liberty is a story that gives no credence to the conceits of secularists. Rather, it is a history written in the language of God's people with the blood of martyrs. The secularist has no valid claim to this legacy. Those of us who speak of the Bible's influence on American constitutional law are often treated to a litany of objections based on supposedly unchristian beliefs and sentiments of our founding fathers. Some of the claims that secularists make may be true. Some are overstated, misinterpreted, or ignore context. More importantly, those who believe in God's providence may see such arguments as simply irrelevant.

The personal piety of magistrates does not diminish the divine unction of their deeds in public office. Saint Augustine settled a similar argument with the Donatists regarding the validity of the sacraments of the church administered by those who later apostatized. He argued that a sacrament's validity is not based on the personal piety of any one individual who performs a sacrament on behalf of the church. Thus, a person who is baptized by someone who later renounces the faith does not need to be baptized again. The validity of the sacrament is not affected by the faithlessness of the one who administers it. The logic of Augustine applies to civil magistrates. The advancement of God's kingdom has never depended on the unanimity of rulers or people. So let the secularists tout the alleged irreligious mindset of a few founding fathers. They speak as if three of four influential deists of that era were the soul architects of the constitution. Those who perceive the hand of God at work in our national heritage view with some puzzlement such grasping at straws.

It remains undeniable that representatives of the constitutional convention were duly elected representatives of a people deeply influenced by the culture of Christianity. The vast majority of those representatives had clear church affiliations that required adherence to doctrinal standards. Some states required all public office holders to be confessing Christians. But this is not nearly as relevant as the seminal origins of the ideals that the founders worked to protect. How many practicing Christians there were within the general population is also irrelevant. What *is* relevant is the undeniable truth that the culture of Christianity profoundly shaped the Constitution. The Bible's enormous influence is too obvious to hide. Its wisdom, its language, and its culture are deeply embedded in the laws, institutions, and governments of the colonies and of the nation. It is not an oligarchy of a few influential men that may claim the ultimate credit for that remarkable document called the US Constitution. Not even the people as a whole may claim it. The power of divine wisdom spoken from the mouth of God gives us freedom. Free countries are God's fortunate benefactors.

The church herself is merely God's unworthy messenger, still seeking that national crown of righteousness.

## IF CHRISTIANS HAD THEIR WAY

What would the country look like if Christians were to become a majority in modern America? Secularist bigots fear a Taliban-style crackdown on non-Christians. This is ridiculous because it is Christians who first championed the concept of tolerance. This is a hate-inspired and ignorance-based fear spread by people who don't know who their friends are in a free society. Christians favor laws that protect the legitimate rights of all peoples, including religious minorities and moral deviants. While Christians disapprove of many forms of behavior that have become acceptable in our culture, we also believe in the sanctity of social boundaries and the strict limits of government control over individuals. Without Christians, the concept of tolerance would not exist. With Christians, the concept of tolerance will always survive. Nobody expects a perfect society as long as it must be made up of imperfect humanity. But by faith we hope for a day that we may at least see sound ideals prevail. It is easy to lose hope of ever seeing such a day. To avoid the grief of high hopes dashed to pieces, it may seem best to become a cynic and renounce all hope of finding a good side of human nature. But cynicism is a faulty religion based on disbelief in God's assurance that there is something redeemable in humanity. I have practiced the religion of cynicism, but I have never been a very good disciple. Cynicism is joyless. Any cynic who cares about pursuing joy must lose his faith in cynicism and embrace the occasional grief that comes with a joyful heart.

Let us imagine a revived Christianized society that would resume the Christian's quest for a national crown of righteousness. It would become a harsh environment for exploiters and tyrants, but it would be a blessing to all people of all beliefs whose means of gratification does not depend on the injury or oppression of others. A revived Christian society will not allow the witness and legacy of the church to be marginalized or written out of history, and it will redeem the arts from the domination of cynics who push their views on society like a godless religion. In those days it will be left to Christian artists to become the guardians of inspiration and enduring beauty, creating art for those of us who have lost faith in cynicism as well as those blessed souls who have never succumbed to it.

Christian writers will create inspiring characters that Christians can model and contemptible characters that nobody wants to resemble. Christian musicians will write music so compelling to unbelievers that it draws them into the culture of the church and exposes them to the gospel. Christian visual artists will rediscover the inherent orthodoxy of excellent craft and will build an artistic legacy that will not allow our culture to forget that God is the author of beauty and of free societies. No longer will Christians fret about how to be relevant to the world, but they will see the *world's* ways as irrelevant and lead the world out of darkness.

## FREEDOM AS THE PRODUCT OF CHRISTIAN FAITH

The free nations of the world are manifestations of the kingdom of God coming to fruition. Free republics represent a progression of biblical idealism that is attained neither completely nor perfectly but is nevertheless unmistakable. Free republics represent a centuries-old progression of enlightenment through generations of churchmen, martyrs, God seekers, and freedom fighters. To see God's hand in all of this may be difficult for those who have no understanding of the providence of God. He has advanced his kingdom through Jews, Gentiles, barbarians, pagans, Christians, heretics, and church fathers. He has established his will through the works of mystics, papists, Protestants, Separatists, Anabaptists, Pietists, Spiritualists, devout people, faithless people, and even the devil himself. Many champions of the kingdom have been imprisoned, banished, tortured, beheaded, hanged, and burned at the stake. Yet through all of this, the kingdom of God has progressed in ways nobody could have imagined.

The British Glorious Revolution of 1688 forever ended the absolute power of the monarchy in Britain. Yet by the mid-1700s, Britain's king and parliament were considered tyrants by American patriots. American Christians fought British Christians in the American War for independence, and they fought each other again in 1812. Then, British Christians led by William Wilberforce fought the British political machine to end slavery in Britain in 1833—a posthumous victory for the devout Wilberforce. In 1861, Christian Americans fought their own countrymen in a bloody civil war in order to bring an end to slavery in America.

After all the wars, debates, movements, and reforms, and many differences that still remain, the free societies of Christian heritage have settled upon a few areas of moral consensus: They must be tolerant of differing views; they must recognize the sanctity of life, the liberty of conscience, and a higher law; they may be governed only by consent of the governed; and they must defend equal justice under the law. Today's near-universal acceptance of such ideals among all thinking people represents a triumph of biblical morality. Even if the Bible's message of salvation continues to be ignored by most, God has given the church a great victory with regard to general cosmology of civic morality. Not every advance of God's kingdom comes in the form of spiritual revival. One of the most important kingdom events in sacred history was God's redemption of Israel from bondage in Egypt. Yet it was not a spiritually strong generation that God led out of Egypt. The Apostle Paul says of that generation, "With most of them God was not well pleased" (1 Corinthians 10:4–6). They were a rebellious and idolatrous people. Yet God's people rightly look back on the exodus as a glorious demonstration of God's providence and a great victory for his covenant people. The progress of God's kingdom may seem to be messy to our eyes, but that progress is real. The church should continue to water her garden and to wait patiently for the Lord of the harvest to make it yield fruit in due season. It is the ultimate goal of all the church's labors. Yet, until that day, the church must attend to many seemingly mundane duties. We must continue to seek that crown of righteousness. Saint Paul speaks of a crown of righteousness that Jesus gives to all who long for his return (see 2 Timothy 4:6–8).

We may look upon our own failings and forever wonder why God would chose such unworthy servants. Yet by God's grace the crown is most certainly ours, and the glory is his alone. Throughout history, much has been done in the name of Christianity that is contrary to Christianity. It is Christ who has taught us the ways of love, charity, liberty of conscience, equality, tolerance, and compassion. Although many Christians have found themselves on the wrong side of history, nobody would know the right side of history but for the teachings of the church. The way of the world is hatred, genocide, intolerance, mercilessness, slavery, and oppression. If not for the pervasive cultural influence of biblical morality, there would be no outrage for such things.

Only Christian societies have shown any seminal capacity for peaceful reform. The Bible not only teaches us what people ought to believe but how we are to maintain peace with those who believe differently. The Apostle Paul wrote, "If it is possible, as far as it depends on you, live at peace with everyone" (Romans 12:18). Many aspects of our moral code are similar to other cultures, but the distinctive mark of biblical culture has always been a deep respect for the life of all mankind.

Jesus commanded us to love even our enemies. But this is not a mandate for pacifism. There are times when evil must be punished. The offenses that are actionable under biblical law are things that pertained to behavior, not to creeds or matters of personal beliefs. All that is necessary for peaceful coexistence is a common respect for a few social boundaries that are essential to any free society. The biblical sanctity of boundaries is foundational to the concept of tolerance. We have a moral imperative to suffer a number of offensive behaviors as long as there is a sacred line of jurisdiction that may not crossed. This is why tolerance is a Christian moral. Secularists, not Christians, force their ways on others. The evils of intolerance and bigotry they think they see in others are usually their own. By the values of radical secularists, all that is right must be imposed on everyone and all that is wrong must be punished. Some things they will tolerate in a capricious way, but they often choose to tolerate things that are injurious to the rights of others while being intolerant of basic civil rights. This is what makes secularism so dangerous. Secularists fear Christians not because they think Christians are so different, but precisely because they think Christians are *not* so different from secularists. Secularists want to dominate and oppress others, so they presume people of faith want to do the same.

But Christianity is not about dominating others. It is about being salt and light in a world that would otherwise be intolerable to civilized people. The advancement of Christianity depends on the power of inspiration, not of compulsion. This is why I remain convinced that art, as a means of inspiration, is so important to our cultural mandate. If we as God's people are to forsake the ways of the world, it is all the more important to tend to God's appointed means of inspiration, such as the arts. Biblical law is about protecting the boundaries that make peaceful coexistence possible with others while protecting liberty. But to believe in the sanctity of boundaries, one must believe in a higher law. This is why a free society must have some biblical influence in its history. Biblical law insists on clear lines of jurisdiction. Among the curses pronounced from Mount Ebal was this one: "Cursed *is* the one who moves his neighbor's landmark" (Deuteronomy 27:17).

Boundaries are not just important with regard to personal property, but also with regard to magisterial jurisdiction. Prosecuting a criminal is important, but only the civil magistrate may do so. Punishing a criminal outside the due process of law is a great crime. Boundaries are also important with regard to the relationship between church and state. In the Old Testament law, it was forbidden for a king to usurp priestly duties. Only those duly called and ordained from the tribe of Levi could serve as priests. In some places in the Holy Scriptures, the sanctity of boundaries seems to trump nearly everything else.

Idolatry is a great offense to God's law, but the boundaries of idolatrous nations were to be respected, as were treaties made with those nations. As the Israelites were on their way to the land that God had commanded them to possess, they came to the land of Moab. God specifically commanded Moses to respect the land of the Moabites. The Moabites were kin to the Israelites, being descendants of Abraham's brother Lot. They had some concept of the God of Abraham, but most Moabites were idolaters who worshiped Chemosh. Their pagan worship sometimes included a horrific practice of child sacrifice. The Moabite king hired a prophet, Balaam, to curse the people of Israel (Deuteronomy 23:5). Moabite women even beguiled the men of Israel and drew them into idolatry (Numbers 25:2). In spite of all this, God had given Moab an inheritance and commanded the Israelites to respect it (Deuteronomy 2:4–9).

What this reveals is that unprovoked aggression against an evil, idolatrous nation is unacceptable according to biblical law. This has a universal application. God's people are to recognize and respect the domain of all who have obtained property by lawful and ethical means, even if they do evil and offensive things within that domain. Only when evildoers violate the domain of others are their offenses actionable by law. The private sins of individuals and the reprobation of nations are things God will judge, but they are irrelevant with regard to the sanctity of property rights and boundaries. God, by his providence, has established the rightful domains of all people, effectively giving all people everywhere an inheritance from God. To violate that inheritance is to violate the sacred boundaries God has established.

The Constitution does not represent some awkward compromise between biblical wisdom and something else. It is not some Hegelian synthesis. The Bible alone, whether by its explicit teachings or implicit principles, is foundation enough for every cardinal principle of the Constitution.

## THE ARCHITECTS OF FREEDOM

Although many secularists are zealous to champion some aspects of the Constitution's wisdom, no aspect of the Constitution is actually a product of secular thinking. The Constitution embraces biblical principles championed through such writings as Samuel Rutherford's *Lex Rex* and popularized by John Locke. Although Thomas Paine proved that these ideas contain much common sense and may be defended by common sense, it would be specious to say that the Constitution is mostly based on common sense. Thomas Paine's contribution was to repackage some essentially theological ideas long held by Protestants and resell them under the label of common sense.

Constitutional freedoms began with the Bible's concept of the magistrate as a public servant whose power was derived from the people. Israel had a king, but God would have the nation of Israel act as a republic. It was the *people* who were to establish a king. God gave Israel these instructions:

> You shall surely set a king over you whom the LORD your God chooses; *one* from among your brethren you shall set as king over you; you may not set a foreigner over you, who *is* not your brother. But he shall not multiply horses for himself, nor cause the people to return to Egypt to multiply horses, for the LORD has said to you, "You shall not return that way again." Neither shall he multiply wives for himself, lest his heart turn away; nor shall he greatly multiply silver and gold for himself. Also it shall be, when he sits on the throne of his kingdom, that he shall write for himself a copy of this law in a book, from *the one* before the priests, the Levites. And it shall be with him, and he shall read it all the days of his life, that he may learn to fear the LORD his God and be careful to observe all the words of this law and these statutes, that his heart may not be lifted above his brethren, that he may not turn aside from the commandment *to* the right hand or *to* the left, and that he may prolong *his* days in his kingdom, he and his children in the midst of Israel.
>
> Deuteronomy 17:15–20

Note the use of the word *you* in the above injunction as in "you shall surely set a king over you." Scripture describes the king as a humble servant of a republic who governs not by the arbitrary laws of men but by the law of God. Much is contained in the Old

Testament civil laws that have become essential for the architects of free societies.

The contrast between biblical and worldly models of magisterial power became well defined during the Renaissance in the fourteenth century. These contrasting views are well represented in the form of two major works: *The Prince* by Niccolo Machiavelli and *Education of a Christian Prince* by Desiderius Erasmus. Machiavelli believed that a prince should guard the appearance of virtue if it serves his political interests, but that he should not otherwise be bound to morals and ethics. He justified consolidation of political power by use of treachery, deceit, ruthlessness, and lies. His book *The Prince* was published in 1513. Erasmus published *Education of a Christian Prince* in 1518 as an antidote to the counsel of Machiavelli and as instruction to the future King Charles X of Sweden. Erasmus gave advice consistent with the biblical model, saying the prince should be devoted to the teachings of Christ. He should be a man of integrity and graciousness. He should commit to doing right, administering justice, and reject bribes. He should be innocent of intrigue and violence. He should not be ruthless or place a heavy yoke of servitude on the people.

Later architects of freedom, like Blackstone and Rutherford, would follow closely in this same spirit of biblical idealism.

Our forbearers sought to enshrine these same biblical values in our Constitution. James Madison wrote, "Belief in a God all powerful, wise, and good is so essential to the moral order of the world and to the happiness of man that arguments which enforce it cannot be drawn from too many sources."[10] In the historical debate that eventually formed the Constitution. There have been many writings and advocates, but the Bible is the indispensable first source for all of it. Our governing principles did not spring spontaneously from the minds of our founding fathers, as if nobody suggested such ideals before the Constitutional Convention was gaveled to order. They developed out of a long history of Christian scholars, invoking biblical principles to uphold basic human rights. Many people think of John Locke as one of the seminal influences on American constitutional ideals, but these ideals were not originally hatched from the fertile minds of men like John Locke. One of Locke's most important earlier influences was Samuel Rutherford. Some scholars believe that John Locke's "Two Treatises on Government" is simply Samuel Rutherford's *Lex Rex* in popular form. *Lex Rex* was a powerful theological work that used the Bible to argue against the doctrine of divine right and to advance the notion that the law of the king must conform to the law of God. This great historical work was dedicated to the memory of Lady Jane Grey.

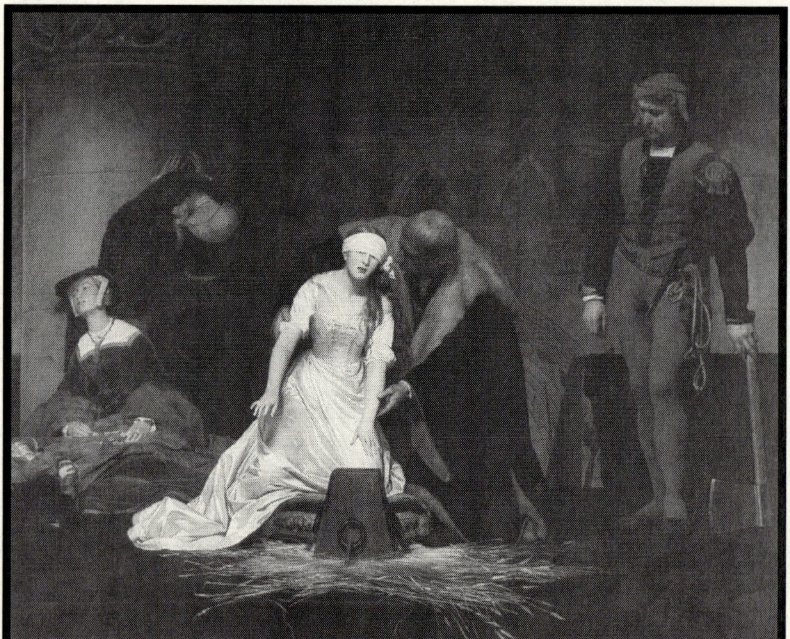

Fig. 22, Paul Delaroche, *Execution of Lady Jane Grey*, 1834

Paul Delaroche depicted the execution of sixteen-year-old Lady Jane Grey, one of the many victims of Bloody Mary's regime. After much persuasion, and on his deathbed, the young King Edward designated his devout cousin Jane as his successor, contrary to the well-published will of his father, Henry VIII. Lady Jane was queen for nine days. She could have saved her life by renouncing her Protestant beliefs. She would not. She represented to the Covenanters and the Puritans all that Bloody Mary was not—the face of a free and just society.

Sir William Blackstone was one of the most commonly quoted authors during the Constitutional Convention. His *Commentaries on the Laws of England* persistently focused on the Bible and on natural law, which in Blackstone's parlance is simply God's law imposed on mankind. He believed that nature and the Holy Scriptures were the two foundations of law.

All of our founding fathers, whatever their individual beliefs, understood that they were standing on the shoulders of great men of faith. Rutherford's and Blackstone's theological concepts of government and human rights flowed from painful historical experience and from a visceral deep-seated foreboding of the corruptibility of man and his institutions. The founders would have been well familiar with horrors of the previous century when the heads of likeminded men of faith were impaled on pikes and publicly displayed. Nobody in the Constitutional Congress wanted to see those dark days again.

Non-Christians in colonial America did not win religious liberty by revolution or protest. They received their liberty as a gift of altruistic Christians fighting on their behalf out of a Christian sense of goodwill and justice. This only happens in Christian cultures. Madison and his contemporaries did not alter the vision of the Christian spirit of religious liberty and tolerance, nor did they discourage the church's moral and cultural influence on the government through its voting citizenry. They simply believed that the only way to ensure *anybody's* freedom of religion was to ensure *everybody's* freedom of religion.

## A RENEWED LEGACY

The next great spiritual revival may well begin, as it has before, with a broader cultural revival and with a visual legacy of that culture. Perhaps some day we will see in churches and public places, large murals depicting the great triumphs of God's people and the sufferings of martyrs. Maybe we will someday see theatrical productions of their lives and times. We may see the images and words of the reformers on our currency. Perhaps the artistic legacy of our fathers will be so ubiquitous in our culture that everyone alive will be compelled to ask, "Who were these people, and what did they do for us?" These should all be remembered. Even when the giants of our faith have appeared to stand alone, they have beheld with eyes of faith great angelic legions of God's army surrounding them. As night falls like a thick veil upon our world of spiritual perception, we strain to hear those voices in the darkness that assure us that we still do not stand alone. We are comforted by the voices of those who have gone before as well as those who remain. We must likewise give assurance to those who stand with us in the darkness that they do not stand alone. Let this sustain us until God's appointed time when we, like Elisha, will once again perceive the chariots of God that surround us. Art that serves a pedagogical role or preserves the history of our faith quickens in us a realization that we are partakers of a powerful spiritual legacy. A great cloud of witnesses surrounds us, and the future we defend is not that of a single nation, but of all free people everywhere. This is Saint Augustine's City of God—our Jerusalem. It is our crown and God's glory. It is what inspires us to say with the psalmist, "If I forget you, O Jerusalem, Let my right hand forget its skill!" (Psalm 137:5).

# OUR WAYWARD **VOYAGE**

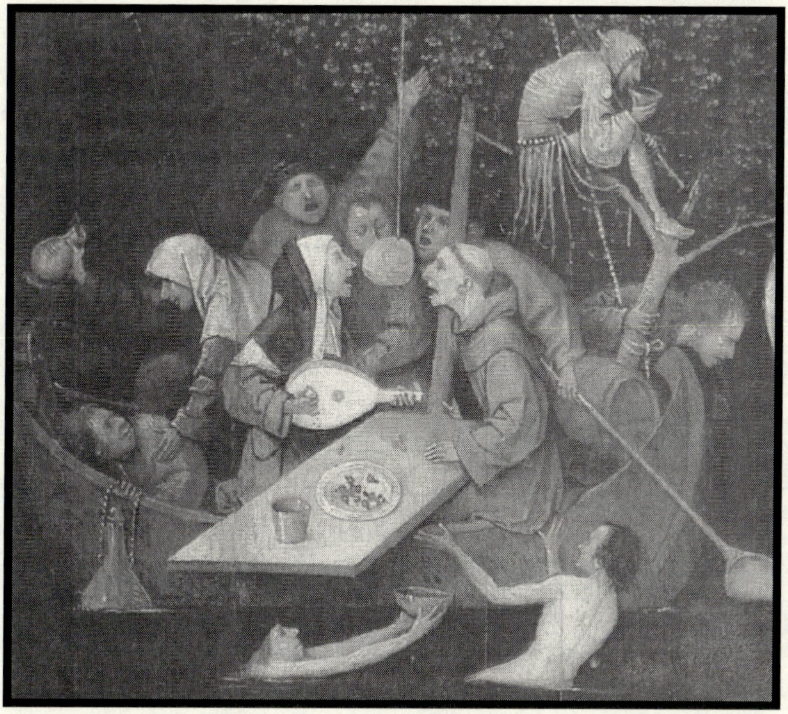

Fig. 23, Hieronymus Bosch, *The Ship of Fools,* c. 1495

## WHO IS AT THE HELM?

Sebastian Brant, a pre-Reformation German theologian, wrote a famous satire called *Das Narrenschiff* ("The Ship of Fools") in 1494. In this allegory of mankind, he lampooned human follies and the corruption of the church. This allegory has appeared in numerous other forms since. Above is part of an altarpiece—a painting by Hieronymus Bosch. It contains symbols of lust, vanity, and frivolity. The crowded ship makes no wake, drifting along. A man holds the rudder but gives no attention to the ship's direction. All of humanity is in a default course of vanity, aimlessness, and frivolity. If the church does not take the rudder, humanity goes nowhere. Who are the people in the water? Perhaps they represent those who choose to abstain from the ways of the dominant culture. Note the bowl held by one swimmer. Another swimmer seems to have snatched something from the ship's table and is placing it in the bowl. Those who cannot abide the ship of fools must tread water and glean what they can from the prevailing culture, or they must take command of the ship.

The Holy Spirit fills the sails of free nations and gives them direction. Those who pilot the ship of state can suffer the presence of wayward simpletons, but the enlightened must maintain control if the state is to remain free. Have we as a people allowed simpletons to take over? Perhaps, to some extent, we have become the problem. Waywardness is, after all, our default condition as sinners. We deserve our fate every time we allow the doctrines of darkness to go unanswered. We should not care what the world thinks, answer according to the world's folly, or seek approval of the world rather than the approval of God. Our faith tells us that we must not be conformed to the world but be transformed by the renewing of our minds. The Puritans were good at that, and we have been unworthy heirs of their vision.

The covenant community has conceded too much over time, and our foundation of constitutional freedoms has begun to erode. Who is at the helm of the ship of state? Tolerance is a Christian value born out of Christian goodwill. It should not surprise us when non-Christians repay goodwill with hatred and intolerance. This merely reflects the normal state of the unenlightened and unregenerate mind.

## RETAKING THE HELM THROUGH ART

When did the church begin to neglect her cultural mandate? We do not obey God if we sequester ourselves in our own Christian world and forget about being an effective light to a world that is lost in sin. It is not true piety to have the church withdraw from worldly affairs. That is the desire of the church's enemies who would use specious arguments of separation of church and state to con the church into silencing herself. The enemies of gospel would have the church defer all issues of art and culture to the children of the world. We have done that, and the effect has been disastrous. Art has become the secularists' most effective way of drawing people out of the church's sphere of influence and of diminishing the church's influence on our culture. To reverse this, the church must seize dominion over every sphere of influence that rightfully belongs to the church—a far larger sphere than what the church has accepted in the postmodernist era.

Is there any doubt that the church should have a hand in shaping the common aesthetics and values of our culture? It is precisely that common cultural ground that God often uses to draw a generation of disbelievers to eventual faith and repentance. If the church can shape the culture with biblical aesthetic values, she will serve an important function as the city on the hill that cannot be hidden. She will be used by God to give to sinful humanity eyes that see and ears that hear the saving message of the gospel. Anything made for a Christian testimony should be aesthetically well done. It should be compelling enough to command the attention of even those who hate us. Beauty itself carries its own important healing message of divine truth, and God has designed beauty as a balm for the unregenerate mind. When the children of the world come to drink deeply of the culture of God's people, it prepares them to receive the more explicit messages of salvation and repentance. Let the godless of our world be held captive by the sheer beauty of the culture of God's people.

The use of artistry to this end cannot be dismissed as gimmickry. It is a means well established by biblical authority. The Bible has established a regulative principle. God said, "You shall not add to the word which I command you, nor take from it, that you may keep the commandments of the LORD your God which I command you" (Deuteronomy 4:2). Certainly, many changes have been made in the manner of worship. These changes are consistent with God's own fulfillment of the law and his own changes in the ceremonial administration of religion. These are changes God has made and changes that the church studies with great care, as the church is not to change capriciously. Art is universal by nature, and it is validated in both the Old and New Testaments. Art does not violate the regulative principle. On the contrary, ignoring the valid use of art should be considered a violation of the regulative principle. The ceremonial law shows us that God clearly delights in using the raw essence of artistry as one of numerous means of grace to affect the hearts of men and to glorify him. It is the church's business to critique and direct any human activity toward righteousness, decency, and enduring beauty.

## THE SISTER MINISTRIES OF LIGHT AND SHADOW

There is a sacred place in the life of God's people for the unambiguous and persistent preaching of the gospel, yet the Bible requires more of us than preaching alone. In the Bible, God chooses the language of shadows to speak to us more often than not. Most of the broader cultural witness of God's people to the world should be—like most of Scripture—somewhat short of an altar call. The Bible contains many examples of those who cannot immediately endure the searing light of the gospel but who are mercifully led by types and shadows into biblical truth. For some, it may be the only way to begin to understand the gospel. God's shadows of mercy come in many forms, quickening and nurturing a conviction of sin and a God-honoring view of creation that leads broken sinners to the light of the gospel. We have a duty to inspire the whole world to honor God. By teaching the world to honor God, some may acquire ears to hear the call of redemption. Consider these words of David: "Therefore I will give thanks to You, O Lord, among the Gentiles, and sing praises to Your name (2 Samuel 22:50). Why is it important to praise God's name among covenant outsiders if not for the sake of sinners? To glorify God is to broadcast his common grace. It is through means that are often inscrutable to us that the Holy Spirit chooses to recreate in dead sinners eyes to see and ears to hear. The ministries of light and shadow are sister ministries that cannot be separated. It is through eyes that are prepared by the ministry of shadows that the searing light of the gospel may be perceived in all of its glory.

## NO SEQUESTERED GLORY

We must not allow ourselves to become culturally isolated and sequestered from the mainstream of civilization. Our goal is to bring all nations to Christ, not just a few individuals. The church is the means by which the whole earth is preserved. But who will preserve us if we lose our effectiveness as a people to preserve a just society? No man places a lamp under a bushel basket. We must let our light shine, for God commands us to do so. Obeying

God by being salt and light to the earth is, in the end, the most effective way of preserving our own savor as a people.

As our culture continues its game of moral limbo, the church is declining right along with the world. When Christians look like the rest of the world, what witness do we have left? Personal piety is not true piety if we see our world headed for damnation and make no effort to stop it. Jesus has not left us the option of retreating to our own cultural enclave as the fabric of a free society rots around us. Our kingdom duties involve more than spreading the abstract knowledge of the gospel. The shepherds of the church must exercise proactive moral leadership for all of humanity and bend our entire culture to the Lord's will. Faith comes by hearing, and it is the culture of the city of God through which God forms ears that are capable of hearing his call to repentance.

Nehemiah is a prime example of proactive leadership. He could have simply denounced apostasy, preached repentance, and hoped that individual believers would eventually become numerous enough to spread revival throughout the land. Instead, Nehemiah aggressively confronted the apostate culture of his time and compelled changes that not everybody wanted. He rebuilt the walls of Jerusalem, revived the religious life and the Sabbath observances, and purged the men of Judah of their pagan wives. As with Nehemiah, it is incumbent upon the shepherds of God's people to extend their influence into the daily cultural experience of Christians and to counter the negative cultural pressures that have been arrayed against us. The cultural backwash of the world is poisoning the church. Yet with God's unction, we can reverse the tide, beat down the gates of hell, and seize our culture for the sake of all of humanity. Without God's redeeming work through his chosen servants, every civil institution will eventually become an instrument of injustice and oppression. Do we truly love our enemies—the atheists, the cynics, the antichristian bigots, and moral deviants? They are all creatures made in God's image, whether they care about it or not. Yet to preserve the dignity and constitutional freedoms of God haters and Christians alike, it is necessary first and foremost to deny God haters the disproportional power and influence that they have usurped by underhanded means. We must deny them their desire for tyrannical control over us for their own good as well as ours. It is the only responsible and compassionate response. It is no act of graciousness to leave the children of darkness in charge of government, academia, and culture. That is like giving a loaded gun to a small child. The children of darkness will eventually use power to create a miserable and oppressive world for themselves and everyone else. To preserve our Christian culture is to preserve the whole concept of human rights.

## CHRISTIANITY: THE PRICELESS SEED OF FREEDOM

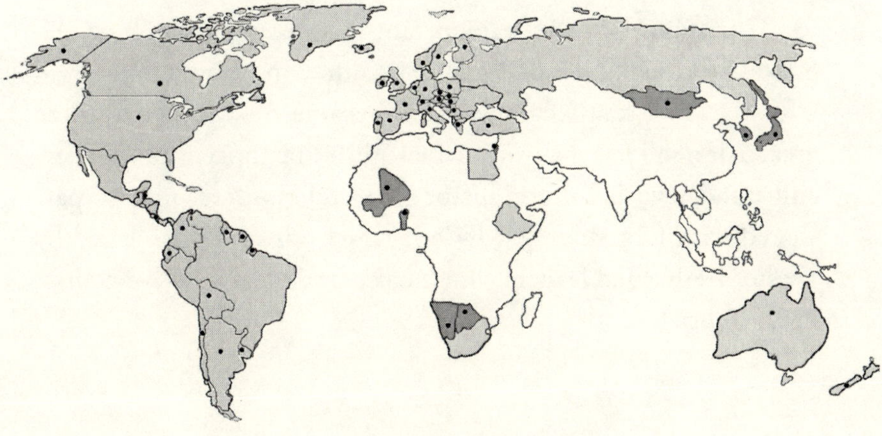

Fig. 24, World Map of Christian Influence

Every free society is based, directly or indirectly, on some historical Christian influence. The map of the world on the previous page shows areas of historically Christianized culture shaded in light gray. The dark shaded areas are client states of culturally Christianized societies. The black dots represent the free countries of the world. There are no dots outside the shaded areas. The map also reflects that having a Christianized culture does not ensure that a nation will be always be free, but free countries are not to be found anywhere in the absence of a Christian influence.

All Western democracies have been deeply influenced by Christianity.

Western values can come through indigenous Christian influence or through imposition by historically Christianized societies. One way or another, that influence must be there.

Japan, Indonesia, South Korea, Australia, New Zealand, Namibia, Botswana, Benin, Guinea, and Ghana are all considered free countries. These are client states or colonies of Western democracies with governments that reflect Western values. Mongolia and Israel are also client states of the West, but these have other compelling links to the culture of freedom. Mongolia has few Christians but a very important historical matriarch named Sorkaktani, daughter of Genghis Kahn. She was a Nestorian Christian of strong character who became the mother of three great Mongolian emperors. Israel is the birthplace of Christianity, and Jewish culture, history, and religion are in large part shared with Christianity. Modern Israel was also established by Western-educated leaders whose cultural and laws are, of course, Judeo-Christian.

## THE THEFT OF A CULTURE

The greatest threat to a free society is not socialism, atheism, paganism, or any other "ism." The threat is the church's abdication of her moral leadership. Enemies of the gospel should be expected to undermine the church, but they cannot overcome the influence of the church if she is faithful to her cultural mandate. Many non-Christians acknowledge Christianity's vital civilizing influence on culture and are glad for it. Some are open to hearing about the gospel and having their minds changed. Others will never believe but are willing to fight alongside Christians for justice, liberty, and the broader interests of free people. The church should not be quick to recognize secular "experts" in matters of government. The church holds the keys to understanding the foundational principles of free societies, and she has the unction of Christ to speak with authority wherever biblical wisdom may apply to matters of civil government. Her authority trumps that of all other claimants, and she should be bold to denounce a civil magistrate if his statements or actions undermine constitutional principles. Nobody can truly be an expert of constitutional law without substantial knowledge of the Bible, for the Bible informs constitutional values. The Bible makes us acutely aware of the corruptibility of rulers and tells us not to put our trust in princes (see Psalms 146:2–4). This is why the framers of the Constitution gave us a system of checks and balances. It is the Bible that teaches us that the one who governs must govern according to the law so that his heart may not be lifted above his brethren (see Deuteronomy 17:15–20).

It was our Christian ancestors who set the table of liberty for us. Where did it all go wrong? Our great Christianized society welcomed the world to feast at her table of social benevolence only to have self-absorbed ingrates belch in her face and insult her chefs. The very people of faith who spread the feast of constitutional freedoms are now being denied the right to partake of it themselves.

There is a distinct pathology to the way that Christian cultures are disenfranchised. On Broad Street (close to Philadelphia's City Hall) stands a wonderful building designed by the great architect Frank Furness. It is the home of the Pennsylvania Academy of Fine Art, the oldest art academy in the Western hemisphere. While I was a student there, I went down the street to visit the library at the Quaker Friends Center. While looking through the books, I overheard a conversation between two ladies, one younger than the other, who were on the library staff. The young lady said, "What if one of our members came in here, read some of the older books, and found out what Quakers used to believe? Somebody could be influenced!" At this, the older lady responded, "What would you suggest?" What I heard after that made it clear to me that these ladies wanted to shelter people from Quaker beliefs of the past. I left to go upstairs to the bookstore, intrigued by what seemed to be the possible beginnings of a plan to suppress some of the very ideas that the Friends Center was established to preserve. When I went into the bookstore, I got a sense of who had stolen the assets of the Quaker church. There were books advocating pacifism, which were generally consistent with historical Quaker teachings. However, there were also books advocating abortion. How did they spin this? William Penn would have considered abortion abominable, but some modern Quakers consider denial of a woman's right to choose a form of violence against the mother. How anyone can cope with the idea of killing an unborn child in the name of non-violence is something I never understood. I was sad for the Quakers of the past that someone had stolen the Quaker assets. Had original Quakers been banished from their local meetinghouse long ago, or did they leave on their own? Are there any real Quakers left? Should it really be my concern? I have many disagreements with the old Quaker view of the world, so why should I care about the views of modern Quakers taking over. Still, I was somewhat sickened at the thought that thousands of old Quakers had given so much financial support to an organization that was established for no other cause than to preserve and protect their particular vision of the truth. The old Quakers were tolerant to a fault, but this tolerance was not reciprocated. The old school of Quaker ideology has now been disenfranchised. The new "Quakers" would abolish the old Quaker beliefs if they could. This seems like a form of grand larceny to me.

This serves as a microcosm of a still greater larceny. The enemies of the church steal institutions that Christians establish. They partake of Christian benevolence, tolerance, and hospitality and work their way into positions of power and influence. Then they use their power to disenfranchise Christians and steal their assets. These interlopers do not stand on the shoulders of giants when they disparage all that we hold sacred. Their view of the world is derived from sitting at the feet of petulant cynics. The true champions of free societies are people of faith. Those that have made freedom possible from the beginning were the kind of people that secularist bigots now utterly despise. The people they mock and deride are the people who have given them the free society that allows them to do so. Antichristian bigots—left to their own devices—would give us a world of darkness, injustice, violence, and oppression. The church is not without faults, but her critics ought to drop to their knees and thank God that the church, however imperfect, has had a profound positive influence on history. They would not be living in a free society without her.

# THE ARTS DON'T LET US FORGET

The message of the gospel saves souls, but the culture of Christianity saves us from cataclysmic humanitarian disaster. It is not just our country's constitution and form of government that makes us a free people. It is also the arts. The arts can teach us alongside spiritual and civic leaders, but most importantly, the arts don't let us forget our lessons as a people. The laws of free nations are only as strong as the character of a free people shaped by common visions and desires, legends, and legacies. This is the substance and domain of the arts. The arts enshrine sacred values that form the moral substance of free people. The arts preserve and affirm the essence of everything we see as beautiful. Consider the music and the literature that shaped the conscience and aspirations of former generations. What informed the values of educated people 250 years ago? Every generation has had to suffer impediments and detractors, but the colonial men of letters in the eighteenth century were all immersed in the same culture, art, and literature. This is what shaped the men who wrote the laws and maintained the commonwealth.

The religious influences of the age are reflected in the arts of this era in England and the American colonies. In 1735, English artist and engraver William Hogarth finished his *Rakes Progress,* a series of biting moral commentaries. Its publication was delayed until the English Parliament passed the first copyright laws as a direct result of Hogarth's lobbying efforts. Hogarth was the most plagiarized artist of his time. He would complete a painting and then produce engravings based on the paintings. His engravings were so popular that forgeries would flood the market before his own authentic engravings were completed and released. He was, for a time, the conscience of England. Hogarth's influence established the concept of intellectual property.

Meanwhile, in Colonial America, Charles Wilson Peale

painted portraits of the statesmen, clergymen, and scientific nature studies. Peale's naturalist obsessions may be thought of as part of the groundswell of Enlightenment thinking, but it fits better with the older Puritan tradition of spiritual stewardship of vocational callings. This is a paradigm that arises from the Reformation concept of the universal priesthood, reverence for nature, and the sanctification of common things. Peale's era was an age of both scientific and social experimentation and of newly discovered possibilities. Franklin, Jefferson, and Peale were all close friends and all cut from the same cloth. When the colonies threw off the weight of the British government, the founders of our new nation perceived an opportunity to establish a lasting hope for a free society, not just for Americans, but also for the rest of the world. Although the American patriots had diverse views of Christian doctrine, the view of the world that informed their political wisdom was uniformly and emphatically Christian.

## THE SEEDS OUR FATHERS SOWED THROUGH ART

The popular literature of the following generation was full of spiritual allegory and soul searching. That was the era of Herman Melville's *Moby Dick,* Nathaniel Hawthorne's *Scarlet Letter,* and Harriet Beecher Stowe's *Uncle Tom's Cabin.* This last book inflamed popular sentiment against slavery to a fever pitch. This is a testament to the need for art. The abolitionists had been arguing against slavery for over two generations in academic and political circles, but abstract debate and consensus among scholars can be quite useless without a broad-based cultural consciousness. It took a work of literature to inflame public sentiment and produce real change. Art has a way of establishing heroes, antiheros, victims, and villains as archetypes. These archetypes are used for the vicarious honor or ridicule, pity or contempt, of real people who seem to fit the same respective character mold. Through the arts, people learn to model the positive archetypes and run from the stigma of those characters designed to be pitiful or contemptible. For instance, one may be admonished regarding the dangers of obsession, but it is a far more effective antidote to read about Captain Ahab and to experience vicariously the torment and ruin caused by his obsession. The Bible uses negative examples to teach us. The Apostle Paul wrote, regarding the rebellion of Israel, "These things happened to them as examples, and they were written for our admonition, upon whom the ends of the ages have come" (1 Corinthians 10:11).

There is, of course, great value in positive living models as well. The Apostle Paul said, "Imitate me, just as I also imitate Christ" (1 Corinthians 11:1). Why would he not say, "Imitate Christ just as I imitate Christ"? After all, Jesus Christ was morally perfect and Paul was a sinner. Would it not make more sense to model the perfection of Christ rather than Paul, who describes himself as the chief of sinners (see 1 Timothy 1:15)? That would be a view consistent with a Neo-Platonic reverence for abstraction and for the ideal. But we were not created to learn spiritual truth by abstraction. We need to see flesh and blood manifestations of positive attributes. In the biblical view, the attribute of being visible is more useful for pedagogical purposes than perfection in the abstract. That is why Paul said, "Imitate me, just as I also imitate Christ." It is the same idea found in the first Epistle of John: "How can you love God whom you have not seen if you do not love your neighbor whom you have seen?" (1 John 4:19–20). God is holy, and those who love holiness will also love God. But God is known through what is visible. The value of character types cannot be overstated. The Christian faith is centered on the idea that through one man, Adam, all have sinned and that through one man, Christ, we are redeemed. The idea of Paul's vicarious pedagogical modeling is not so different from this. It is why the communion of saints is so important. For communicating spiritual truth, living among God's people is more effective than sermons. We are to model Christ to each other. However imperfect our model, we will occasionally get something right and the attributes of Christ become visible. This has more pedagogical value than a hundred catechism lessons.

It is the same with regard to the tragic flaws of the characters of art and literature. These are engraved into our memory through stories told to us over and over, along with countless allusions heard in day-to-day conversations. We have a mini-sermon run through our minds whenever we hear any reference to a Good Samaritan, a prodigal son, or a David and Goliath. It is one thing to hear, "It will cost you far more than it's worth in the long run." It is more foreboding to hear, "That sounds like a Faustian bargain." It may be good advice to say, "Be careful with those special credit card offers," but it is more instructive to say, "Beware of Greeks bearing gifts." Such expressions evoke the memories of whole stories with all of the character development and life lessons they reveal with poignant clarity. It is a way of gaining wisdom without the hardship that breaks youthful souls of their foolish and naïve ways. Those who will not learn wisdom by art and literature may be forced to learn by hardships revisited over and over. Fools do not see hardships as the fruit of bad choices, but simply of bad fortune. Fools don't see the need to change their ways. They believe that only their luck needs to change. However, those who immerse themselves in great literature are made aware of every thread of the pathology that is woven into a fate that has nothing to do with luck, but with wise and foolish choices.

This is why a liberal arts education is so important to the general welfare of individuals and to culture in general. It is a noble pursuit to learn math, science, medicine, law, engineering, and other useful disciplines. Such studies create a more useful people. But the arts—properly taught—can create a wiser people. To rest control of the arts is to lay siege to the gates of hell and to infuse the air of free lands with the intoxicating aroma of cultural enlightenment and liberty. Even the Church's harshest critics will gladly breathe in the sweet fragrance of her beautiful culture. They may remain unmindful of the Church's indispensable influence on free cultures. They may never acknowledge that this priceless gift has been laid at their feet by the people of God. Nevertheless, having tasted it, they may be persuaded of the need to defend it.

# THE SUBLIME **JOURNEY**

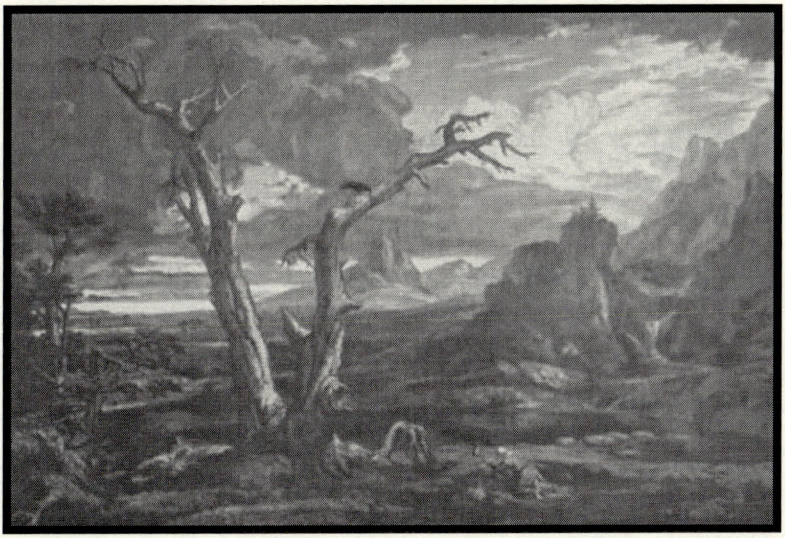

Fig. 25, Washington Allston, *Elijah in the Wilderness*, 1818

The above image by Washington Allston depicts Elijah as a small figure in a vast wilderness. He could easily go unnoticed in this landscape. Look closely for Elijah to the right of the base of the tree, about halfway between the base of the tree and the lower-right corner. He is the small form of a man on his knees. God has sent the ravens to feed him. Elijah felt quite alone at one point in his ministry, and he serves as an example for those who must sometimes stand alone in what they believe. When we are inclined to declare with Elijah that we are no better than our ancestors and give in to despair, God sustains us with the most unlikely creatures of the wilderness.

Much in the story of Elijah is relatable to frustrated artists, but the sublime journey of an artist is unlike that of Elijah, who was driven to the wilderness by an evil king. The still, small voice heard by an artist speaks not of the affairs of kings and prophets but of a special place for understanding the desires of the heart. We journey through the wilderness in search of that place. As a young Christian, I found fine art to be a world of undecipherable value. The allure of art was intoxicating to me, and I perceived that God had placed in art the key to something important. Through a still, small voice or a vaguely familiar scent, I perceived that my calling had meaning. Yet to identify that meaning in rational terms was impossible. My Christian friends told me that my artistic aptitude was a gift from God and that I should be a good steward of my talent. Yet I could not begin to know what God expected of me as an artist. Did the world really need another artist? The self-doubt and frustrations were great. I envied those who had clear callings in ministries that were well validated such as doctors, pastors, and missionaries. Finding such clarity in art was important to me, but it was an enormously frustrating task. Art became an excruciating burden at times yet, in the end, yielded unimaginable personal rewards.

Why do people associate the word *talent* with artists? In the parable of the Talents, Jesus makes no mention of artists. A talent was something of known value—something of value measured by weight. And there were clear expectations for those given the talents. What does the work of an artist have to do with known value and clear expectations? The ultimate value of art is *not* known, and the expectations are *not* clear. Art is a wonderful thing, but artists are given a foreign currency of *unknown* value. It is a currency that can only be redeemed in the unknown country where it was minted—somewhere in the heart. A good steward is a good investor, but a currency of unknown value yields unpredictable returns. The stewardship of an artist should be measured by means other than his art alone if there is to be a just accounting of his stewardship. But with regard to the value of his calling, he must take a journey to discover the value of his gift. The artist seeks a sanctuary of goodness and beauty in the heart of humanity where his currency is highly valued. For me, that place has been hard to find, but it is there. Only through this arduous journey can we know the value of what we hold or how to invest it as good stewards.

My path seemed rather lonesome and poorly marked at first, but as my path has become clear, my journey has become gratifying. I found that country. It is now clear to me that the value of an artist's strange currency is substantial. My calling now seems clear. Those of us who have taken this journey to its end know that there is great value in the journey itself. Perhaps such sojourners may persuade those with talents to come and trade in this wondrous place where artists come to redeem their strange currency. Here God's people may invest their talents wisely. The destination is great, and the journey itself is almost as good. Let all who take this sublime journey testify to the truth of the things discovered along the way.

The people of God are the guardians of truth. They are called to fight a spiritual war amid a predominant culture of ideas and influences that seek to beguile them. Beauty is the most compelling witness of truth, and all enduring beauty is born of truth. How we value beauty is the essence of culture, and how we celebrate beauty is art. Our perception of beauty develops from a view of ourselves and of God, who gives us a framework for judging what is knowable and what is good. Our view of the world influences art, and art has a reciprocal influence on our view of the world and our reasons for believing all that we recognize as truth. The guardianship of truth has many challengers, and in the resulting war of ideas, the final measure of victory will be evidenced over the course of centuries.

To the casual observer, the tapestry of ideas that constitute the body of scriptural wisdom may seem like so many separate and lovely threads. But the committed seeker of divine truth will perceive relatively few and common threads that run throughout this glorious tapestry. These are the basic principles that direct our knowledge of God and help us perceive his image in our own being. Ironically, this simpler vision of spiritual truth will seem most inscrutable to the mind of fallen man because he seeks in this tapestry a different image that will not appear. He seeks the image of a god that is made in man's image. He is terrified at the image that does appear—the image of the one true God who is the sole author of law.

For those of us who do not fear this tapestry's image, it is time to define a clear and vital role for the arts and to revive the distinct culture of the city of God for the people of God and for society as a whole. We are called to spread the gospel to the whole world, but the gospel of Jesus is not spoken with words alone but through the *culture* of God's people. Our culture is the candle on a lamp stand that gives light to the whole house. It is the city on the hill that cannot be hidden. It was never God's design to represent the gospel with words alone. The unregenerate mind does not respond to words alone. Most of the changing power of the gospel makes its mark on the unregenerate heart through its various life-changing expressions—the beauty of holiness, the restored dignity of man, the sacraments, and the fellowship of the saints. These are the means that the Holy Spirit chooses to convict and convert the soul, and they are just as important as the spoken word. These are also the shadow ministries of the church. Like any other form of beauty, the beauty of holiness can only be revealed through what is knowable to sinful flesh. When the allure of enduring beauty dies, the soul becomes reprobate. Conversely, it is vain beauty that lures the children of darkness to their ultimate demise. The abstract ideologies of darkness are a small threat compared to the perverse art and culture of the world. The Church should ignore the experts that have led the entire culture down a dark road. They have no genuine authority declaring what is beautiful.

The mantel of authority must fall to whoever is able to form and defend a cogent body of logic in matters of culture and beauty. The theologian, as guardian and conservator of the truth, is the heir apparent to a place of authority in the study of beauty, more so than any artist who is a stranger to the things of God.

The ugly and inane may now be placed alongside the exquisite and sublime as equals for their vaunted ordination as "art." Some artists and critics seem to venerate concept before all else, while classical standards of art validate craftsmanship and natural form and effect—principles of beauty that imply a divine cause. Many artists are torn between an intuitive awareness of the divine order and an ideological denial of that order that is imposed upon them. It sometimes seems to be a war against the very idea of beauty. There was a time when man affirmed absurdity in one area of his thoughts while repudiating absurdity in his love of beauty. But now the absurd is accepted even in art. The artist, in his fallen state as the autonomous partaker of the knowledge of good and evil, is becoming more consistent with his credo. He has embraced the inevitable death that results. It is all part of the broader anti-gospel that is preached to us rather consistently, corrupting the church and mankind as a whole. Its end is utter reprobation. Even the darkest cultures of the past have retained some remnant of divine light. The love of beauty has been the godless man's single token of common value with the people of God. But the war against beauty itself is utterly unprecedented. Its negative effect on culture and on the soul of humanity is likewise unprecedented. It is time for the people of God to uphold the hand of Moses and restore this cultural form of God's light that can no longer be taken for granted.

What shall the battle look like if the people of God are to

rise up to reclaim their culture? What divine authority should the Church bring to bear upon the largely enigmatic field of art? As the war against enduring beauty becomes more intrusive, our theologians should eventually have much to say about art whether they realize it now or not. The Bible provides a solid foundation for understanding art and culture. With a bit of effort, church leaders can learn to speak with confidence, unction, and authority on such matters. I am convinced that only God's Word can provide a logical philosophy of aesthetics. If the artist fills certain spiritual needs, it is the Church's duty to guide and direct the arts as it would any other morally sensitive endeavor. The ministry of the artist is exceptionally spiritual in nature. If the Church leaves the artist to his own devices, she has allowed a *de-facto* moral authority to rest with secularists who have no official calling, approbation, or guidance. This should not stand. It is like a usurpation of the pulpit from someone who has received no calling or ordination.

What shall our spiritual criteria be for distinguishing between good and bad art? Which forms of artistic expression are hurtful and which forms are helpful? How are we to understand and recognize the differences? Who is there to teach us? If the search for beauty and truth can be made into an exacting discipline, the Christian artist must certainly take a large degree of responsibility to embrace that discipline. The final guardianship for all matters of spiritual truth inevitably belongs to the Church. Christian artists must reject the present inane authority structure of secular art scholars and look to the Church for help in creating a new one. Is beauty an issue we will leave in the hands of a secular class of aesthetically enlightened gods who, by virtue of their subtle intellect and artistic prowess, are exclusively qualified to judge good art from bad? There is a foul odor to this view.

But finding a voice of authority in any field is not without problems, especially regarding the disciplines of art and aesthetics. In disciplines such as medicine and law, a layman may use the ultimate guidepost of tangible results—empirical evidence—for achieving universal desirables. A doctor's goal is to heal patients. A lawyer's goal is a judgment or settlement favorable to his client. These are universal desirables, and the measures of success are clear in these fields. But for the expert in the study of beauty, the results of professional achievement are much less tangible and the desirables by which success is measured are not universal. One artist may love God, and another may hate him. Such basic differences create entirely different worlds regarding one's perception of beauty and truth. Therefore, let not the laymen in the things of beauty quickly cede his judgment to any so-called expert. For in the pursuit of truth, there should be no such thing as a layman. Those who know and love the truth are better qualified to recognize the eldest daughter of truth—beauty—than some celebrated expert who is a stranger to the things of God.

So what shall we say to the potential agents of change? You spiritual leaders must understand the weapons of your spiritual warfare. Do not overlook any part of the arsenal that God has given to you for the advancement of his kingdom. Let the embers of the communal hearth never burn out in your congregation. An order of worship may be discerned from the Holy Scriptures, and the ministries of light and shadow are well established in the preaching of the Word, the sacraments, the hymns, and the visual environment of public worship. Notwithstanding the obvious importance of the abstract ministry of words, the power of words is severely undermined without the ministry of shadows. The ministry of light is reductive by nature, consisting of sharp contrast, bold lines, clear guideposts, and doctrines. These are the kinds of things that we love after we believe, but it is not what the Holy Spirit typically uses to draw those locked in unbelief. It is the shadow ministries of creative expression that sets forth a full and compelling vision of the kingdom. By way of the shadows, God draws sinners to his cleansing ministry of light.

God has indulged us to drink deeply of his revelation through every sensory avenue. The Church has a rich cultural history, but her coat of many colors has been taken and held forth by some as false evidence of her demise. The Church's enemies have dulled senses concerning the true and enduring beauty, which is the image of God in the life of humanity. The legacy of the world's darkness is the stench of death to God's people, and only the dead can tolerate it. The children of darkness have sought to impose upon us an ugly world, but God can reverse the tide of reprobation that has afflicted our culture. In fact, our long spiritual drought may soon be over. A cloud about the size of a man's hand has appeared over our parched and contorted cultural landscape that has been invaded by the kingdom of darkness. The thunder we hear is the sound of the reprobate's world being crushed under the weight of its own absurdity. Perhaps the earth will quench its thirst with tears of repentance. The Church has once again begun to care about her kingdom responsibilities. If the Church retakes the culture, there may soon be no army left standing as strong as the warriors of truth.

The challenge for understanding the nature of beauty and the importance of creative gifts is more acute than ever. Let us not fear to undertake that sublime journey that is the ministry of art. Let the church be a faithful steward of the shadow ministries, which God has given to her. The Bible gives us plenty of reasons to believe that through the arts the Church may present its best challenges to the deadly doctrines of a corrupt culture and to prepare the world for the inevitable advance of the gospel. You Christian artists must live and labor in the shadow of an enduring beauty that is the shadow of Almighty. You must not take your duties lightly. Wisdom has mixed her wine and furnished her table. She calls for us to come. May all glory be to God! We shall indeed come!

# ENDNOTES

1. Isaac Newton's *Principia, General Scholium,* 1687
2. *Westminster Confession of Faith,* Larger Cat., Chapter 1, Part VI
3. *Westminster Confession of Faith,* Larger Cat., Q. 4
4. *Life sermons of Dr. John Tauler,* Eng. tr. by Susana Winkworth, (Smith, Elder, and Company, 1857)., p. 5
5. Ibid, p. 8
6. William Blake, *Book of Urizen*
7. *Leonardo da Vinci,* quoting *Cod. Arund. Fol. 24 r.,* page 33. Reynal & Company and William Marrow & Company, New York. Copyright by Instituto Geografico De Agostini, Novara, Italy.
8. Leonardo de Vinci, page 167, quoting Treatise, fol. 68
9. Of the Manner in Which the Persecutors Died, Lacantius, Chapter 1
10. (Letter to Rev. E. Beasley, Nov. 12, 1825; *Letters and Other Writings of James Madison Vol. III,* pp. 503–504; 1865, J.B. Lippincott & Co.)

# APPENDIX

The history of Christianity has been turbulent and full of conflict and strife. Yet its shadow of beauty cast upon the free societies of Europe and the west is too obvious to be disputed. Although many citizens of western style democracies have become faithless, there remains a distinct Christian imprint upon the culture of these free societies. Let not the numbers of the faithless discourage those who labor for the gospel. God will call his elect in due season. Meanwhile, the culture of Christianity continues to progress, with noteworthy spiritual victories over the past two centuries:

Namibia is a free country today because of its Western and Christian influences. It became independent from South Africa in 1990, and it has many Lutherans and Roman Catholics. Botswana was a long-time protectorate of Britain. It is mostly Catholic, and has a constitution that was brokered by the British. Mali has been a long-term democracy project of the United States. Benin is now governed by an evangelical protestant, Yayi Boni. Guinea began as a French province and a protectorate. Ghana is a client state of Britain with several other European interests. America's CIA helped to topple the corrupt Nkrumah regime and establish democracy in Ghana. Ghana's president from 2001 through 2008 was John Kufuor, a Roman Catholic. The current president of Ghana is John Atta Mills, a Methodist.

Mongolia is considered a free country today and is like an island of freedom landlocked by two oppressive states, Russia and China. After the recent fall of Communism in Mongolia in 1990, it became a parliamentary republic. Reformed Mongolia actively courted and received the help of the United States and other Western democracies, and its reforms were inspired broadly by the free-world ideological victories of that time. For this reason, one may speak of modern Mongolia as a client state of the West, but such a description deserves an asterisk. Modern Mongolia's affinity for Western values might be more attributable to a unique indigenous Christian influence in its ancient history. Mongolia's first Christian influences came through Nestorian Christian missionaries from Persia. In the thirteenth century, Genghis Kahn married a Nestorian Christian woman, Ibaka-beki. One of Khan's daughters-in-law, Sorkaktani, also a Nestorian Christian, was a woman of strong character—a matriarch who became the mother of three great emperors, including Kublai Khan. The Nestorian Christian influence is reflected in Mongolian law, in which it is still written that all people on earth are created by one Creator.

America's client state of Israel also needs an asterisk. It is a small country that could be covered by a dot on the world map. Israel has certainly been influenced by Western allies, but it might be argued that Israel may well have achieved a free society on its own. Judaism shares the same essential view of humanity as Christianity. The Jews have the Old Testament moral and civil law that is foundational to the laws of free, Christianized societies.

Societies with no historical connection to the biblical law could never construct a free society on their own. Douglas MacArthur proved, however, that such a culture could be taught. Few Japanese have accepted Christianity itself, but the Japanese have absorbed many of the Judeo-Christian values of the West—enough to maintain a stable democracy. Indonesia was governed and colonized by the Dutch until after World War II. In 1949, the Dutch yielded to pressure from the United States to grant independence to Indonesia. South Korea came under United States administrative control in 1945 after World War II, and it is a United States protectorate to this day. Australia began as a British penal colony in 1788, and the free colonies of South Australia and Victoria were established in 1836 and 1851 respectively. Australia became its own commonwealth in 1901, adopting the same Westminster system of parliamentary democracy as the British. Missionaries brought Christianity to New Zealand's indigenous Māori people in the 1830s. Many of them converted, and Christian missionaries maintained an advocacy relationship with the Māori against lawless European visitors. New Zealand became an official British colony in 1851 and became a separate dominion in 1907. Regrettably, South Africa is not free. It has a recent deplorable past with racial apartheid, and the world will not soon forget the labors of Episcopal archbishop Desmond Tutu to end it. Regrettably, the South African people have lost their quest for freedom through another form of oppression called socialism. This shows that a Christian culture does not guarantee that a nation will always be free. The freedom and righteousness of a culture is something the church must continually work to maintain. Is there a free nation on earth whose laws have not been profoundly influenced directly or indirectly by biblical culture? No, there is not one example. God's shadow on enlightened cultures is absolutely essential to freedom, and it is maintained through the laws, morals, ideals, and arts of a free people.